Trading with Pariahs

Trading with Pariahs

Trade Networks and the Failure of Economic Sanctions

Keith A. Preble and Charmaine N. Willis Ward

LEXINGTON BOOKS
Lanham • Boulder • New York • London

Published by Lexington Books
An imprint of The Rowman & Littlefield Publishing Group, Inc.
4501 Forbes Boulevard, Suite 200, Lanham, Maryland 20706
www.rowman.com

86-90 Paul Street, London EC2A 4NE

British Library Cataloguing in Publication Information Available

Library of Congress Cataloging-in-Publication Data

Names: Preble, Keith A., 1975- author. | Willis, Charmaine N., author.
Title: Trading with pariahs : trade networks and the failure of economic sanctions / Keith A. Preble and Charmaine N. Willis .
Description: Lanham: Lexington Books, [2024] | Includes bibliographical references and index
Identifiers: LCCN 2024023798 | ISBN 9781666903737 (cloth) | ISBN 9781666903744 (ebook)
Subjects: LCSH: Economic sanctions.
Classification: LCC HF1413.5 .P728 2024 | DDC 327.1/17—dc23/eng/20240605
LC record available at https://lccn.loc.gov/2024023798

To Keith's father, Richard, who encouraged him
to persevere through life's challenges.
To Ron Willis, who inspired Charmaine's love of politics,
fostered her curiosity, and encouraged her at every turn.

Contents

Acknowledgments

This work initially started as a standalone paper on the failure of economic sanctions to rollback North Korea's nuclear weapons program (Preble and Willis 2024b). Our conversations around that initial paper pushed us to look at other "hard targets," and we began to see some interesting patterns with international pariah states and economic sanctions.

We wish to thank several people for their various comments and support throughout the lifespan of this project. First, we thank Joseph Parry and the editorial team at Rowman and Littlefield for the opportunity to publish our book and for their guidance throughout this process. Second, we also want to thank the anonymous reviewers who provided useful feedback that has helped shaped the work.

We also wish to thank several people who gave feedback on this project at various phases of its development: (in alphabetical order) Joel Campbell, Charles Crabtree, Jennifer Cyr, Jon DiCicco, Bryan R. Early, Laura García Montoya, Benjamin Habib, Justin Hastings, Nakissa P. Jahabani, Jangai Jap, Jeehye Kim, Young-Im Lee, Elizabeth Menninga, John Oakes, Morten Pedersen, Kaitlyn Robinson, Jay Song, Jiakun Jack Zhang, and organizers and attendees who facilitated and attended our presentations at the Asian Politics Online Seminar Series (APOSS) (2021; 2022), the International Studies Association (ISA) Annual Meeting (2021), the ISA-Northeast Annual Meeting (2021; 2022), the Pacific International Politics Conference Online Speaker Series (PIPCOSS) (2021), the Political Networks Conference (PolNet) (2022), and the Southwest Workshop on Mixed Methods Research (SWMMR) (2022). Keith also wants to thank his father, who passed away before the publication of the book, for encouraging him to see it through, and his family for their support. He also thanks Bryan R. Early for his continuing mentorship and contributions to international relations, much of which is featured prominently throughout the book. Keith would also like to thank David Kearn Jr. for his help and guidance in the final stages of the manuscript. Charmaine is grateful to Bayley, Dad, Scott, Whitney, Uncle JJ, Lynda, Emily, Bryan, Kate, Anne, Todd, Jelly Bean, and Norah for all of their love and support during this project.

We approached this project with unbridled enthusiasm as we sought to learn and understand the role of sanctions in this high-stakes game of world diplomacy and international intrigue. We experienced several obstacles over the course of writing this book, both personally and professionally. Nonetheless, we persisted as we feel that social network analysis and descriptive approaches can provide a much-needed broad visual overview of the impacts of sanctions on the trading networks of target states and even sanctions senders. We also believe that the concept of weaponized interdependence provides important insights into when and why sanctions are able to compel changes in states' behavior—and when they fail to do so. In closing, beyond the key empirical conclusions in the book, we want researchers, especially early career scholars, to be the champions of getting your own ideas over the finish line. Always know that there's space for new ideas, new ways of thinking, and new approaches to understanding political science problems. Descriptive work, often taken for granted in our discipline, can open the door for theory development about political phenomena of interest, which we hope that this book ultimately accomplishes. As a discipline seeking relevance in an era where higher education and social science research are constantly besieged by dwindling political and financial support, let's engage with new ideas rather than crush them, even at the expense of our own contributions to the discipline.

Introduction

Trading with Pariahs

Queen Elizabeth II, the United Kingdom's longest-reigning monarch, passed away on September 8, 2022. Her funeral, which took place eleven days later on Monday, September 19, brought royal families, heads of state, former UK prime ministers, and a whole host of "who's who" in international politics to Westminster Abbey. While this solemn affair brought together politicians and the powerful from around the world, there were some notable absences of world leaders. Leaders from six countries—Syria, Venezuela, Afghanistan, Russia, Belarus, and Myanmar—did not receive invitations. North Korea curiously enough *did receive* an invitation, but the British invitation was extended only to the ambassador level and not directly to the Kim family (Dasgupta 2022). What do these six uninvited countries plus the snubbing of Kim Jong Un have in common?

These countries represent a unique "club" of *pariah states*, states that have remained isolated and ostracized by the international community. Such states are often economically and diplomatically sanctioned as well as isolated and some pariahs have also felt the full force of the US military. Harkavy (1981) has linked the pariah status of states to nuclear proliferation, although the term is quite often used more broadly and across a number of issue areas, especially by US officials. "Pariahs" may also refer to states who develop or possess other forms of weapons of mass destruction as well as those who are gross violators of human rights norms.

Pariah states, according to Harkavy (1981, 136), often have "precarious . . . sole sources of conventional arms supply . . . [and] very vulnerable in a crisis to cutoffs of space parts or to denial of weapons resupply." As nations "faced with adversaries having sold support from a major power" (1981, 136), pariah states are clearly exposed to the impact of trade-centered economic sanctions and arms embargoes. As research on sanctions busting has shown

(Barry and Kleinberg 2015; Caruso 2003, 2005; Early 2015; Early and Spice 2015), target states, even pariah states, are often capable of attracting sanctions busting economic support from third-party state governments and their respective firms. Pariah states are not always impoverished states with small-sized economies; most states hit with economic sanctions are target states with medium-sized economies, which tend to attract greater levels of sanctions busting support (Preble 2023). Even seemingly isolated "pariahs" like North Korea and Myanmar are medium-sized economies. A key puzzle that motivates our research is, if pariahs are so ostracized, how is it that they remain capable of resisting comprehensive and targeted sanctions from an array of sender states? While we agree that sanctions busters are critical to this discussion, the networks of support and the ways in which these networks adapt and change when sanctions are imposed is a critical intervening variable.

Economic sanctions play an important role in international relations by the ways in which these policies seek not only to bring about policy and behavioral changes but also in the way that they signal when countries violate norms and seek to undermine the liberal international order led by the United States and Western US allies. Pariah states represent a challenge to that order, yet remain extremely resilient to sanctions policies developed by the United States and other senders in the international system.

Yet there is evidence that policymakers are aware that efforts to use sanctions against pariah states is often difficult and futile. States impose economic sanctions with the intent of not only changing offending states' policies but also drawing attention to norm violators. When the United States sanctioned Myanmar during the Clinton Administration, the late Secretary of State Madeline Albright admitted that US policymakers had designed economic sanctions primarily to draw attention to the offending military junta's violations of international norms related to the deterioration of democracy and the treatment of political prisoners (Steinberg 2007), such as 1991 Nobel Peace Prize winner Aung San Suu Kyi.

Economic sanctions are not the only means that policymakers can use to draw attention to the norm violations of pariah states. During his first State of the Union address before Congress on January 29, 2002, President George W. Bush introduced the phrase "Axis of Evil," a reference to several international pariah states that frequently violated international norms through their quest for weapons of mass destruction, their state sponsorship of terrorism, and the threats these pariahs posed to world peace:

> States like these, and their terrorist allies, constitute an axis of evil, arming to threaten the peace of the world. By seeking weapons of mass destruction, these regimes post a grave and growing danger. They could provide these arms to terrorists, giving them the means to match their hatred. They could attack our

allies or attempt to blackmail the United States. In any of these cases, the price of indifference would be catastrophic. (Bush 2002; Glass 2019; Wagner 2002)

Two of the countries that formed Bush's "Axis of Evil," Iran and North Korea, feature prominently in our study on the effectiveness of economic sanctions. Both Iran and North Korea have proven to be inscrutable challenges to US administrations. Myanmar (Burma) has similarly been a sanctions target for several US administrations (Anguelov and Bryant 2015, 33–5). The United States has imposed blistering unilateral sanctions on these states for decades, and Iran and North Korea are or have been the target of United Nations (UN) sanctions along with sanctions imposed by the European Union (EU) while Myanmar has not been subject to UN sanctions. Despite decades of unilateral and multilateral economic sanctions against these international pariahs, North Korea (also known as the Democratic People's Republic of Korea, DPRK) has continued to develop, enhance, and grow its nuclear arsenal and ballistic missile capability. Iran has remained steadfast in the face of unilateral economic sanctions as it seeks, according to the United States and Israel, to develop nuclear weapons through its continued efforts at uranium enrichment (Kroenig 2018). And although Myanmar took steps toward democracy in the 2010s (one of the sanctions goals), hopes for Burmese democratization were dashed when the military staged a coup in 2021.

North Korea and Myanmar on the one hand and Iran on the other represent two sides of the same coin. These states have been the target of US sanctions and have successfully—but with difficulties and through different means—resisted those sanctions. Our book seeks to show how economic linkages and the structures that states find themselves in are necessary conditions for sanctions to be effective (and successful). While North Korea's (Frank 2015) and Myanmar's (Anguelov and Bryant 2015, 51–4) economic linkages to the West are meager, Iran's linkages, especially to European countries are vast and, prior to the imposition of the Joint Comprehensive Plan of Action (JCPOA), were much deeper.

For decades, Europe had been Iran's most important trading partner (European Commission 2022). Once European trade and financial sanctions against Iran increased dramatically to support negotiators seeking Iran's commitment to the Joint Comprehensive Plan of Action, Iran had little choice but to sign it. As Adam Tarock notes, the West got significantly more from the deal than Iran (Tarock 2016), and Iran has since learned from its experience negotiating the JCPOA. This experience has shown the Iranians that their exposure to the EU and EU member states' economies is a vulnerability. Since the agreement collapsed following the Trump Administration's cancellation of US participation, Iran has reconfigured its network of licit trade away from Europe (European Commission 2022). Data from the *Atlas of Economic Complexity* show that Iran has pivoted much of its trade away from Europe toward more sanctions busting supporters, notably China, India, and Syria (Growth Lab at Harvard University 2021). This post-JCPOA shift in trade reflects the extent to which target states can adapt as they seek to evade sanctions.

North Korea, on the other hand, has far fewer linkages and is much less susceptible to weaponized interdependence outside of Asia. North Korea's dearth of ties with the West means that it is far less susceptible to economic and financial sanctions imposed by Western states. Whereas Iran's dependence on the West has made it much more susceptible to multilateral economic sanctions, North Korea has refashioned its network of licit and illicit trade to maintain trading relationships with countries willing to do business with it. It has sought greater engagement with those countries either unwilling or unable to enforce economic sanctions against the Hermit Kingdom (Preble and Willis 2024b).

Myanmar is also less susceptible to any weaponized interdependence that the United States or any other Western has attempted to wield. Prior to the first rounds of Western-led sanctions in the late 1980s and early 1990s, Myanmar's economy was already largely focused on trade with other Asian states, notably those within Southeast and East Asia, though it did trade with the United States and EU member states. However, as the sanctions regime continued and increased, Myanmar became much more economically dependent on its traditional trading partners in Asia as well as new trading partners such as China and India. In this case, Asian countries largely chose to continue trading with Myanmar for commercial reasons as well as to try to address Myanmar's human and civil rights issues without isolating it.

Our work draws upon the research on *weaponized interdependence* developed by Henry Farrell and Abraham Newman (2019) to understand when sanctions *can work* and why they have failed against pariah states. Weaponized interdependence refers to the ways in which states with political authority over key nodes in the international network of money, goods, and information create policies that in turn generate panopticon and chokepoint effects. Panopticon and chokepoint effects emanate from policymaking conducted by states in privileged positions (these *key nodes*) in a network.

Panopticon effects emerge from policies that leverage states' informational advantages against adversaries and assist states in monitoring the activities of states that utilize their network. These informational advantages emanate from policy choices that states make in their domestic and foreign policies. Foreign policy decisions that favor diplomatic and/or economic engagement over isolation can bring significant informational advantages. Many states in the international system resist calls for sanctions and seek to preserve not only economic benefits from trade and investment but also use those benefits as a means of persuasion and coercion. For example, Japan's decision to ignore

US requests to isolate and sever relations with Myanmar reflected its foreign policy prerogative to seek eventual policy change in Myanmar through engagement and dialogue. Panopticon effects can emanate from legislation and regulations that countries pass, as well. The United States Patriot Act and Bank Secrecy Act are examples of policies that generate panopticon effects. Both pieces of legislation (and others) permit US agencies to monitor activity in the US financial system and collect information on users. UN Security Council Resolutions, global policies passed by the UN Security Council, can also generate panopticon effects. Resolution 1718 (2006), for example, provided for the creation of a UN Panel of Experts to oversee the implementation of UN sanctions against the DPRK. These experts are charged with collecting information from member states' governments that evaluate and study the effectiveness of UN targeted sanctions. These reports provide information on whether UN economic and financial sanctions are having their intended effects and provide the Panel of Experts with critical information needed to evaluate and monitor the effectiveness of the UN member state compliance with UN sanctions. The information gathered through panopticon generating policies provides the "ammunition" to construct and design policies that subsequently generate chokepoint effects.

Chokepoint effects emanate from policies that endeavor to isolate and sever a user's connection to critical nodes in the network. These policies restrict and limit interactions between the target states and the chokepoint effect-generating sender state. Economic and financial sanctions generate chokepoint effects. The multitude of US legislation and regulations promulgated by agencies such as the US Departments of Treasury and Commerce are examples of policies that generate chokepoint effects, as are UN economic sanctions that apply to all member states (Farrell and Newman 2019, 45–6). Economic sanctions can take a variety of forms—targeted, sectoral, or comprehensive—or can also involve blacklists, such as the United States' Specially Designated Nationals (SDN) listings, travel bans, and, in some cases, diplomatic isolation.

We posit that panopticon and chokepoint effects play an important role in whether economic and financial sanctions are effective at achieving the interests of senders imposing them. We argue that there must be a balance between panopticon and chokepoint effects that domestic and foreign policies operating in key nodes within a given network generate. Senders must also balance the need to punish and isolate through chokepoint effects with the vast data and information captured through panopticon effects, which provide the necessary resources for the implementation of the *correct* policies that generate potent yet measured chokepoint effects.

In our estimation and research, North Korea and Iran represent failure and success cases of economic sanctions, respectively. What differentiates these two countries' ability to weather the hardship of economic sanctions is their ability to refashion networks of trade in the face of an economically globalized and interdependent world. For North Korea, its ability to weather the onslaught of economic sanctions meant relying on illicit networks developed prior to the imposition of sanctions and eschewing trade ties with US allies and sanctions-implementing states in East Asia. For Iran, its reliance and dependence on the EU and EU markets, which sanctioned Iran more comprehensively in the run-up to negotiations of the JCPOA, meant that it had nowhere else to turn once its access to EU markets diminished. Iran had little choice but to agree to signing the JCPOA for sanctions relief and saw working with the West as a necessary step in gaining access to frozen assets and important trade linkages. The Myanmar case is similar to the North Korea case in many ways; the military junta created new trade ties and deepened existing ties, mostly with other Asian states, in the face of Western-led sanctions. At the same time, however, the Western-led sanctions regime was successful at keeping the junta's human and civil rights violations in the international spotlight.

CONCEPTUALIZING AND OPERATIONALIZING PARIAHS

The term "pariah state" is one that academics and policymakers often use but rarely define. Niblock (2001) notes that US and Western governments have referred to them as "rogue states" and "states of concern" that needed to be restricted or contained until the domestic political systems within the "pariah states" themselves "removed the leadership that had inspired the state's delinquency" (2002, 12) (2001, 12). The political organization within the state is intimately connected to renegade behavior that is itself a function of the methods of rule, specific policy goals, and questions of legitimacy of the regime (Nincic 2007, 12–14).

Harkavy (1981) details various characteristics of what a pariah state usually possesses including: "widely questioned" origins and/or legitimacy and meager supply and production capability of weapons (1981, 136). Additionally, they are typically "weak" states with few resources of their own (Chow and Easley 2019, 505). Perhaps pariah states' most notable characteristics are their relationships with and connectivity to other states.

First, the term "pariah" is often used, though rarely explicitly defined, as a state that has violated international norms. Of course, norms change over time; a state may become a "pariah" if it continues to engage in behavior that the international community no longer deems acceptable. One normative realm in which many states appear to be referred to as "pariahs" is that of human rights, a set of norms that has changed significantly over time. As Sikkink (2008) notes, "since the 1980s, democratizing states throughout the world have begun to hold individuals, including past heads of state, accountable for human rights violations" (2). A classic example of a state labeled a "pariah" for human rights violations is South Africa when it was under Apartheid (Harkavy 1981; Vale and Taylor 1999). It is perhaps unsurprising then that the three countries we profile in this book—North Korea, Myanmar, and Iran—are all accused of human rights violations.

However, violating human rights alone does not appear to make a state a "pariah." For example, Amnesty International's 2021/2022 annual report found that 43 percent of countries "have introduced new laws to stop people peacefully expressing their rights," 55 percent "use excessive or unnecessary force against demonstrators," and 54 percent "arbitrarily detain human rights defenders" (Amnesty International 2022). Of course, there are many different aspects of human rights beyond these measures, but clearly, nearly half the countries of the world are not labeled "pariahs." Even the United States is a violator of human rights by some metrics, such as its unwillingness to ratify the UN Convention on the Rights of the Child or ban the corporal punishment of children in schools, the only one of 140 signatory countries not to do so (Sorensen et al. 2024).

Earlier studies on pariah states have tended to be case-based approaches that use the pariah concept or label but describe pariahs rather than delineate the boundaries of the concept. For example, Sicker's (1987) analysis focuses on Libya and the "adventurous politics" of Muammar Qaddafi, especially the way in which his regime frequently flouted international norms. Sicker (1987) describes in detail the use of repressive tactics to achieve national unity and cohesion given the dearth of leadership potential in Qaddafi's revolutionary regime (5). International norms that pariah states may disregard go beyond weapons of mass destruction and human rights violations, though. Such norm violations may also include the use of state sponsorship of terrorism as a tool for achieving foreign policy objectives and pariah state leaders' vanity projects for states stringently isolated from the international stage and having few supporters (Sicker 1987, 31, 131).

This brings us to another key aspect of pariahs: they often face (what pariah states perceive as) acute internal or external threats that may encourage them to build up their military capabilities and/or develop weapons of mass destruction (Harkavy 1981, 135; Chow and Easley 2019, 504). While the former may draw international condemnation, the development of weapons of mass destruction, such as nuclear weapons, violates international treaties, such as the Treaty on the Non-Proliferation of Nuclear Weapons (NPT). Two of the states in this study, North Korea and Iran, have repeatedly violated international norms regarding the proliferation of nuclear weapons.

As a result of pariahs' insecurity, they often try to find a more powerful patron state (or "black knight" in sanctions literature parlance; see Hufbauer et al. 2009 and Early 2011) that can help them survive in an international environment full of adversaries through political, military, and/or economic means (Harkavy 1981, 136; Chow and Easley 2019, 505). However, the asymmetric relationship is often risky for both parties. For more powerful states, a relationship with an international pariah often has little benefit and, indeed, may be a "liability" (Harkavy 1981, 136). The relationship can bring the patron into conflict with other members of the international community for supporting the pariah (Chow and Easley 2019, 505). As discussed in chapters 2 and 3, one source of tension between the United States and China is the latter's support of North Korea despite US and UN sanctions. For pariahs, they may "risk abandonment, loss of autonomy, and domestic backlash for compromising sovereignty," and pariahs "are expected to comply with their patrons' interests" (Chow and Easley 2019, 505). Furthermore, pariahs often have little recourse as their isolation from the international community limits their options (Chow and Easley 2019, 505). As we discuss in chapters 2–4, China has been a key patron to many international pariahs (Chow and Easley 2019, 502) profiled in our book.

Overall, this discussion suggests that pariah states are countries that are often weak with few resources. They violate international norms in areas such as human rights and/or non-proliferation. Because of their weakness and isolation from the international community, they often seek out a more powerful patron state who can support the pariah militarily, politically, and/or economically. However, measuring "pariahtude" is challenging. While the possession of nuclear weapons (with the exception of the five exempt states under the NPT) will likely make a state an international pariah for violating non-proliferation norms, this is not a *necessary* condition for pariah status. And while violating human rights may earn a state the "pariah" label, it is not a *sufficient* condition. How, then, can we identify international pariahs? Harkavy (1981) offers several measures that can identify international isolation:

> the number and identity of nations with which [pariahs] maintain formal diplomatic relations, the outcomes of critical UN votes (particularly those pertaining to the legitimacy of pariah regimes), membership in intergovernmental organizations (IGOs), and overall trade relations are good indices, at least when used in combination. (140)

In his study of four "pariahs" (Israel, South Africa, South Korea, and Taiwan), Harkavy (1981) finds, however, "all of the pariahs have far wider trading networks than those of diplomatic relations; each conducts extensive trade with numerous nations with which it does not exchange ambassadors"

(141). As we found in our recent study, that pattern seems to hold with the "pariah" North Korea, which conducts trade with many more states than it maintains diplomatic relations (Preble and Willis 2024b). Beyond North Korea, the "pariahs" Iran and Myanmar have also, at times, had a vast array of trading partners despite international condemnation (and economic sanctions). We argue that economic sanctions, on the other hand, provide a useful metric, albeit an imperfect one, for identifying international pariahs. At most, members of the international community impose sanctions to attempt to create some kind of change in the target state's behavior. At minimum, sanctions send a signal to the target, the international community, and a sender's own domestic constituents that the target is engaging in "bad behavior." As we discuss in chapter 4, for example, US policymakers have sometimes employed sanctions for the purposes of signaling, as they did toward Myanmar.

In this book, we conceptualize "pariah states" as states who have violated either the codified rules or norms of the neoliberal world order led by Western states such as the United States, Western European states, and their allies. Sanctions are often imposed by Western states on pariah states when they violate this order. Figure 0.1 shows the number of senders of sanctions (both states and international organizations) per target from 1988 to 2022. We focus on this period that encompasses the years immediately preceding the "Sanctions Decade," during and after where states began imposing sanctions on others at an unprecedented rate (Cortright and Lopez 2000; Felbermayr et al. 2020; Yotov et al. 2020). We include only target states that have been sanctioned by twenty or more senders. We contend that an international "pariah" is not likely to be sanctioned by only a handful of senders. Since pariah states are known for engaging in deviant behaviors (Nincic 2005)—such as human rights violations (North Korea, Iran, Myanmar), threats to the status quo (Russia), WMD proliferation (North Korea, Iran)—then we would expect to see senders implementing sanctions in response to two or more deviant behaviors. Raising the deviant behavior bar means that a country like India, for example, which was sanctioned for its nuclear weapons program, would not necessarily be considered a pariah state because sanctions were not applied for other types of deviant behaviors. Thus, states who have been sanctioned by many senders are more likely to be labeled as pariahs since they are not only frequently cut off from international trading networks and isolated by international community more generally but also engage in a mix of deviant practices that undermine the neoliberal world order.

As Figure 0.1 shows, there are many states that have been the target of sanctions over the past 30+ years by a multitude of senders. It is important to note, however, that while there is certainly strength in numbers, some of these sanctions are multilateral (vis-à-vis international organizations like the UN and the EU) and, arguably, bring more pressure on the target as more

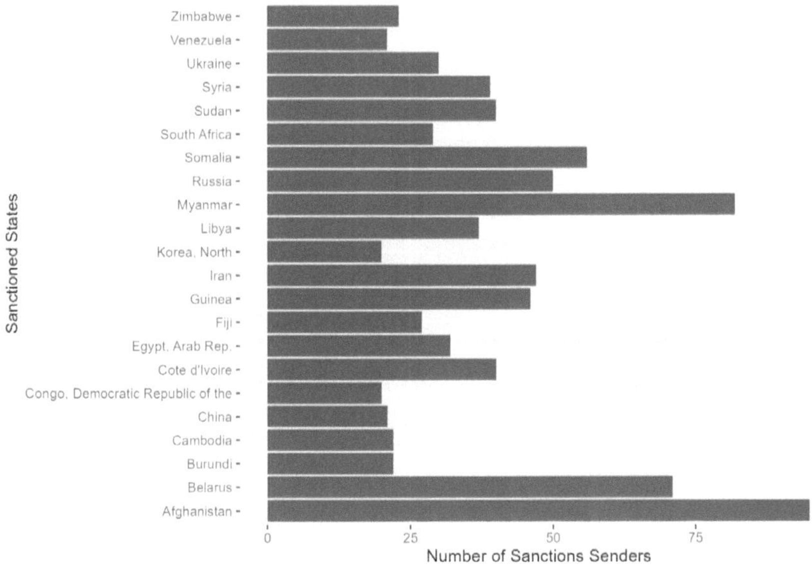

Figure 0.1 Number of Sender States per Target, 1988–2022. Note that all senders who sanctioned a target via a multilateral agreement (such as a UN Security Council Resolution) are counted together as an international organization sanction. If UN, EU, or other multilateral sanctions were broken down by sender state, the count would be much higher. *Source*: These data come from the Global Sanctions Database (Felbermayr et al. 2020).

nodes in their network impose sanctions at once but can be less effective under some conditions (Kaempfer and Lowenberg 1999). For example, while Myanmar has one of the highest counts of senders sanctioning it, most of the sanctions are from individual states. Although the EU has sanctioned Myanmar, the UN never has. Conversely, while Figure 0.1 suggests that North Korea has a lower count of senders, many of the sanctions against it are multilateral including a series of UN sanctions, meaning that the number of senders is much higher. For its part, Iran has a variety of sanctions issued by both individual states and international organizations such as the EU and the UN. Despite this multitude of sanctions, with a few notable exceptions such as South Africa, economic sanctions have generally been unsuccessful in coercing pariah states to change their behavior.

While there are several "pariah" states, we chose to focus on North Korea, Myanmar, and Iran as they all present important puzzles and insights for both sanctions scholars and policymakers. North Korea has been sanctioned by the UN for decades and by the United States for even longer. However, the Hermit Kingdom continues to defy predictions of its collapse and its nuclear and WMD weapons programs continue to thrive. Why has North Korea been so resilient to international pressure? Iran has also been heavily sanctioned, often mentioned in the same breath as North Korea in US policy circles. As mentioned, it was only when EU and UN sanctions coincided with the US sanctions that Iran began to acquiesce to sanctions pressures. Is the combination of US, EU, and UN sanctions the right "recipe" for sanctions success in some cases? And finally, sanctions appeared to work toward pressuring Myanmar to democratize when the military junta consented to the country's first elections in 20 years (Kudo 2011). However, that optimism was dashed when the junta returned to power in early 2021 after waging a coup d'etat (*BBC News* 2021). Thus it is unclear what role, if any, sanctions had in Myanmar's recent foray into democracy.

EFFECTIVE OR SUCCESSFUL SANCTIONS: A RARE EVENT?

Tools of economic statecraft, especially economic sanctions, have received much less attention from international relations scholars as Baldwin (1985, 2020) notes in his seminal work *Economic Statecraft.* In evaluating the effectiveness of any policy, scholars and analysts must be cautious in judging the success and failure of an instrument and labeling a policy as "working" or "not working" can be "slippery" (Baldwin 2020, xiii). To focus solely on measures of effectiveness while failing to consider costs has the potential to mislead, and success or failure may be in response to the use and implementation of policy alternatives rather than the original policy in question (Baldwin 2020, xii–xiii).

Understanding when and why sanctions work has inspired intense debates among sanctions scholars and practitioners. Debates in the 1990s sought to explore and challenge the success and effectiveness of economic sanctions (Baldwin and Pape 1998; Elliott 1998; Pape 1997, 1998). Hufbauer et al.'s (2009) systematic study and classification of sanctions events, first published in 1985, sought to understand the utility of economic sanctions across a multitude of different variables while also studying the success and impact of economic sanctions cases involving a multitude of senders (those states imposing economic sanctions).

While the United States has been the principal sender and much scholarship has been devoted to its use of economic sanctions (Demarais 2022; Drury 2001; Early 2012), additional attention is now being paid to the EU's use of economic sanctions. Scholars have sought to show the impact of EU autonomous sanctions as well as the efficacy of those sanctions across a number of cases of critical importance to the EU's Common Foreign and Security Policy (Drulakova et al. 2010; Eriksson 2011; Giumelli 2013a, 2013b; Portela

2005, 2011). The rise of China and its growing economic clout both in East Asia and globally has also drawn the attention of scholars who have sought to understand the use of economic sanctions with Chinese characteristics (Nephew 2019; Reilly 2012; Poh 2017). As sender state variation increases, the debate over whether sanctions are effective at achieving the foreign policy interests of states remains a critical question as the goals, objectives, and processes for designing, implementing, and enforcing economic sanctions vary considerably across the multitude of senders using economic sanctions in their statecraft toolkit. The duration and scope of economic sanctions also vary considerably across senders. Between 1990 and 2018, just over a quarter (26 percent) of all sanctions imposed across senders (United States, EU, UN, and regional organizations) ended due to target acquiescence with the remainder ending due to sender capitulation (Attia and Grauvogel 2023). This dynamic highlights the challenges that senders face in designing sanctions that achieve their goals.

For sanctions to be successful, Hirschman argued (1945) that the target state needs to be vulnerable to the economic pain caused by the sanctions. The existence of vulnerabilities ultimately requires some economic dependence or interdependence between the target and sender states. Therefore, when such interdependencies *do exist,* target states would and should rationally seek to avoid economic sanctions to avoid disrupting their national interests (Allen 2005, 120). For the target state to take the imposition of sanctions seriously, the sender must feel some pain, too (Lektzian and Sprecher 2007). If the target sees that the sender state is willing to bear a burden in order to change the target's behavior, concessions on the part of the target state are more likely (Drezner 1999; Martin 1992, 1994). Otherwise, the target state would simply have little reason to cave to the coercive power of the imposed economic sanctions (Blanchard and Ripsman 2013).

It is also important to explicate the underlying logic behind sanctions. First, it is important to recognize that sanctions are inherently coercive and invoke what Schelling (1977) terms "the power to hurt." Economic sanctions in particular do not invoke the threat of military force but rather the threat of harm to a state's economic well-being. However, they may well undermine a state's military power since military strength depends on states' military expenditures. Thus, the "hurt" here is "restrictions maintained by a government with respect to economic activity with foreign countries or persons [. . .] [consisting] of trade/investment and financial sanctions" (Frank 2006, 9). It is this threat of economic hurt that, in theory, influences a state to act according to whatever the sanction demands.

Schelling's discussion of the distinction between deterrence and compellence is also instructive regarding sanctions. Both require a threat, clarity around what the object needs to do to diminish the threat, and follow-through of the threat if the object does not acquiesce. At face value, economic sanctions seem to be a form of compellence as they threaten to continue an action until the target state does what the sanctions require: "blockades illustrate the typical difference between a threat intended to make an adversary do something [compellence] and a threat intended to keep him from starting something [deterrence]" (Schelling 1977, 69). For example, in the case of North Korea, abandoning its nuclear weapons program would theoretically end the multilateral economic sanctions against it. However, if compellence fails, it becomes deterrence. In the case of economic sanctions, even if a state does not acquiesce to compellence, it may refrain from actions that would elicit further sanctions.

Baldwin (1999) has argued that the choice of economic sanctions is just one of many policy options governments make when confronted by a policy challenge requiring some instrument of coercion or persuasion. Much of the debate on sanctions success and effectiveness requires also identifying those policies that might have potentially worked better at achieving a given policy goal. To evaluate sanctions' effectiveness, they must be situated among the menu of policy options available to states rather than considering sanctions in isolation in evaluating their effectiveness and ultimately whether they are successful. Sometimes, though, as Bapat and Kwon (2015) argue using data from the Threat and Imposition of Economic Sanctions (TIES) data set (Morgan, Bapat, and Krustev 2009; Morgan, Bapat, and Kobayashi 2014), sanctions are likely to be employed under conditions in which they are not predicted to succeed. This may occur when governments impose sanctions for political reasons but firms within their country are unlikely to comply for commercial reasons, or when the economic exchange between the sender and the target states is weak.

Research on the use of economic sanctions has highlighted their versatility and range as policy instruments. James Barber (1979) and Margaret Doxey (1987/1996) were the first scholars to move beyond seeing sanctions as mere tools of punishment. Doxey noted that sanctions were often employed in achieving eight unique goals: deterrence, compliance, punishment, destabilization, limiting conflict, solidarity, symbolism, and signaling (Charron and Portela 2022, 5; Doxey 1987, 54–8). Different actors within a multilateral coalition may perceive different purposes for the sanctions. Further, international cooperation has been shown to be a key ingredient to sanctions success with the likelihood of success increasing as cooperation increases (McClean and Whang 2010). When the UN Security Council imposed sanctions prohibiting the export of luxury items to the DPRK, it was hardly constraining the activities of the regime or anticipating that the measures would result in the termination of its nuclear program, but rather was signaling the unacceptability of its actions contrary to international non-proliferation norms

(Biersteker, Eckert, and Tourinho 2016, 21). This, however, may also be a matter of states' perception. It is likely that some members of the Council, such as the United States, perceived sanctions on luxury goods to the North Korean political elite as coercive and meant to pressure elites to change their behavior while other members, such as China, saw the sanctions merely as a warning to the regime. When evaluating sanctions' efficacy, these perceptions play an important role in the *perceived* effectiveness of economic sanctions.

It is also necessary to distinguish between the types of sanctions. First, they may be unilateral or multilateral. Frank (2006) notes that multilateral sanctions were rare before 1990 at least partially due to UN restrictions on the use of Security Council sanctions: "According to Article 39 of the UN Charter, the Security Council is allowed to impose sanctions only to maintain or restore international peace and security. . . there must be genuine 'international concern' behind the sanctions" (Frank 2006, 10). Multilateral sanctions are theoretically more effective as they entail coercion by a large number of states, thus magnifying the "hurt" and making the pain more palpable for the object of the sanctions and depriving target states of additional avenues for trade and support (van Bergeijk 1989). The UN and the EU are not the only international organizations that impose economic sanctions. Charron and Portela (2015) found in their study on the UN and regional sanctions imposed throughout Africa that other multilateral regional organizations also play a role in implementing and imposing economic sanctions to manage regional security concerns.

However, in practice, multilateral sanctions are often less effective than unilateral sanctions for two major reasons. As the case of the UN Security Council illustrates, it is difficult for states to even agree upon sanctions. States and their leaders have different foreign policy goals, domestic considerations, and even different perceptions of international events (Jervis 2017). While the United States has been in support of UN sanctions against North Korea since the 1990s, UN Security Council sanctions were not issued until the mid-2000s when China got on board and stopped its threat to use its veto power as one of the five permanent members of the Security Council. Second, multilateral sanctions present a coordination problem: they are often not implemented uniformly. The Panel of Expert reports published by the UN Security Council in monitoring economic sanctions against North Korea and Iran profile a plethora of cases of UN member states abdicating their responsibilities to implement and enforce economic sanctions through their respective legal systems. Returning to Schelling's argument, threats are thus only effective if the object believes that the threat is credible. If states do not follow through on implementing the sanctions, the target of the sanction might not conform to them because it does not see the sanctions as threatening.

Sanctions may also be comprehensive or targeted. The goal of comprehensive sanctions is to impact both the political elites and the population at large to exert maximum pressure on the government to comply with the sanctions. Such sanctions may include those focused on the transportation sector or a core economic sector (Biersteker, Eckert, and Tourinho 2016). In both democratic and authoritarian regimes, leaders would theoretically be responsive to public pressure: democratic leaders rely on popular support to be elected and authoritarian leaders rely on social stability to remain in power. However, comprehensive sanctions raise humanitarian concerns: is the suffering of a country's population worth potential sanction acquiescence? As Haggard and Noland (2017) point out, authoritarian regimes may not be concerned with the public's well-being, thus rendering comprehensive sanctions ineffective. Thus, comprehensive sanctions are becoming internationally taboo (Biersteker, Eckert, and Tourinho 2016), especially as scholars have shed light on the humanitarian issues and human rights concerns resulting from the use of economic sanctions (Batmanghelidj and Moret 2022; Moret 2015; Daher and Moret 2020).

Additionally, their logic may simply backfire, especially if comprehensive economic sanctions, in particular, seek regime change. When the international sector of an economy is hit, there is the risk of inhibiting the growth of a domestic middle class and thereby slowing the indigenous process of democratization. In many cases, there is a high risk that sanctions actually strengthen the regime that they were supposed to weaken. A typical response of a people in the face of sanctions is to "rally around the flag," and support the leadership in the face of foreign coercion (Frank 2006). As several scholars have argued, this was the case in Myanmar, where the military junta blamed the country's economic struggles on the Western-led sanctions regime (Nyun 2008, 484–5). The "rally-round-the-flag" effect is most prominent in authoritarian states where target states often have a mere modicum of economic and social connections to the sender. As such, "strong claims to legitimacy help a regime to withstand external sanctions pressure" by strengthening the cohesiveness of the elite (Grauvogel and von Soest 2014, 643–4; 648). In other words, comprehensive sanctions often do not have their desired effect, especially against regimes that can successfully link legitimation to the regime's very survival.

In other cases, nondemocratic regimes may also be resilient to economic pressures from sanctions. The pressure to capitulate to the imposition of economic sanctions fails because the economic pain often fails to generate political costs (Lektzian and Souva 2007, 849), although there is likely variation in the nature of the authoritarian regime with personalist regimes more susceptible to the costs of sanctions coercion (Peksen 2019b). The variation and potential of sanctions pressures and costs are present across the use of economic sanctions against North Korea, Myanmar, and Iran, our study's three major cases.

The use of multilateral targeted sanctions emerged in the 1990s in an effort to limit the humanitarian effects of economic sanctions, although even smart sanctions impose what Cortright and Lopez call "social pain" (2002, 6; 1995, 2000). Targeted sanctions are intended to focus their impact primarily on the political elite and quite often specific individuals within the elite. These can also include diplomatic sanctions as well as arms embargoes and sanctions on commodity goods (Biersteker, Eckert, and Tourinho 2016). While targeted sanctions avoid the humanitarian issues incurred by comprehensive sanctions, they can also be difficult to implement because they require a thorough knowledge of the targeted country's domestic politics: who are the people that should be targeted and what kind of sanction will force them to act? As Schelling mentions, it is important to know what the object values and fears in order for "the power to hurt" to be effective (Schelling 1977, 4).

Finally, it is important to note that the literature on economic sanctions tends to identify three distinct purposes for economic sanctions. First, coercing a change in behavior is the most common purpose for sanctions. However, economic sanctions may also be used to a second or third purpose: to constrain or to signal (Biersteker, Eckert, and Tourinho 2016, 20–22; Giumelli 2011; Giumelli 2013b, 3). Sanctions can be used to constrain a target's activities, such as making it difficult for the target to construct nuclear weapons. Sanctions can also be used to signal an actor's violation of an international norm, such as nuclear testing violating international non-proliferation norms or violations of human rights that are occurring domestically. Biersteker et al. (2016) find that, out of the three, sanctions used to signal are the most effective: signaling sanctions work 56 percent of the time while constraining and coercive sanctions work 44 percent and 20 percent of the time, respectively (Biersteker, Eckert, and Tourinho 2016, 32). These statistics cast doubt on the effectiveness of economic sanctions.

While the literature's shift to studying the differences in the implementation, perception, and success of targeted, sectoral, or comprehensive sanctions has been important for sanctions research, sanctions, even when "done right," may be undermined by interloping third-party states or sanctions busters. Although sanctions busting received scant attention by sanctions scholars in the past, there is a vast and burgeoning research program around this highly policy-relevant facet of economic sanctions (Early 2009; Caruso 2003, 2005; Demarais 2022; Barry and Kleinberg 2015; Preble 2023; Su 2020; van Bergeijk 1989). Sanctions busters are third-party states that often have trade relations with both the sender and target of the economic sanctions; the trade and foreign aid they provide undermines the effectiveness of economic sanctions by mitigating the economic harm sanctions are meant to impose (Early 2009, 2015; Early and Jadoon 2016; Early and Spice 2015).

Our study specifically explores the role of sanctions busters in helping targets ameliorate the negative impacts of economic sanctions. North Korea, for example, has received sanctions busting trade and foreign aid from not only China, but also Soviet Union/Russia, South Korea, and Japan. European and EU member states have provided significant sanctions busting support to Iran, especially through the provision of oil exports to European customers. Europe/EU had been Iran's largest trading partner for decades prior to the imposition of economic sanctions by the EU. Myanmar, the third pariah state we study, received significant aid and trade from other ASEAN member states as well as aid and trade from China and Japan.

While the role of sanctions busters in undermining the effectiveness and success of any potential economic sanctions is well-known, target states also have tools at their disposal to evade sanctions pressures. Neo- and neoclassical realists, for example, argue that when states are presented with threats that they have the potential to *internally* balance, creating security using domestic resources at their disposal, what Lobell terms "internal resource extraction" (2018, 597; also see Taliaferro 2006). Internal resource extraction taps into a state's existing resource endowments, capabilities, and capacities to generate resources lost when sanctions are imposed. While states targeted by sanctions can seek out new trading partners (i.e., sanctions busting support), states do not rely solely on external substitution—that is, new trading partners. States also have the ability to engage in internal substitution, which reflects a state's domestic production capabilities and ability to produce goods it imports domestically, thus obviating its need for potentially sanctioned goods (Kavaklı, Chatagnier, and Hatipoğlu 2020).

Economic sanctions can only be as effective as the resources sender states devote to enforcing their policies. Businesses are routinely faced with weighing the costs and benefits associated with a firm's pursuit of profits or its compliance with economic sanctions. In some cases, firms play little active role in shaping government policy in areas of foreign policy seen as being beyond their ability to control and influence. Firms may simply perceive complex sanctions environments like those impacting North Korea, Myanmar, and Iran as too problematic and de-risk from these markets (Giumelli and Onderco 2021). Changes in US regulations and a more aggressive pursuit of sanctions busters, especially by European financial institutions (Early and Preble 2020b), have certainly helped to contribute to firms' overcompliance with sanctions to avoid civil and criminal enforcement actions by US regulators or removing risky sanctioned markets from their business portfolios. These efforts to de-risk and overcomply have impacted humanitarian assistance to targeted states impacted by the "comprehensivization of sanctions"

(Mallard, Sabet, and Sun 2020, 124), which makes it difficult for aid providers to finance aid provisions to targeted states as banks are unwilling to risk running afoul of US sanctions regulations (2020, 125). Sanctions enforcement actively seeks to thwart sanction evasion activities, but in doing so has unintended consequences on humanitarian outcomes in target states.

While sanctions busting third-party states explain why economic sanctions are a beleaguered foreign policy tool, sanctions busters are effective at undermining economic sanctions because of the nature of the networks in which trade target states find themselves embedded. One of our principal contributions is the contention that *these networks not only matter but are a necessary condition for understanding why economic sanctions are ineffective.* More importantly, to understand why bargaining with states like North Korea and Myanmar has failed or why the P5+1 successfully negotiated a nuclear deal with Iran, the structure of these networks and the interactions that take place across these linkages must first be understood.

Our research makes two important contributions. First, our study adds to the debate on sanctions' effectiveness and success through our application of the weaponized interdependence framework. Weaponized interdependence highlights how the lack of interconnectivity, and the transience of a target state's trade network complicates efforts by sanctions senders to influence a target's behavior in meaningful ways. This suggests that sanctions may be self-defeating in some cases; by weakening or severing trade network ties, senders may relinquish any economic leverage over target states using panopticon effects, effects generated by policies that gather information and data and monitor the interactions between nodes. The network visualizations we create provide empirical evidence of these network effects and how the target's network of trade can make dramatic shifts (but not always!) at critical junctures when sanctions are imposed by senders. Second, target states have sometimes considerable agency in devising responses to economic sanctions but also in devising policies that change the target's connectedness in the network, demonstrating how targets can adapt to sanctions pressures in a variety of ways.

Our insights have implications for the use of economic sanctions against "hard targets" like North Korea, Myanmar, and Iran. First, economic sanctions should be used in concert with other tools of statecraft, especially diplomacy. Failure to do so may doom sanctions to fail or, worse, lead to humanitarian crises. The use of diplomacy should not involve only the target states but also states that have the potential to undermine the effectiveness of economic sanctions, such as China in the case of North Korea sanctions. The inability of the United States to negotiate with Iran, Myanmar, or North Korea may help to explain why US economic sanctions, adept at causing economic harm to large segments of those countries' populations, have done little to motivate the governments to acquiesce. Second, economic sanctions are unlikely to move the needle of policy change when the sender has little economic leverage over the target or when the target purposefully minimizes its connectedness to portions of the network dominated by sender states. While the United States, for example, can apply financial and economic sanctions against targets, many targets have over time adapted and found ways to evade sanctions, especially with the help of sanctions busting states. The design of economic sanctions should anticipate the ways in which states will resist economic sanctions.

As Farrell and Newman (2019) rightly point out, focusing solely on bilateral dependencies results in a significant loss of information as no target or sender trades with a single state. States exist within vast networks of trade, but also of finance and foreign aid, among others. Across these vast global networks, information and data pass through network nodes, with some nodes being inherently more capable and powerful militarily and economically (like the United States and EU member states) while others are at a disadvantage given their asymmetric position within the network's hierarchical structures of power and opportunity. As discussed in the next section, a weak position within the international community and asymmetrical relationships with more powerful states are key characteristics of so-called "pariah" states. For us, these networks are key intervening variables that can explain the effectiveness or ineffectiveness of sanctions regimes, especially the long-running layers of sanctions that have been imposed on pariah states like North Korea, Myanmar, and Iran.

CASE SELECTION AND RATIONALE

Our book examines three cases of economic sanctions against pariah states: North Korea, Myanmar, and Iran. While there are a multitude of pariah states that have been sanctioned unilaterally or by the EU and UN, our choice to explore North Korea, Myanmar, and Iran as our major cases highlights variation on the spectrum of sanctions success and effectiveness. More importantly, in developing the notion here that network structures matter, identifying variation in the structures of these networks is necessary in understanding the limits of panopticon and chokepoint effects in achieving policy change.

North Korea is our foundational case that provided our initial inspiration for the book. North Korea represents the quintessential "hard target" (Haggard and Noland 2017), but it also represents one of the few sanctions cases that involved economic sanctions imposed on it by myriad sender states and international organizations ranging from the UN to the EU.

Myanmar mirrors North Korea in many ways, especially the regionally focused trade profile. Also, Myanmar has often eschewed greater international linkages in favor of reducing their exposure to the influence of other countries. One clear difference is that Myanmar lacks nuclear weapons, and economic sanctions have been imposed mainly for human rights abuses and violation of democratic norms after elections were overturned by the country's military juntas. Myanmar is a case of sanctions that could have worked if the right senders had imposed them, and many of those countries in East and Southeast Asia refused US entreaties to impose economic sanctions, preferring engagement to isolation.

Iran is a case where interconnectedness and interdependence matter a lot, and it is this interdependence with key actors that makes Iran highly susceptible to Western sanctions when the right actors impose them. Up until the EU member states joined with the United States in imposing an oil embargo and limiting Iran's access to the Society for Worldwide Interbank Financial Telecommunication (SWIFT) and financial markets in the EU, Iran had largely been able to weather US unilateral economic sanctions. Once the UN Security Council imposed economic sanctions on Iran, the EU followed suit and bolstered UN targeted sanctions with its own autonomous sanctions. These multilateral and autonomous UN and EU sanctions coupled with US unilateral sanctions proved too much for an already struggling Iran.

SUMMARY OF FINDINGS AND IMPLICATIONS

We argue that the structure of networks that target states find themselves in is a key variable for understanding the effectiveness and success of economic sanctions. We test our propositions across three cases by looking at the decades-long sanctions regimes levied against North Korea, Myanmar, and Iran. North Korea is a case where the network structures are malleable as North Korea not only adjusts its connections to trading partners for its licit trade but generates new connections to illicit trading partners. Our analysis of North Korea shows that too much isolation and too little engagement and monitoring, which bring vital information to more powerful states in the network, undermine the ability of economic sanctions to achieve their goals. We further explore North Korea's agency and the complexity of its interactions with key trading partners through an in-depth case study.

In the case of Myanmar, we find that targets whose commercial interests are largely regional will have limited connectivity within the network. Myanmar shows that its ties to Southeast Asia, China, Japan, and India limit the ability of nodes outside the region, namely the US and EU member states, to effectively wield their economic power through sanctions to effect policy change.

The largely symbolic use of economic sanctions served as a form of "public relations" that drew attention to the plights of Nobel Peace Prize winner Aung San Suu Kyi, her National League for Democracy (NLD), and the suffering of everyday Myanmar citizens under a brutal regime. The case of Myanmar demonstrates that economic sanctions work best when the actors with the greatest interdependence and leverage are engaged in generating chokepoint effects. Myanmar's neighbors, especially other members of ASEAN, opted, we argue, to generate panopticon effects through policy choices that brought Myanmar into ASEAN rather than choke off commercial ties with Myanmar.

The final case of Iran shows the power of weaponized interdependence. Decades of US economic sanctions had little impact on Iran. While the humanitarian impacts and problematic economic developments in the country (namely inflationary pressures) harmed the country, the regime remained steadfast. The EU, despite US secondary sanctions, remained Iran's largest trading partner for decades before the imposition of economic sanctions. The EU, well-placed to weaponize its interdependence, employed well-timed targeted sanctions that isolated Iran from the European financial system along with a near total embargo on Iranian oil. Our study of Iran's network and associated measures of degree and strength centrality demonstrate high levels of interdependence that the EU successfully weaponized through coordination with the United States. These pressures compelled Iran to return to the negotiating table, which led, thanks to European efforts of engagement early on, to the creation and adoption of the JCPOA on October 18, 2015.

Because network configurations and structures matter, policymakers would do well to explore the full extent of licit and illicit trade and commerce of target states. Sanctions, we argue, are more likely to work when there are not only the right policies but also the right actors taking part. US policymakers should consider using their vast resources to put together sanctioning coalitions of the proper actors rather than relying solely on the use of unilateral comprehensive economic sanctions, efforts that have pushed many countries to develop creative ways to avoid US economic sanctions pressures.

PLAN OF THE BOOK

Our book proceeds with the following six chapters. Chapter 1 introduces the weaponized interdependence framework developed by Farrell and Newman (2019) and situates our argument within that framework. We see the structure of networks as a critical intervening variable for understanding the potential for effective sanctions and successful sanctions and discuss how we employ tools of social network analysis (SNA) to test our propositions. Chapter 2 introduces our flagship case of North Korea, which, in our estimation, represents one of the most challenging implementations of economic sanctions against a target state. We explore the network structure and dynamics of North Korean licit and illicit trade. Chapter 3 introduces a detailed case study of North Korea's relationship with key trading partners within its network: China, South Korea, Japan, Russia, and the United States. The case studies highlight North Korea's agency in response to US economic sanctions and how other trading partners have interacted with North Korea as it has sought to develop its WMD program. Chapter 4 turns to the case of Myanmar, which explores how its key trading partners opted to generate panopticon effects through policies of engagement. We explore how Myanmar's membership in ASEAN provided its members with access to information and data as well as with channels to monitor developments in Myanmar. Chapter 5 explores the case of Iran, our "success" case. We explore how Iran's historical interdependence and commercial ties with the EU made Iran highly susceptible to EU targeted sanctions. We argue that the EU's engagement and ties to Iran and US cooperation provided the EU with the means to bring about the realization of the JCPOA. Our final chapter introduces two shadow cases, Russia and Cuba, which show how trading network structures impact the effectiveness of economic sanctions. We then conclude our book with policy implications that emerge from our analysis.

Chapter 1

Theorizing Trade Network Linkages and Sanctions

Our study seeks to understand why US economic sanctions are ineffective in bringing about policy change in cases where sanctions are applied to countries it sees as pariahs. This unique "club" of states has included: Cuba, Iran, Iraq, Libya, Myanmar (Burma), Nigeria, North Korea, Panama, Russia, Serbia/Yugoslavia, South Africa, Sudan, and Zimbabwe. Each of these states has been not only heavily sanctioned by the United States but also features prominently in US foreign policy discourse in both Congress and the Executive Branch (Woolley and Peters 1999). A puzzle that motivates our study is the power asymmetry between the United States and these pariahs: US economic and military power should provide the United States with a significant advantage in bringing about policy change yet often fails to do so. While the United States has been successful in bringing about significant change in a few of these pariahs, such as Panama and South Africa, other pariahs have withstood United States and, in some cases, EU and UN economic sanctions and resisted efforts to capitulate to the senders' demands. Why have economic sanctions been unable to break the *status quo* and bring about policy change?

Our research has identified three types of trade networks (table 1.1). Each of these networks represents a particular pattern of trade and features unique structural properties that allow us to distinguish them from one another. It is important to note that these networks are not mutually exclusive, remembering that networks are dynamic and that a target state's network may encompass any of these types across time.

The *Black Knight* network is one in which the target state is highly reliant on a single state (or perhaps even two states) for a significant majority of or, in some cases, nearly all of its trade and economic transactions. While the target state in such a network may trade with dozens of other states,

Table 1.1 Network Configurations

Network Type	*Properties*
Black Knight	Target state relies on a single trading partner for trade and political support.
Isolated	Target state's trade is largely regional even before the imposition of economic sanctions.
Interdependent	Target state's economy and trade are highly dependent on global trade and financial networks.

Source: Created by Authors.

the share of trade tends to concentrate in a single state while the remaining share of trade is distributed across the remaining potential trading partners although such shares tend to be minuscule. The DPRK's network, for example, after the imposition of economic sanctions largely resembles a *Black Knight* network as nearly all of its trading and economic activity comes from or involves China. *Isolated* networks are those in which the target state's trade is largely regional with the lion's share of economic activity occurring among the target state's regional partners. DPRK trade prior to the imposition of sanctions with its trade split largely between China, Japan, and South Korea represents such a network. Myanmar's trade is also typical of an *Isolated* network as most of Myanmar's economic engagement remains squarely in Southeast and East Asia, becoming even more regionally focused over time. The last network type we identify is an *Interdependent* one. An *Interdependent* network is one like Iran's in which the target state's trade and economic activity are highly dependent on global trade and financial networks. Target states that trade with sanctions imposing sender states or require financial and trade networks to carry out vital economic activity tend to have networks of this type. States within *Interdependent* networks are highly susceptible, we argue, to weaponized interdependence under the proper conditions.

Using the weaponized interdependence framework developed by Farrell and Newman (2019), we theorize that the structure of the networks and the connections between the senders of economic sanctions are critical intervening variables; the targets of these economic sanctions and their connectedness to the bevy of third-party states trading with both the sender and target *matter*. The networks in which targets find themselves—either by design (North Korea) or by circumstance (Myanmar)—have unique structures and qualities that make it difficult for economic sanctions to impact the target state. Conversely, states with greater connectedness, like Iran, are much more susceptible to panopticon and chokepoint effects due to the structure of their network and the nature of the trade linkages between the target and its major trading partners (such as Iran and the EU).

When targets are able to reshape the very structure of the network in which they reside, by canceling and creating new linkages or "walks," they are able to withstand and ameliorate the "pain" of economic sanctions, as in the North Korea case. In other cases such as Myanmar, the target state finds itself in a network where senders are minimally engaged with them. This lack of economic engagement gives the sender not only very little economic engagement "to choke off" but also means that there are few opportunities for panopticon effects to gather information and monitor targets. In cases where sanctions are *effective*, like the Iran sanctions regime, economic engagement provides the means through which interdependence can be effectively weaponized (Table 1.2).

The sender's use of economic sanctions creates an imbalance between the *panopticon* and *chokepoint effects* it generates (Preble and Willis 2024b). This imbalance occurs because the chokepoint effects created by the implementation of economic sanctions undermine the ability of sender states to gather the information necessary to monitor target states and collect necessary and critical data. These necessary and critical data provide policymakers with the necessary "raw materials" to construct and adapt effective economic sanctions.

As chokepoint effects increase, cut off, and isolate target states from key nodes in the network, the potential of panopticon effects to collect information and monitor the target state's activities diminishes and, in some cases, even disappears. These panopticon effects emanate from policies implemented by governments over the key nodes they control, policies that are often created to capture information and monitor traffic within the network. This traffic can take many forms, such as cellular phone data and calls and financial flows, which impart tremendous amounts of information (Farrell and Newman 2019, 55). We also see licit and illicit trade as another form of traffic integral to interstate relations where flows of goods (and services) can tell a lot about the nature of a relationship between two nodes within a network.

Panopticon effects are generated by policies that are designed to monitor and collect information on how other nodes in the network are engaging with the node generating the panopticon effects. In the United States, the implementation and passage of the Patriot Act (2001) and Bank Secrecy Act (1970) allow the government and financial institutions, respectively, to collect information on constituents within and outside the United States that make use of the United States' financial system. The joint economic projects between the Republic of Korea (ROK) and North Korea (DPRK) are another example of a panopticon effect by providing ROK businesses and officials with important information, critical due to the scarcity of information and data exiting and entering North Korea. Diplomatic engagement may also generate panopticon effects. The presence of an embassy

Table 1.2 Summary of Sanctions Success and Trading Networks in North Korea, Myanmar, and Iran

Case/Country	Dependent Variable	Independent Variables	Intervening Variable	Target Behavior
North Korea (DPRK)	Sanctions failure	Comprehensive and targeted US, EU, and UN trade and financial sanctions. China as "black knight."	Network type: isolated, black knight Network structure that *adapts* due to NK's agency in finding new licit trading partners and tapping into illicit trade network.	Dramatic changes in the structure of the trading network.
Myanmar (Burma)	Sanctions failure	Modest trade and financial sanctions by the US, EU member states. Lack of chokepoint effects generated by key trading partners in Southeast Asia and China.	Network type: isolated Network structure that prioritizes regional trade with other Association for Southeast Asian Nations (ASEAN) member states, China, and Japan and shields Myanmar from Western efforts to punish it.	Network remains relatively stable. Myanmar's connectedness outside its region is minimal.
Iran	Sanctions success	Comprehensive and targeted trade and financial sanctions involving the US, EU, and UN. Iranian agency with efforts to increase trade ties with UAE, Turkey, European countries, and China.	Network type: interdependent Network structure that is highly dependent on connections to key nodes in Europe makes Iran susceptible to chokepoint effects.	Network makes minor adjustments but reliance on key trading partners makes eschewing such connections difficult.

Source: Created by Authors.

and diplomatic engagement may also provide states with an opportunity to collect and gather information on the states in which they are located. ASEAN countries' decision to admit Myanmar to the regional organization is another example of diplomatic (and economic) engagement generating panopticon effects. This information—regardless of its form and medium—captured through myriad panopticon effects generated by key nodes is itself a source of power. More critically, the information gleaned through the generation of panopticon effects provides key nodes with the necessary resources to create "blueprints" for the design of effective and potent chokepoint effects.

Chokepoint effects emanate from the policies of powerful nodes in the network that isolate other nodes within the network by prohibiting the ability of other nodes to connect to it. Farrell and Newman posit that supply chains, for example, can be weaponized (2019, 44). Firms can stifle competition by choking off competitors by limiting their access to key suppliers. States and firms in concert or in opposition can implement policies or make business decisions, respectively, that isolate and sideline rivals and competitors. Chokepoint effects can also be generated by the imposition of strategic trade controls whereby one state limits the ability of competitor states to purchase particular types of dual-use goods or high-tech goods. Some states may also impose investment bans by limiting the amount of firms' investment from certain countries in an effort to protect nascent domestic industry or for political motives. Banks may also generate chokepoint effects through business operations, which are shaped by risk and compliance imperatives. In high-risk locales, banks may generate chokepoint effects by developing business policies that limit the ability of foreign banks to make use of correspondent banking. Economic sanctions are one type of policy that generates chokepoint effects, a potent economic weapon fashioned from the "blueprints" from the data and information captured by key nodes' panopticon effects.

"Economic sanctions" is a broad term that can encompass a number of different policy provisions: travel bans, blacklisting of individuals and companies, import and export bans, as well as a multitude of financial sanctions that limit the use of another state's currency or financial system. They are just one type of policy that states and some international organizations like the UN and EU employ that generate chokepoint effects. The United States, one of the principal senders of economic sanctions, generates numerous chokepoint effects through the implementation of economic sanctions against states around the world. Diplomatic isolation is another policy that generates a chokepoint effect through limiting target nodes' ability to participate in international organizations or operate an embassy or consulate in another node. Russia's recent invasion of Ukraine has shown the ways in which states' policies that have sought to isolate Russia diplomatically have limited the ability of Russia's diplomatic representatives and their staff from fulfilling their mandates (Gijs 2022), which often works in tandem with other chokepoint effects.

The form and intensity of sanctions regimes are dependent upon data and information captured by panopticon effects. Yet, once chokepoint effects isolate and sever connections, the ability of panopticon effects to capture the same level and intensity of information and data likely diminishes. As we discuss in chapters 2 and 3 on North Korea, for example, economic sanctions, which generate chokepoint effects, limited the ability of states like South Korea and Russia to continue joint economic projects that generated panopticon effects through not only the provision of information and data but also through the ability to monitor the DPRK.

Target states like the pariahs in our study actively resist economic sanctions by relying on and encouraging sanctions busting trade (Early 2009, 2015; Early and Spice 2015) or on the support of a "black knight," third-party states that provide significant sanctions busting aid for political rather than solely commercial reasons (Early 2011; Hufbauer et al. 2009). The Soviet Union and China are two prominent black knights, having provided Cuba and North Korea, respectively, with substantial aid to help the regimes of both states counter and undermine US economic pressure and efforts to bring about regime and policy change. Only states with significant economic resources close to or on par with those of the United States have the potential to play such a role and are likely to do so even because the benefits of providing politically fraught support outweigh the costs. Yet when a black knight appears, sanctions regimes must be altered to account for this economic support that undermines the effectiveness and potential for the sanctions to succeed.

Without updated and steady streams of data and information, adjustments to economic sanctions policies become difficult. Sender nodes—nodes imposing economic sanctions on target states (or nodes)—must make some "best guesses" on how to alter their sanctions regimes as the ability to acquire or capture information and data diminishes as nodes targeted by economic sanctions are denied access to the sender node. Key nodes, which once employed policies that generated vital panopticon effects, have now lost the ability to collect updated data and information on target states. Information that was vital for the initial policy design is now missing as these designs need to be restructured. This dynamic, we argue, diminishes the effectiveness of economic sanctions and their potential for success.

Our study focuses primarily on economic linkages (or "walks") through licit (and, in some cases illicit) trade between nodes (i.e., states) to show how the structure of these networks helps us to understand why economic sanctions fail to bring about behavioral changes in these pariah states. The economic linkages we study take the form of trade flows between countries, which provide a useful measure of economic dependence and interdependence among states in the network.

When economic sanctions are implemented on target states that trade significantly with key nodes in the network, there is likely to be a reduction in trade as states, firms, and constituents weigh the costs and benefits of maintaining trading relationships. We theorize that economic sanctions are likely to be the most effective at achieving their goals when the target state's connections within the network are vast and unchanging. Our case study in Iran provides an excellent example of how it remained susceptible to Western coordinated efforts to bring about a resolution to its budding nuclear program with the eventual signing of the Joint Comprehensive Plan of Action (JCPOA) in 2013. When states are able to refashion their trading networks, like North Korea, or have regional foci, like Myanmar, the ability of economic sanctions to result in policy or regime change is unlikely.

Our argument *is not* premised on the logic that sanctions have *no effect* on these pariah states. In fact, the economic and humanitarian costs borne by states targeted by economic sanctions can be severe and damaging to societies, impacting public health and other humanitarian outcomes (Moret 2015; Batmanghelidj and Moret 2022; Peksen 2011). Yet, despite the pain that economic sanctions bring to many states, target state governments often develop capabilities to resist the impacts of economic sanctions. We show that these pariahs have significant *agency* by seeking out ways to resist and mitigate the impact of economic sanctions. We seek to operationalize agency through the use of social network analysis (SNA), which we address in the next section. Our study is motivated by two key questions. First, why are many pariah states positioned to avoid the pain of economic sanctions? Second, why is it that Iran found itself susceptible to coordinated economic sanctions by the United States, EU, and the UN, while North Korea and Myanmar have largely evaded sanctions pressures? We see the structure of these networks as critically important intervening variables that help to explain why economic sanctions often fail with pariah states. To understand the ability of countries to evade sanctions, we must first understand the structure of the licit and illicit networks of trade these states have constructed.

The cases detailed in this book represent a range of sanctioned states' trading networks. The DPRK case highlights the failure of economic sanctions. Some observers have argued that China provides critical "black knight" support, which explains why and how North Korea has been able to resist US and UN economic sanctions. *Our study on North Korea demonstrates the limitations of economic sanctions when states lose access to flows of information and data, muting the effectiveness and success of the chokepoint effects generated by the economic sanctions.* While China's role is prominent in helping North Korea mitigate the pain of economic sanctions, China's role obscures the efforts of other sanctions busting third-party states seeking to capitalize on emergent commercial opportunities from the imposition of the economic sanctions even when such countries *support UN sanctions* against North Korea, such as Russia and India. Focusing solely on China's role also ignores North Korea's agency, emboldened by its country's *juche* (self-reliance) philosophy. As our analysis shows, North Korea has been able to not only refashion its trade network but has also grown a complementary network of illicit trade developed in the 1970s to further undermine US economic sanctions. North Korea has developed an unrivaled playbook of sanctions evasion that has allowed its nuclear weapons and ballistic missile research to continue stridently. Economic sanctions, we argue, have largely failed as North Korea's pursuit of nuclear and ballistic missile technology capable of carrying nuclear warheads to the United States continues.

Iran, on the other hand, represents a sanctions success story by showing the power and potential of both panopticon and chokepoint effects. The case demonstrates the ways in which the E3 (Germany, France, and the UK) worked to bring about policy change and then worked with the larger European Union (EU) and the United States to deploy a blistering array of economic sanctions against Iran. Their combined efforts left Iran with little choice but to negotiate the JCPOA in an effort to push the West to roll back a significant portion of economic sanctions levied against it (Cronberg 2017a, 2017b; Tarock 2016). While US economic sanctions have been relentlessly applied against Iran, the E3 (the original three EU countries that worked to negotiate with Iran) and the collective grouping of EU member states have taken a much more targeted approach by privileging diplomatic and economic engagement over isolation. The balance struck between the EU's ability to generate panopticon effects through Iran's use of SWIFT and the linkages delivering Iranian energy and oil to Europe allowed it to refine and target economic sanctions much more potently and effectively with the United States than either sender could do individually. Iran's ability to wield agency like North Korea is limited by its reliance and dependence on key exports to European partners as well as China, Russia, and regional players such as the United Arab Emirates (UAE). Iranian dependence on European revenue and access to EU financial markets makes it much more susceptible to economic sanctions, which played a key role in resolving the nuclear standoff with Iran by providing the US and EU partners with the ability to weaponize the EU's interdependence with Iran.

Finally, the case of Myanmar, a case in which sanctions largely failed to achieve senders' objectives, demonstrates how the structure of the network matters in whether economic sanctions have the potential to be impactful. This case shows United States and international sanctions against Myanmar are limited when sender states' economic linkages are meager, and the target's network of trade is largely concentrated regionally and remains "unglobalized." While Myanmar had some trade to the West and trade and investment from the West throughout the period of sanctions under study (1988–2012), Myanmar's principal trading partners, countries well-placed to collect information and monitor through the generation of panopticon effects, failed to exercise leverage through the imposition of economic sanctions and failed to generate chokepoint effects (Jones 2015). The inability and unwillingness of Myanmar's key trading partners—China, India, Japan, and ASEAN members Singapore, Thailand, Malaysia, Indonesia—to weaponize interdependence and leverage their economic linkages meant that the country was largely numb to sanctions pressures. Sanctions from Western states such as the United States and members of the EU did not make much of an impact in terms of Burmese policy or regime change as these senders were largely detached from Myanmar's trade profile. The imposition of economic sanctions had little impact on Myanmar's human rights violations and reinforced Myanmar's commitment to regional trade and economic engagement with neighbors. To explore the dynamics of weaponized interdependence and sanctions ineffectiveness and failure, we utilize SNA to develop several hypotheses that test the validity of our theory across these three cases.

SOCIAL NETWORK ANALYSIS

Social science and international relations more broadly have been slow to embrace SNA. SNA can be both descriptive and inferential through the use of exponential random graph models (ERGMs) and their respective variants. Such models can be difficult to implement, although a number of packages in R and other statistical software have helped to make SNA less arduous to implement.

Our study utilizes UN Comtrade (United Nations 2021) data, as well as Inter-Korean trade data (East-West Center and National Committee on North Korea 2019) for our case on North Korea. We employ SNA to develop and analyze undirected networks of the target states to explore our hypotheses by first generating geospatial visualizations using UN Comtrade data (Knapp 2017). These figures visualize the ability of states targeted by economic sanctions to insulate themselves from economic sanctions by changing the structure and form of their trading network and increasing their connections throughout the network. To understand the effect of economic sanctions on our target states, an analysis of the social network based on trade linkages (imports and exports in any given year) demonstrates how these relationships can change across time as economic sanctions are implemented and imposed on target states—in some cases leading to dramatic shifts while in others having little to no impact at all.

SNA relies on three key assumptions. First, structural relations are key to understanding what "observed behaviors"—in this case, trade flows—occur between actors in the network (Knoke and Yang 2020, 8). For example, the trade network in which North Korea operates helps to explain not only how and why North Korea behaves the way it does toward its trading partners but also helps to explain those observed behaviors of other states connected to North Korea within the network. In the case of Myanmar, the trade network helps to explain why Western sanctions had little impact as well as the potential for chokepoint effects on the part of Myanmar's Southeast Asian neighbors.

Second, the direct contacts within these social networks are the result of social interaction (Knoke and Yang 2020, 8–9). In other words, the linkages or walks that connect one node to another is a result of some interaction. In considering the cases presented here, it is through social interactions that North Korea, Myanmar, or Iran can influence and be influenced by its trading partners. Given the preponderance of trade that North Korea has conducted in the past with China, Japan, and South Korea, the trade linkages between these states would indicate that these three countries potentially have greater influence and leverage over other aspects of North Korean foreign policy than the United States, whose "walks" or linkages to North Korea are minimal at best.

Lastly, the network in which these countries trade, behave, and interact is dynamic. Such networks are said to be constantly changing, forming, and reforming as social relations between these states alter the network (Knoke and Yang 2020, 9–10). The fact that the structure of networks can adapt, shift, and change reflects the agency of the nodes or actors present in the network, severing ties and creating new ties as the political and policy contexts between nodes in the network fluctuate. As we argue here, the structure of the network serves as a key intervening variable that determines the limits and potential of economic sanctions. We rely on two key measurements that are common in SNA, degree and strength centrality measures, to which we now turn.

DEGREE CENTRALITY

Degree centrality captures the total number of connections or walks for each node in the network. It demonstrates not only the number of ties for nodes in the network but also the overall size of the network (Borgatti et al. 2022, 171). The more linkages a node has, the higher the degree centrality that node will possess. Our study utilizes an undirected network that counts a linkage or walk as any time imports or exports are exchanged between the target states in our study and their respective trading partners. Degree centrality

Figure 1.1 Comparison of North Korea's Degree Centrality (Share of Trading Partners) and the Number of Trading Partners, 1990–2017. *Source*: Created by Authors.

thus represents the number of trading partners our given target states have in any given year.

Degree centrality can be misleading. Figure 1.1 shows North Korea's degree centrality over time as the share of trading partners in each year (left *y*-axis) along with the count of the Hermit Kingdom's unique trading partners in the bars for any given year (right *y-axis*). North Korea's trading partners have increased over time, yet the measurement fails to convey the *depth* or *strength* of the trade linkages between North Korea and these trading partners. In many cases, as our analysis in chapter 2 explores, many of these linkages lack depth. An increase in the number of trading partners might give the impression that North Korea's global reach through trade is growing, yet, as our measures of strength centrality demonstrate, many of these linkages are superficial, representing only a meager fraction of North Korea's total annual trade.

STRENGTH CENTRALITY

Strength centrality measures the depth or intensity of the linkage between two nodes in a network using the volumes of trade rather than trade linkages (De Benedictus et al. 2013, 25). For our study, we construct two measures of strength centrality (Table 1.3).

Table 1.3 Description of Strength Centrality Measures

Measure Name	*Description*	*Calculation*
Measure of Strength Centrality 1 (MOSC1)	Trading Partner's Share of Target's Total Annual Trade	(trading partner's imports + exports with target)/ *Target's total annual trade*
Measure of Strength Centrality 2 (MOSC2)	Target's Share of Trading Partner's Total Annual Trade	(target state's imports + exports with trading partner) / *Trading partner's annual trade*

Source: Created by Authors.

MEASURE OF STRENGTH CENTRALITY

These measures of strength centrality capture the intensity of the connection between two nodes in the network, the state targeted by economic sanctions and one of its trading partners. The first measure of strength centrality (MOSC1) captures the intensity of the sanctions busting conducted by the target state's trading partners. In other words, how important the target state is to the target's trading partner (and potential sanctions buster). MOSC1 is a useful measure of sanctions busting trade and is analogous to commercial dependence.

As De Benedictus et al. (2013) note, strength centrality is synonymous with trade share or commercial dependence. It provides us with a measure of the depth of the commercial linkage and dependence on trade conducted with the pariah state by a third-party sanctions busting state. More importantly, it allows us to compare not only the level of interdependence between the target and a trading partner but also the level of interdependence among competing trading partners. Figure 1.2 shows five of Myanmar's trading partners and their respective trade share or commercial dependence. As Figure 1.2 shows, during the period in which Myanmar is sanctioned by the West, many states maintain ties via sanctions busting trade to Myanmar despite the human rights abuses by the military junta.

The second measure of strength centrality (MOSC2) operationalizes our concept of agency, efforts through which the target state seeks to change its circumstances in the face of economic sanctions by avoiding and evading them, isolating their trade to a particular region, or seeking support from a 'black knight.' It captures the importance of the target's trade to any given trading partner (and potential sanctions buster) of the target state. Target states change their circumstances by seeking to increase their trade with trading partners willing to sanctions bust to compensate for the negative effects of economic sanctions. MOSC2 captures the target state's share of any given trading partner's total annual trade (Figure 1.3). Figure 1.3 shows the MOSC2 values between Iran and key trading partners, UAE, Turkey, Greece,

Figure 1.2 Myanmar Trading Partners and Their Respective Trade Shares (MOSC1), 1980–2017. *Source*: Created by Authors.

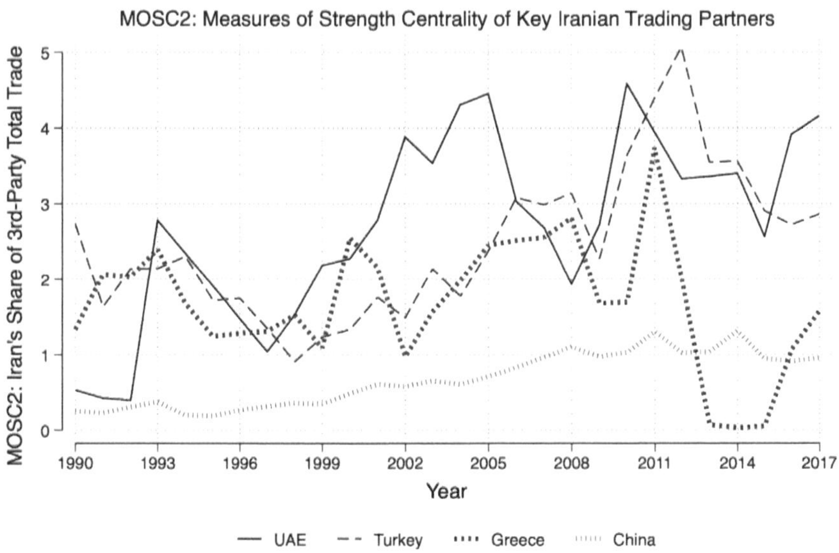

Figure 1.3 Target State's Share of Any Given Trading Partner's Total Annual Trade (MOSC2). We argue that MOSC2 represents a way to capture a country's agency. We posit that as this value increases, the sanctioned state seeks to create greater dependence and independence with its trading partner. *Source*: Created by Authors.

and China. We expect this value to be low or even zero for the sender state, which, in wanting to impose the toughest sanctions possible, will reduce or even eliminate its exports to and imports from the target state. However, for the four states profiled here, Iran's economic engagement with each rises as sanctions against Iran increase reflecting Iran's efforts to avoid the pain of economic sanctions. Greece represents an exception where Iran's ability to trade with Greece is severely diminished by the imposition of EU sanctions, reflecting the effectiveness of EU autonomous sanctions.

The relationship between MOSC1 and MOSC2 can shed light on the nature of the ties between two nodes or states in the network. In our case study on North Korea, we show how China's share of North Korea's annual trade grows substantially as the number and intensity of economic sanctions increases and prominent sanctions busters Japan and South Korea withdraw their economic engagement.

North Korea's commercial dependence on China grows considerably (right *y*-axis) while there is a steep decline of DPRK's share of China's total trade (left *y*-axis) that plateaus and grows slightly as international sanctions against North Korea increase after each nuclear and ballistic missile test (Figure 1.4). Figure 1.4 shows not only that economic sanctions are not impacting licit trade but also reflect the "black knight" trade dynamics. Even as North Korea's trading partners increase over time, China serves as a critical lifeline for North

Figure 1.4 DPRK's Strength Centrality Measures with the People's Republic of China (PRC). *Source*: Created by Authors.

Korea as economic sanctions imposed by the United States and other key former trading partners—such as South Korea and Japan—generate chokepoint effects that isolate and limit North Korea's access to other nodes in the network.

CONCLUSION

As the case studies which follow demonstrate, North Korea represents a case of extreme agency. As one of the most heavily sanctioned states in the world, North Korea has developed impressive capabilities in evading economic sanctions by shifting to trading partners willing to engage in trade-based sanctions busting while also leveraging illicit networks of trade and finance and other activities to mitigate the effects of economic sanctions. Myanmar, on the other hand, is relatively "immune" to the impact of economic sanctions due to its regional trade profile. While the economic effects harmed the general population of Myanmar considerably, the military junta that has dominated Myanmar has been relatively untouched by the impact of economic sanctions (Jones 2015; Nyun 2008). The very states that could have had an impact on Myanmar through the generation of chokepoint effects sought instead to generate panopticon effects through diplomatic engagement with the military junta that culminated in bringing Myanmar into ASEAN in 1997.

Of our three cases, Iran represents an important success case. Iran's dependence on these markets for trade (especially energy exports to Europe) provided Europe with significant leverage that helped bring Iran to the negotiating table. Iranian interdependence with European countries and the EU allowed them to generate panopticon effects that provided useful data about Iran. More importantly, these effects were generated by diplomatic and economic engagement. SWIFT, for example, which collects information on how banks utilize the European and global financial system, captured significant quantities of data that could then be leveraged against Iran to undermine its efforts to develop nuclear weapons as the EU negotiated sanctions packages to target the regime and ultimately weaponized its interdependence with Iran to help Washington lead to the eventual signing of the JCPOA.

While the literature has made strides in studying and understanding the impacts and effects of sanctions busting (Barry and Kleinberg 2015; Caruso 2003, 2005; Early 2009, 2015, 2021), the efforts and maneuvers of target states have not been as sufficiently explored. How states respond to and cope with the imposition of economic sanctions varies considerably with some states more well-placed to make adjustments to their trade networks and exercise *agency*. We seek to move beyond the sender bias in the economic sanctions literature (Peksen 2019a) by exploring the ways in which target states *actively* seek to undermine and avoid economic sanctions rather than be seen as mere captives to great powers.

Chapter 2

De-weaponized Interdependence

The North Korea Sanctions Regime

North Korea is one of the most heavily sanctioned countries in the world and is considered by many to be a pariah state, states that are often estranged from the international community or great power support (Harkavy 1981, 136). Like Venezuela, Myanmar, and Iran, North Korea has endured decades of economic sanctions by a multitude of senders, from the United States and the EU to the UN. North Korea's first nuclear test in 2006 led the UN Security Council (UNSC) to pass a series of resolutions sanctioning North Korea for its provocative behavior. The passage of the first resolution, UNSCR 1695, was particularly notable because it was the first time that China, a permanent member and a long-time ally of North Korea, voted in favor of a resolution sanctioning North Korea. Since UNSCR 1695, the UNSC has imposed increasingly stringent sanctions on North Korea, corresponding with North Korea's subsequent nuclear and ballistic missile tests, in an attempt to rein in North Korea's nuclear development program and provocative behavior. These sanctions, which range from sanctions of trade and finance to arms embargoes, have culminated in a total ban on nearly all trade that have limited not only North Korean exports but also imports into the Hermit Kingdom.

Despite the multitude of unilateral and multilateral sanctions levied on North Korea, North Korea's nuclear and ballistic weapons development program has continued largely unabated, and the Kim regime lives on with regime collapse unlikely. North Korea's resilience is remarkable. It has endured famines and natural disasters and has been undeterred by efforts of great powers to coerce it into abandoning its nuclear weapons program. Why has North Korea been so adept at avoiding the pressures of economic sanctions? Several scholars have engaged with this question. Most recently, Haggard and Noland (2017) argued that a key reason is that the North Korean government has been able to insulate itself by shielding "key bases of political support" within North Korea (29). We agree that domestic politics provides a critical lens for understanding North Korea's resilience, but we find that this is only part of the picture. We argue that the implementation and enforcement of economic sanctions by senders led North Korea to alter its trading network, reallocating its trade to other countries, or nodes, within its network. North Korea operates with considerable agency and does not remain passive in the face of blistering economic sanctions imposed on its economy, allowing North Korea to readjust its connections within the network, which limits the ability of senders to weaponize effectively the interdependence between them and North Korea. It is not solely about passing the pain of economic sanctions onto the populace but also insulating the regime from the coercive potential of senders targeting North Korea (Preble and Willis 2024b).

Employing social network analysis (SNA) using UN trade data from 1990 to 2017, we find that a key reason North Korea has been able to evade sanctions pressures is that economic sanctions represent a paradox: they have been successful at isolating North Korea but less effective in meeting their objectives of regime change or undermining North Korea's military readiness, denuclearization, and inhibiting the country's ballistic missile development. Our SNA helps visualize the empirical evidence of this paradox. From our analysis, we find that the structure of North Korea's network of licit trade changes in notable ways as senders of economic sanctions reduce or restrict their economic engagement, isolating North Korea from international networks of trade, finance, and investment. First, as this isolation deepens, the breadth of North Korea's trade profile expands, and we attribute this expansion to its need to replace lost markets due to the imposition of economic sanctions.

Second, as the breadth of North Korea's trade profile grows, North Korea begins to rely almost exclusively on China for its conventional trade, which results in a "black knight" pattern of trade. Black knights are states whose efforts at undermining and busting sanctions is driven less by commercial opportunities and more for political purposes (Early 2011; Hufbauer et al. 2009). Black knight trade patterns emerge when a trading state facing economic sanctions seeks relief and support from a major trading partner; this pattern of trade is evidenced when a majority of a country's imports and exports come from a single source, as is the case with North Korea and China. More critically, the ability of other states to weaponize interdependence with a target state wanes as the black knight becomes central to the former's network of trade.

As we illustrate, North Korea's trade network shows remarkable pliability as it adapts to international pressures of economic sanctions that countries within and outside the region impose on North Korea. SNA highlights the ways in which economic sanctions can induce changes in the very structure of the network over time as target states adapt to sanctions costs, creating the necessary conditions for a black knight to emerge. As economic sanctions are imposed, North Korea has shifted its trading relations to countries less willing to enforce sanctions (such as China) while becoming less economically dependent on trade partners who do enforce sanctions (e.g., Japan, South Korea, and Western countries).

THE RATIONALE (AND FAILURE) OF SANCTIONS AGAINST NORTH KOREA

Both individual countries, such as the United States, and multilateral institutions, such as the EU, whose restrictive measures aimed at North Korea have largely aligned with the United States (Giumelli 2023, 390–1), and UNSC, have imposed sanctions on North Korea. Sanctions have involved varying objectives from slowing down the development and growth of its military and to bringing about regime change and later—via UN sanctions—halting the development of its nuclear and ballistic missile programs. Sanctions can be both positive and negative (Baldwin 1985), and most analyses of negative sanctions imposed on North Korea conclude that they have failed by several metrics, as evidenced by the continuity of these programs (Frank 2006; Habib 2016; J. Park and Walsh 2016). Peksen and Peterson (2016), though, argue that senders are more likely to threaten or impose economic sanctions when there is significant dependence on the target but conditional on the target's *limited ability* to redirect trade to third-party states. A state like North Korea where North Korea demonstrates nearly zero dependence on the United States while also having access to the enormous Chinese market calls into question the strategic motives of US economic sanctions against North Korea, potentially undermining US credibility in successfully implementing and enforcing sanctions against the Hermit Kingdom. Such dynamics may also reflect the ineffectiveness of economic sanctions as suitable costly signals (Whang and Kim 2015), which may underscore how US economic sanctions fail to resonate with the DPRK elite.

The success of sanctions often requires credible and costly commitments. In the cases of the South African and Libyan sanctions regimes, for example, the international community's credible commitment facilitated their effectiveness (H. Kim 2014, 93). Conversely, a major reason why the sanctions against North Korea have not been effective is that some states in the international community have not credibly committed to the sanctions regime. For example, while UNSC members China and Russia eventually agreed to impose UN sanctions on North Korea following its first nuclear test in 2006 in theory, they have been reticent to enforce them in practice and are two of North Korea's most prominent sanctions busting trade partners (Noland 2009); 77; Panel of Experts 2020, 2019, 2018, 2017b, 2017a, 2016, 2015, 2014, 2013, 2012, 2011, 2010). Sanctions have had little, if any, impact on North Korea's trading relationship with China and more recent analyses suggest that sanctions have increased the trade between the two partners, effectively offsetting trade restrictions from other countries (Lee 2018, 34). The inability of sanctions to warn off potential sanctions busters is hardly unique to North Korea as few countries enforce economic sanctions consistently like the United States, and the UN lacks effective enforcement mechanisms when countries fail to implement economic sanctions properly, as Panel of Expert reports consistently highlight. Sanctions busters have helped North Korea engage in counter-strategies to ameliorate the negative effects of economic sanctions, which can range from import substitution, smuggling, and/or engaging in illicit trade (Hovi, Huseby, and Sprinz 2005, 481). Sanctions have also compelled North Korea to seek other trading partners who "do not pose sanctions risks, or with whom its nuclear and missile interests are aligned, most notably Iran, Syria, and potentially Egypt" (Haggard and Noland 2010, 541).

Defining whether sanctions are successful or even effective depends on the goals of sanctions when implemented. The sanctions imposed on North Korea have not only varied by sender but also in the goals associated with the different sanctions programs imposed since 1950. Longstanding US economic sanctions imposed in the 1950s, for example, which have sought to curtail the development of North Korea's military and trigger regime change, have had mixed results on North Korea. North Korea's military, while being the fourth largest in the world, operates outdated equipment (Albert 2020). While it still poses a threat, North Korea's inability to modernize its conventional military has meant it must rely on more expensive and complex forms of deterrence, such as nuclear, biological, and chemical weapons. Regime change and denuclearization are much more complicated issues and may be more insulated from the economic pain that sanctions inflict. Sanctions may not have achieved the goals that senders initially associated with the economic sanctions, but economic sanctions may have had at least a minor impact on the ability of North Korea to further test and develop its nuclear arsenal. UN sanctions that have targeted North Korea's ability to export commodities or import luxury goods have also seen mixed results, as Panel of Expert reports since 2011 demonstrate (Panel of Experts 2011, 2012, 2013, 2014, 2015, 2016, 2017b, 2018, 2019). Yet at the same time, economic sanctions and threats of further sanctions have only emboldened the regime to resist and find ways to undercut the sanctions, which may make success even more elusive for US and UN sanctions. Recent ballistic missile tests provide further empirical evidence that unilateral and multilateral sanctions are doing little to stop weapons testing in North Korea (Zwirko 2021; Sang-Hun 2021).

Beyond the lack of credible commitments, the literature also posits that domestic political costs play an important role in the success of economic sanctions; without them, the likelihood of compliance on the part of the target state is low. Autocracies like North Korea are less likely to cave from the imposition of economic sanctions given that "authoritarian leaders have little incentive to concede to economic coercion [. . .] leaders of these rogue states are willing to stand firm in the face of sanctions pressure indefinitely" (Allen 2005, 133). The audience costs (Weeks 2008) are likely low or easily ameliorated in a country like North Korea where Kim Jong Un has assassinated those who create dissent or fail to tow the party line. However, authoritarian governments may also tolerate domestic dissent to signal their intentions to an international audience (Chen Weiss 2013). Interestingly, the North Korean government has tolerated and even organized mass protests against the sanctions imposed on the country (Kim 2009). While we are not arguing the leader of North Korea faces no political pressures, the Kim regime is less beholden to sanctions pressure than what is typical in democratic states and even some authoritarian states (Pak 2020).

In authoritarian regimes, "comprehensive sanctions [create] the opportunity for target governments to allocate rent-seeking opportunities to [their] supporters. This policy response, [. . .] if anything, increase[s] an authoritarian regime's grip on power" (Drezner 2011, 100). Indeed, North Korea is no exception to this pattern. When sanctions are imposed on North Korea and resources are limited, elites with political and/or trade and manufacturing connections are more likely to receive them than the general population and are therefore insulated from sanctions pressures (Lee 2018, 48). International trading relationships are also dominated by State-Owned Enterprises (SOEs), the military, and other gatekeepers (Haggard and Noland 2010, 567). Furthermore, this concentration of resources is more likely to be in Pyongyang, manufacturing centers, or areas along the Chinese border that witness increased trade than in other regions in the country (Lee 2018, 35).

Typically, the pain from economic sanctions occurs not only due to the loss of trade but also through civil and criminal enforcement and compliance efforts, especially by the United States, which aggressively pursues financial and non-financial firms for sanctions violations (Early and Preble 2020b). The reduction in licit trade with North Korea, however, has reduced the number of potential violators that regulatory agencies in the United States, such as the Office of Foreign Assets Control (OFAC), are likely to detect, further limiting the pain that the US economic sanctions can bring to bear on would-be sanctions busters. The United Nations Panel of Experts on North Korea (Panel of Experts 2010, 2011, 2012, 2013, 2014, 2015, 2016, 2017a, 2017b,

2018, 2019, 2020) has documented dozens of instances of North Koreans selling their coal to overseas buyers by delivering cargo on the open seas or bypassing trade through third-party states, such as China, whose economic and trade ties are substantial. It should be noted, however, that the Chinese entities involved in North Korean trade are not SOEs (Haggard and Noland 2017). Rather, they are often private Chinese companies (Early 2015).

At the same time, sanctions disproportionately impact the North Korean populace. While the political and economic elite receive what few resources come into the country under sanctions, the general population receives less than usual (H. Kim 2014; Park and Walsh 2016). This is especially problematic in a country like North Korea with a history of famine and where over 60 percent of the population lives below the poverty line (Crespo Cuaresma et al. 2020). As previously mentioned, sanctions may impact different regions differently: areas with high numbers of political or economic elites (such as Pyongyang) may feel the effects of sanctions less severely than more rural areas (Lee 2018, 35). Additionally, North Korean women may be disproportionately impacted by sanctions for several reasons. First, sanctions bring economic pressure that is associated with higher rates of domestic and sexual violence, female trafficking, and female prostitution (Féron et al. 2019, iv). Second, North Korean women are expected to be both caretakers and workers, made more difficult when sanctions target industries such as manufacturing that have relatively high numbers of female workers (Féron et al. 2019, iv). Given the disproportionately large impact of sanctions on the North Korean people versus the elite, "if pressure exerted through economic, political, or military means increases to a level that is high enough to trigger a qualitative change such as regime collapse, we might end up with a successful surgery, but a dead patient" (Frank 2006, 34).

Thus, the consensus among analysts and academics is that economic sanctions against North Korea have been largely unsuccessful (Brewer and Terry 2021; Hudson and Francis 2016; Salisbury 2017a; Watterson 2020). This is partially because political elites remain isolated from sanctions pressures (Haggard and Noland 2017) and because the country has found ways to adapt and circumvent sanctions pressures through licit and illicit means (Preble and Willis 2024b). While these are important insights, we argue that another part of the picture is the trade networks in which North Korea is included. We argue that North Korea's network is initially isoldated (Table 1.1) and is not sufficiently economically integrated into licit global trade networks with sanctions-enforcing countries, such as the United States, European countries, or the United States's regional partners such as Australia and New Zealand, for sanctions to be effective.

Networks highlight not only the limits of economic sanctions but also allow us to observe North Korea's agency. As a target state, North Korea actively seeks out new trading partners. SNA also provides insight into who is willing to trade with North Korea. North Korea represents an untapped market for commercial opportunity, and the risks of tapping into these commercial opportunities can equate to significant rewards by those willing to brave the economic and political risks of doing so. Using strength centrality measures for both the target (North Korea) and third parties (its trading partners will to help it evade and bust sanctions) demonstrates both the agency and the allure of these economic opportunities.

SHOOTING BLANKS OR JUST BAD AIM? WHEN SANCTIONS FAIL TO HIT THEIR TARGET

The United States has generally been able to leverage its central position in the global financial and trade system to weaponize interdependence effectively (Farrell and Newman 2019). As Wertz (2013) explains:

> To many global financial institutions, the risks of bad publicity, increased regulatory costs or fines, or the possibility of losing access to the U.S. financial system outweigh the potential profits to be made from doing business with an entity that may be linked to proliferation, terrorism, or other illicit activities [. . .] ready access to the U.S. financial system is the lifeblood of most global financial institutions. (70)

Therefore, the potential cost of access to the US financial system if caught violating financial sanctions is simply too high for many businesses, especially foreign financial institutions, which are often targeted by US regulators like OFAC (Early and Preble 2020a, 2020b). Additionally, a lack of access to the US-dominated financial system is damaging for states and businesses targeted by US sanctions that rely heavily on the US dollar. While US financial sanctions have made it difficult for the regime in North Korea to finance its ambitions, those sanctions have largely been ineffective in coercing North Korea to cease its nuclear program or upending the political order as North Korea has found other ways to earn money. As Drezner (2011) argues, “By punishing ordinary market activity, sanctions give entrepreneurs a strong incentive to take the criminal route—and they usually earn higher-than-usual profits in the bargain” (98). More problematically, even targeted financial sanctions seem to have little impact on both the wealth disparity between North Korean elites and the civilian population and the development of North Korea’s nuclear weapons program, as evidenced by the various nuclear and ballistic tests under the sanctions regime (Wertz 2013, 78).

To understand why North Korean sanctions have failed, we agree that it is important to look beyond “bilateral interdependencies” and “aggregate market share” (Farrell and Newman 2019, 43). Weaponized interdependence relies on countries’ policies that, when implemented, generate two kinds of effects: panopticon and chokepoint. Panopticon effects come from policies that states controlling key nodes in the international trading network enact that enable information collection and monitoring. Chokepoint effects are policies that sever nodes (states) from accessing other nodes and limit the ability of other states "to walk" through the network across various connections. Economic sanctions can, for example, generate chokepoint effects that limit the movement of information, people, goods, weapons, and finance. Comprehensive US economic sanctions against North Korea, Myanmar, and Iran are excellent examples of chokepoint effects where US regulations and foreign policies isolate target countries from not only engaging with the United States but also attempts (and sometimes successfully) of pushing other countries throughout the network of following US policies. Our application of weaponized interdependence considers mainly government policies, which we see as playing a greater role in North Korea's actions than informal sanctions individual firms may impose via supply chains or derisking.

When there is weaponized interdependence to wield, the asymmetrical networks between the sender and target states can be a highly effective coercive instrument. When European countries cut Iran off from SWIFT and imposed a near-total embargo on Iran's oil exports to Europe, Iran lost an important financial and economic lifeline. The complex interdependence between Iran and key EU trading partners left Iran exposed as the EU sanctions deprived Iran of a critical source of revenue. The lack of access to the EU's financial system made trade settlement exceedingly complex, raising the costs of goods and generating significant inflation for Iran's already battered economy (Batmanghelidj and Moret 2022). What the Iran case demonstrates is that building new "walks" through the network is both costly and time-consuming. North Korea, by contrast, has remade its network over time, severing "walks" and forgoing trade with former trading partners despite the many layers of economic sanctions imposed on it by the UN, United States, and EU.

However, target states are not passive to panopticon and chokepoint effects as they are able to create new network connections to avoid probing and coercive senders. They may also realign their connections in the network by seeking out alternative trading partners. North Korea has demonstrated agency in regards to sanctions is consistent with its Juche ideology, the principle of "self-reliance" that has anchored North Korean policymaking and propaganda since founder Kim Il-Sung first used the term in the 1950s (Kang 2007). Through its various state-run news agencies, the North Korean government has repeatedly denounced sanctions against it, especially from the United States, and asserted that it will not acquiesce to sanctions pressures. For example, a 1998 article from the Korean Central News Agency (KCNA) stated that North Korea has "done all we want to in face of dozens of years of U.S. sanctions. We do not mind if the U.S. continues sanctions against us. We will live on and advance socialism through self-reliance" (*KCNA* 1998b). More recently, the North Korean government emphasized in a 2017 Rodong Sinmun article that North Korea has been able to "bolster" its military capability "despite the US-led vicious sanctions" (*KCNA* 2017). Given North Korea's public statements about the US and UN sanctions regime and assertions that it will survive through "self-reliance" despite sanctions, it is unsurprising that North Korea has found creative ways to circumvent them as it continues to identify potential trading partners.

One avenue is the development of a black market. As Drezner (2011) argues, "by punishing ordinary market activity, sanctions give entrepreneurs a strong incentive to take the criminal route—and they usually earn higher-than-usual profits in the bargain" (98). In the case of North Korea, targeted financial sanctions may push those enterprises determined to do business with the country, both legitimate and illicit, to black-market activities such as money laundering (Wertz 2013, 71) or, as recently noted by investigations, illicit activities may be ignored by regulators (Leopold et al. 2020). One such example of illicit market activity involves "exports" of labor to other countries to work on a multitude of defense and infrastructure projects (Sieff 2017; U.S. Department of Treasury 2020; Yoon 2019). These workers then bring back currency to North Korea once they are repatriated by the countries where they are working once the UNSC becomes aware of such activities (Hui 2020; Pattison 2014).

North Korea has adopted other creative approaches to funneling money into its market in the face of sanctions pressures. It has, for example, also resorted to selling away its fishing rights to fishing enterprises (Town and Yozell 2020), namely in China. The sale of such rights is hard to stop or capture through economic sanctions and provides North Korea with significant amounts of hard currency. North Korea is also able to smuggle in hard currency that eschews the use of the global financial system, demonstrating the difficulties the United States faces in weaponizing its place in the asymmetric network that might have some positive impacts on North Korea's behavior.

Perhaps most problematically, North Korea is willing and able to find trading partners who are willing to ignore sanctions in exchange for access to North Korean markets and products. Third-party states, like the target, may simultaneously build new walks through the network to the target state to benefit from the commercial opportunities created by the network effects created by economic sanctions. As the chokepoint effects generated by senders cut off North Korea from access to critical goods, terms of trade become much more favorable to third-party states. Firms in sanctions busting states may be tempted to seek out these lucrative commercial opportunities despite the political and economic risks associated with such trade. Further, third-party sanctions busting states may also seek out these new commercial opportunities to avoid a sender state's (or the UN's) panopticon effects that collect information and monitor economic activity with target states (Preble and Willis 2024b). Such activities may involve transshipment via third or fourth countries or the use of front companies and brokers to mask the true nature of the buyer and seller. Sometimes, the trade is not hidden and operates out in the open. For example, North Korea, a country rich in anthracite coal, is still able to export the commodity despite UNSCR 1718, which bars the export of North Korean coal. What once used to occur on the open seas away from potential observers now happens brazenly as sanctions busting third-party states like China no longer hide their attempts at providing support to North Korea via trade-based sanctions busting by docking in North Korean ports or allowing North Korean vessels to dock in Chinese ports (Warrick 2018).

We offer three hypotheses that address reasons for the failure of the North Korea sanctions regime related to its trading networks. The imposition of long-term economic sanctions has spurred North Korea to both reshape and (re) structure its network. One of its myriad adaptation strategies that demonstrates North Korea's agency in combating economic sanctions has been to establish stronger trading relationships with countries that ignore or neglect to enforce UN sanctions. Thus, we posit that North Korea's licit trading network will shift when more stringent international sanctions are applied, weakening trading linkages with countries who enforce the sanctions and strengthening others that fail to enforce them, especially in sanctions busting states where firms seek to take advantage of lucrative commercial opportunities. Specifically, we expect that North Korea's trading network will shift significantly after the UNSC began formally sanctioning the country in the wake of its first nuclear weapons test in 2006 and subsequent sanctions. At the same time, we also expect North Korea's network to change, albeit less dramatically, when there is less international condemnation, as it will be more politically feasible for a wider range of states to engage in licit trade with North Korea. For example, North Korea's relationships with several countries, especially in East Asia, improved after the signing of the Agreed Framework in 1994, a negotiated resolution to the First Nuclear Crisis.

H_1: The structure of North Korea's trade network changes over time as economic sanctions are imposed.

Because economic sanctions created lucrative commercial opportunities, we developed two measures of strength centrality (MOSC). Our first strength centrality measure (MOSC1) captures the importance of North Korea's market to third-party sanctions busting states (Table 1.3). As Early (2009, 2011, 387) notes, "most cases of extensive sanctions-busting are commercially driven" and are more likely to receive support from the global marketplace (Early 2011, 388). Given North Korea's isolation within the global marketplace and its renunciation of trading partners providing significant support (South Korea, Japan, for example), commercially driven sanctions busting still occurs.

> *H_2: The presence of economic sanctions increases third-party commercial engagement with North Korea.*

Our second strength centrality measure (MOSC2) captures North Korea's agency and efforts to mitigate the pain caused by economic sanctions. As a measure of strength centrality, it measures the importance of North Korean trade to the third-party's total annual trade (Table 1.3). As this measure's value increases, it reflects North Korea's agency at seeking out third-party states and their respective constituents willing to trade and engage economically with the Hermit Kingdom. If we fail to reject our hypothesis, then chokepoint effects imposed by nodes in North Korea's network push North Korea to isolate itself and rely on key nodes within the network for support. This isolation limits the ability of key nodes in the network to weaponize interdependence and also forces the regime to reconstitute its network by insulating it against the negative impacts generated by the chokepoint effects.

> *H_3: The presence of economic sanctions compels North Korea to rely on China as a black knight.*

ANALYZING TRADE NETWORK DATA

Our study utilizes UN Comtrade data (United Nations 2021) as well as inter-Korean trade data (East-West Center and National Committee on North Korea 2019) from 1990 to 2017 in exploring trends in trade between North Korea and its key trading partners. We employ SNA to explore our hypotheses in two distinct ways. First, we use the trade data from the above sources to operationalize H_1 by generating several geospatial visualizations of North Korea's trading network (Knapp 2017). These visual networks are descriptive, but they are important nonetheless in showing two effects: North Korea's ability to insulate itself from economic sanctions by changing its trading network and increasing its connections throughout the network. In order to understand the effect of economic sanctions on North Korea, an analysis of the social network based on trade linkages provides a look at how these relationships have changed across time as economic sanctions from not just the United States but other states in the international system have influenced trade flows and trade linkages. We created several network graphs that show North Korea's trade linkages with states in the international system in 1990, 1995, 2003, 2007, and 2017. We selected these temporal windows as they capture the first and last years of our study (1990 and 2017) and years in which we expect North Korea's network to shift in response to important international events (the Agreed Framework in 1994, a series of high-level talks in the early 2000s, and North Korea's first nuclear test in 2006). We then use SNA to show descriptively the share of the trade conducted with North Korea (indicated by the size of each node) but also the geographic distribution of that trade across the international system by mapping the network geospatially. While the number of North Korea's trading partners has increased over time (Haggard and Noland 2017), the concentration of trade within the network has shifted considerably as states, such as China, account for a preponderance of trade with North Korea while other countries, such as Japan, cease trading with North Korea. The geospatial network visualizations demonstrate that, while North Korea's trading network has diversified, the concentration of trade and the structure of its network has also shifted across time.

To test our hypotheses, we utilize three measures common to SNA. Our first measure, degree centrality, captures the number of trading partners and measures the change to the network with North Korea at the center of this network and is useful for testing our first hypothesis. Degree centrality refers to the number of connections each node has in the network and reflects the number of North Korea trading's partners. As we show (Figure 2.1), North

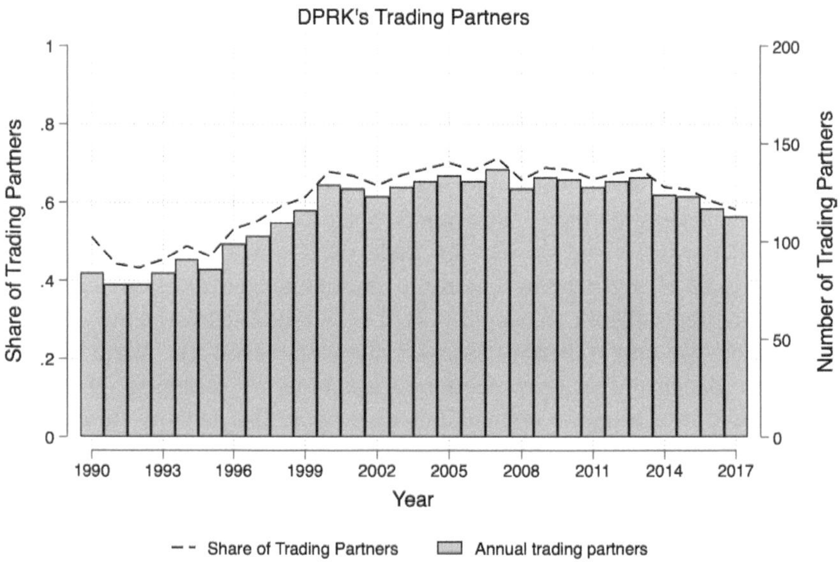

Figure 2.1 North Korea's Degree Centrality (1990–2017). Bar graph shows the number of trading partners each year. Solid line represents the share of total possible trading partners or DPRK's degree centrality. Source: Created by Authors.

Korea's trading partners increase and diversify across time. Previous studies have highlighted North Korea's increased portfolio of trading partners over time, and this measure seems to indicate an increased centrality among North Korea's trading partners (Haggard and Noland 2017). While this may be true, the strength of the relationship between these trading partners and North Korea varies considerably, especially as North Korea's share of trade has remained regionally focused over time.

To test our second and third hypotheses, we develop two measures of strength centrality, both of which are weighted by the total trade conducted by North Korea or its trading partner. These two measures of strength centrality, MOSC1 and MOSC2, are used to capture the commercial interest of third-party sanction busting states and North Korean agency, respectively. These measures of strength centrality are similar to trade share measures, which is not unusual when working with trade data (De Benedictus et al. 2013). We provide the MOSCs for North Korea and its trading partners in Tables 2.1 and 2.2.

Table 2.1 MOSC1 (Strength Centrality Measure) for Key Nodes Ranging from 0 to 100 Percent. Values of 0.0000 Reflect Trade Share < 0.0001. Missing Cells Indicate Years Where No Trade Was Reported

	Measure of Strength Centrality (MOSC1)				
	Trade partner's total share of DPRK's annual trade				
	1990	*1995*	*2003*	*2007*	*2017*
Angola	0.0000	0.0000	0.0000	13.2495	0.0000
Australia	1.6367	0.0323	0.1988	0.099	0.0000
Austria	1.3648	0.0000	0.0998	0.0681	0.0188
Brazil	0.0008	1.9987	4.184	3.0076	0.09
China	29.0729	21.6108	31.4842	26.223	93.0654
France	1.4979	1.3278	0.3606	0.2002	0.0206
Germany	7.7396	3.192	2.8119	0.6848	0.1165
India	2.8404	2.5676	3.9814	10.5845	1.7401
Indonesia	5.0309	1.2325	0.0732	0.0394	0.0404
Italy	1.5257	1.2084	0.9581	0.1353	0.0078
Japan	27.7383	22.7298	8.0213	0.1209	0.0000
Mexico	2.0302	7.7035	0.9257	0.6007	0.1175
Russia	0.0000	0.0000	3.498	1.8222	1.4535
S. Arabia	0.1685	1.4889	0.1927	0.4585	0.0000
Singapore	2.5914	1.8375	1.8804	0.8376	0.0094
S.Africa	0.0000	0.0718	0.221	1.8605	0.0413
S. Korea	0.811	20.4291	22.287	23.8555	0.0187
Thailand	2.3114	1.6232	7.7705	2.8696	0.0000
USA	0.0019	0.1969	0.2473	0.0229	0.0000
Venezuela	0.0009	0.0013	0.0002	2.6736	0.0000

Source: Created by Authors.

Table 2.2 MOSC2 (Strength Centrality Measure) for Key Nodes Ranging from 0 to 100 Percent. Values of 0.0000 Reflect Trade Share < 0.0001. Missing Cells Indicate Years Where No Trade Was Reported

	Measure of Strength Centrality (MOSC2)				
	DPRK's total share of trade partner's annual trade				
	1990	*1995*	*2003*	*2007*	*2017*
Angola	0.0000	0.0000	0.0000	1.8718	0.0000
Australia	0.0368	0.0008	0.0043	0.0026	0.0000
Austria	0.0253	0.0000	0.0018	0.0016	0.0003
Brazil	0	0.0502	0.1074	0.0758	0.0012
China	0.5363	0.206	0.1229	0.0954	0.1313
France	0.0056	0.0061	0.0015	0.0013	0.0001
Germany	0.0172	0.0084	0.0069	0.0022	0.0002
India	0.1153	0.0973	0.1105	0.2102	0.0138
Indonesia	0.179	0.0357	0.0019	0.0013	0.0006
Italy	0.0076	0.0074	0.0055	0.0010	0.0000
Japan	0.0929	0.0789	0.0317	0.0007	0.0000
Mexico	0.0422	0.1359	0.0092	0.0085	0.0007
Russia	--	--	0.0505	0.0219	0.0131
S.Arabia	0.004	0.051	0.005	0.0085	0.0000
Singapore	0.0421	0.0209	0.0225	0.0123	0.0001
S. Africa	0.0000	0.0037	0.0092	0.0849	0.0012
S.Korea	0.0114	0.221	0.2052	0.261	0.0001
Thailand	0.0723	0.034	0.1655	0.0745	0.0000
USA	0.0000	0.0004	0.0004	0.0001	0.0000
Venezuela	0.0001	0.0001	0	0.1982	0.0000

Source: Created by Authors.

MOSC1 captures the third-party state's trade dependence on North Korea, which is calculated by dividing the third-party's total bilateral trade with North Korea each year by the target state's total annual trade that year. As this value increases, we see North Korea as being commercially important to the third-part state's firms and constituents. MOSC2 captures the importance of the third-party state to North Korea's trade network, which is calculated by dividing the total bilateral trade North Korea conducts with a trading partner by trading partner's total annual trade that year. As this value increases, it reflects North Korean agency in seeking out trade partners willing to help it evade economic sanctions. Higher values of strength centrality also potentially indicate not only the importance of a particular node but also an increased ability to influence others in the network (Yan and Ding 2009, 2108). Countries that share borders with North Korea, such as China, South Korea, and Russia, should ostensibly have higher values in relation to other trading partners given their geographic proximity.

NETWORK ADAPTATION: DYNAMIC SHIFTS IN NORTH KOREAN TRADE

Using a series of geospatial network visualizations that map nodes onto their geographic coordinates, we show how North Korea's network of trade changes across time. The narrative that we develop provides visual evidence of North Korea's isolation as it seeks to insulate itself from the effects of potential weaponized interdependence, as the structure of North Korea's network changes (H_1) We then conclude this section by discussing the measures of strength centrality to show the impact of sanctions busting (H_2) and the North Korea's reliance on China as a black knight (H_3).

In 1990, the lion's share of trade with North Korea involved China, Japan, Germany and other western and eastern European countries, Mexico, along with Australia, Thailand, Singapore, and Indonesia (Figure 2.2). The only economic sanctions targeting North Korea in 1990 were US economic sanctions imposed during the Korean War (Chang 2006b; Wertz 2020). China and Japan were clearly North Korea's two largest trading partners in the

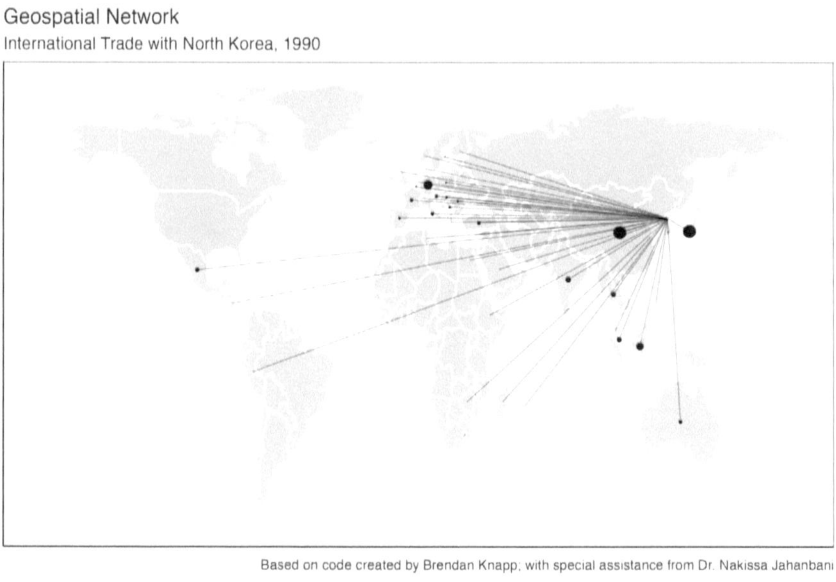

Figure 2.2 Trading Partner Distribution. Ties between North Korea and trading partners in 1990. The ties between North Korea and its trading partners are indicated with solid black lines. We only consider North Korea's trading relationships when total aggregate trade exchanged is greater than or equal to $1 million current USD, which we argue are more significant trading ties. Black filled circles are nodes or states in the international system. The size of the nodes increases as that country's trade share with North Korea increases. *Source*: Created by Authors.

early 1990s. The former is perhaps unsurprising given its historical support for North Korea. Furthermore, the collapse of several eastern European states and the Soviet Union in the late 1980s and early 1990s meant that North Korea lost major political allies and economic partners, thus making it even more dependent on China for support. Japan's key position in North Korea's trading network during this period was driven by rapprochement between the two countries at the beginning of the 1990s. The collapse of the Soviet Union and other former communist states drove North Korea to find new trading partners while greater access to North Korea's market was alluring for Japanese business interests (Hagstrom and Soderberg 2006, 3; Okano-Heijmans 2010, 379).

By 1995, North Korea's relative diversification of trade interests changed (Figure 2.3). China, Japan, and now South Korea became North Korea's dominant trading partners followed by Mexico and Germany. Western Europe, Saudi Arabia, and Brazil also took on a greater share of trade with North Korea. US trade with North Korea exceeded $1 million dollars as it began exports to North Korea after it relaxed economic sanctions in the wake

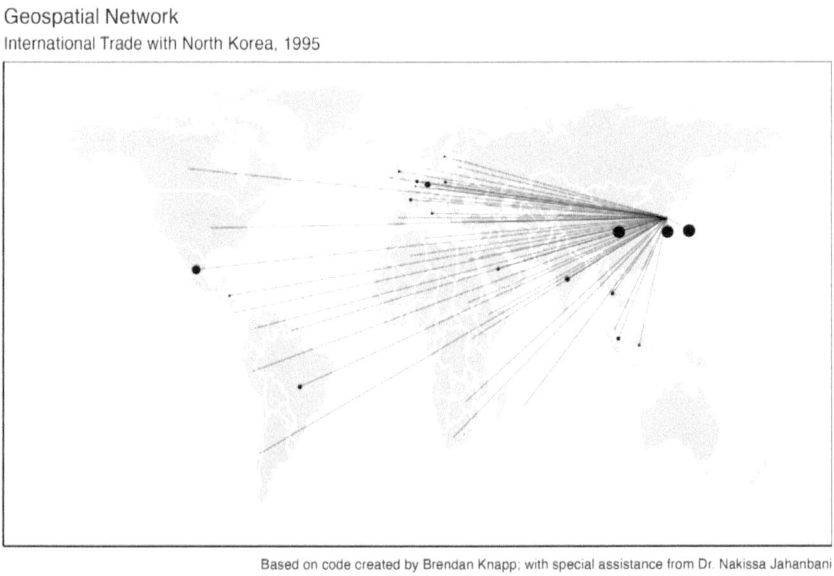

Figure 2.3 Trading Partner Distribution. . Ties between North Korea and trading partners in 1995. The ties between North Korea and its trading partners are indicated with solid black lines. We only consider North Korea's trading relationships when total aggregate trade exchanged is greater than or equal to $1 million current USD, which we argue are more significant trading ties. Black filled circles are nodes or states in the international system. The size of the nodes increases as that country's trade share with North Korea increases. *Source*: Created by Authors.

of the Agreed Framework in October 1994 during the Clinton Administration (Chang 2006b). Furthermore, the Agreed Framework and the Great Famine in North Korea encouraged regional partners such as Japan, China, and South Korea to maintain or increase trade with the country.

While Japan remained an important trading partner with North Korea throughout the 1990s, its trade share declined to 8 percent in 2003, corresponding with key developments in their bilateral relationship. Russia returned as a key trading partner by 2003 along with increasing trade with Southeast Asian trading partners (Figure 2.4). The early 2000s saw several rounds of normalization talks between Japan and North Korea, including the high-level meeting between Koizumi Junchiro and Kim Jong-Il in 2002 (Blomquist and Wertz 2015; Hagström and Söderberg 2006, 4). Initially, the summit between the two leaders appeared to herald in a new era of positive relations between the two countries. However, North Korea's admission of abducting Japanese citizens proved to be a domestic bombshell in Japan and facilitated the deterioration of the countries' relationship (Blomquist and Wertz 2015; Hagstrom and Soderberg 2006, 4).

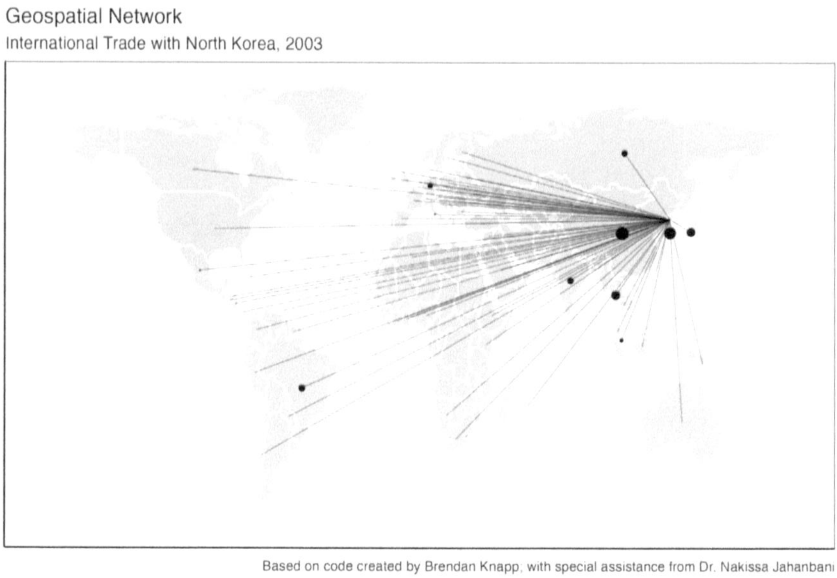

Figure 2.4 Trading Partner Distribution. . Ties between North Korea and trading partners in 2003. The ties between North Korea and its trading partners are indicated with solid black lines. We only consider North Korea's trading relationships when total aggregate trade exchanged is greater than or equal to $1 million current USD, which we argue are more significant trading ties. Black filled circles are nodes or states in the international system. The size of the nodes increases as that country's trade share with North Korea increases. *Source*: Created by Authors.

Additionally, North Korea's revelation that it had been enriching uranium, in defiance of the Agreed Framework, drew international condemnation. As the international community condemned North Korea, China became North Korea's top trading partner (31 percent) in 2003 followed closely by South Korea (22 percent), which was in the final years of Kim Dae Jung's presidency, who sought to encourage inter-Korean relations through his "Sunshine Policy." US exports to North Korea also dropped (to about 0.25 percent), perhaps driven by concerns of North Korea's uranium enrichment program and the Bush administration's inclusion of North Korea in his "Axis of Evil" speech as a state that may provide weapons of mass destruction to terrorists (Wagner 2002).

By 2007 (figure 2.5), North Korea's trading network shifted again after it conducted its first nuclear weapons test in 2006. China (26 percent) and South Korea (24 percent) occupied the two top trading spots followed by Angola (13 percent), India (10 percent), Brazil (2 percent), Thailand (2 percent), Congo (2 percent), Venezuela (2 percent), South Africa (1.9 percent), and Russia (1.8 percent). There was not only a concentration of trade in these

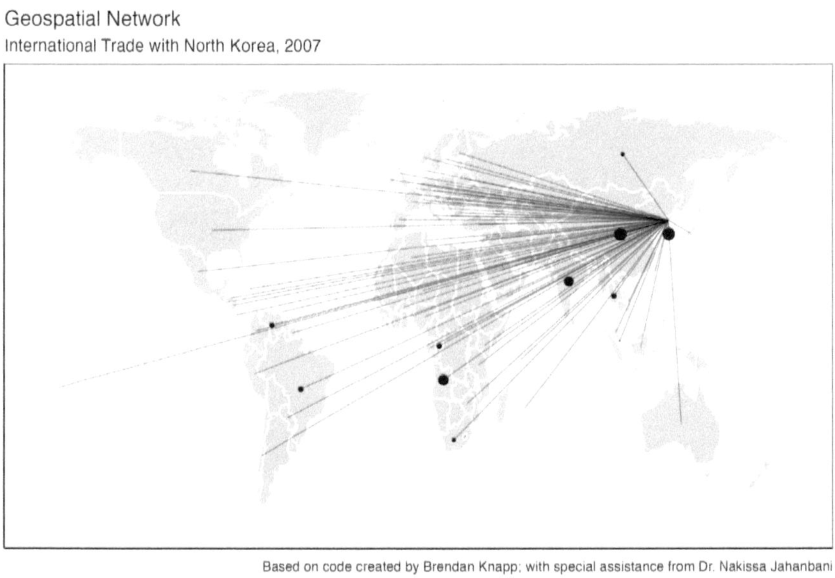

Figure 2.5 Trading Partner Distribution. Ties between North Korea and trading partners in 2007. The ties between North Korea and its trading partners are indicated with solid black lines. We only consider North Korea's trading relationships when total aggregate trade exchanged is greater than or equal to $1 million current USD, which we argue are more significant trading ties. Black filled circles are nodes or states in the international system. The size of the nodes increases as that country's trade share with North Korea increases. *Source*: Created by Authors.

countries but an increase in the number of total trading partners during this period (Haggard and Noland 2017). The breadth of North Korea's network of trade increased, yet the country continued to rely heavily on its neighbors, China and South Korea. After the test, the United States's already limited share of North Korean trade declined to insignificant levels (0.02 percent). North Korea's trade linkages to Western Europe fell to levels on par with the United States. Additionally, Japan's trade (and influence) with North Korea continued to decline: in 2003, Japan and North Korea exchanged $261,000,000 in trade but by 2007, Japanese trade with North Korea declined by 97 percent to a low of $9,114,584. This shift in Japan's trade with North Korea was a reflection of increased domestic support for economic sanctions and greater policy congruence with the United States. UNSC Resolution 1718, issued in the wake of the 2006 nuclear test, also induced member states to cut back trade with North Korea, and the United States and Japan imposed their respective unilateral sanctions.

By 2017, China dominated North Korea's trade network, accounting for 93 percent of North Korea's total trade. Japan and South Korea, who, once along

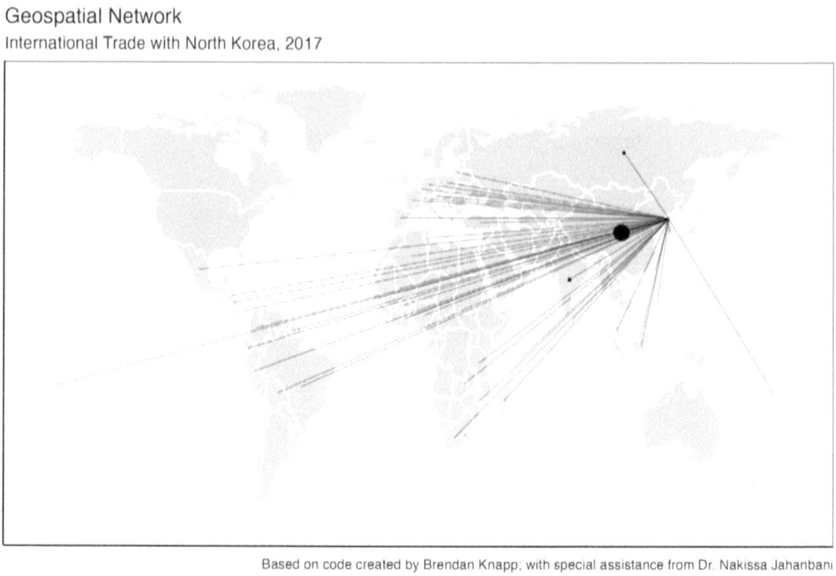

Figure 2.6 Trading Partner Distribution. Ties between North Korea and trading partnres in 2017. The ties between North Korea and its trading partners are indicated with solid black lines. We only consider North Korea's trading relationships when total aggregate trade exchanged is greater than or equal to $1 million current USD, which we argue are more significant trading ties. Black filled circles are nodes or states in the international system. The size of the node increases as that country's trade share with North Korea increases. *Source*: Created by Authors.

with China, each accounted for about 20 percent of North Korea's trade, were no longer connected to North Korea's trading network, at least partially due to shifts in domestic opinion and foreign policy toward the North. The United States by 2017 lost its own tie to North Korea and no longer had a "walk" to North Korea through its key allies, Japan and South Korea. Furthermore, South Korea's connection to North Korea dropped to its lowest level since the resumption of inter-Korean trade of $1 million, just under 0.02 percent of North Korea's total trade. India and Russia accounted for an additional 3.1 percent of North Korea trade (Figure 2.6). The remaining 3.9 percent of North Korean trade came from a smattering of countries around the world. The discussion and description of these changes provides support for our first hypothesis (H_1): over time, North Korea's network adapts to isolate itself from the effects of weaponized interdependence. These adaptations created a trade network that by 2017 relied almost exclusively on China. Our discussion provides evidence for our first hypothesis (H_1) that the structure of North Korea's trade network changes over time as economic sanctions are imposed. As the number and severity of sanctions increase after the first nuclear test, the network of trade adjusts and reacts to these developments.

Figure 2.7 shows a plot of the two measurements of strength centrality (MOSC1 and MOSC2). MOSC1 refers to China's share of North Korea's

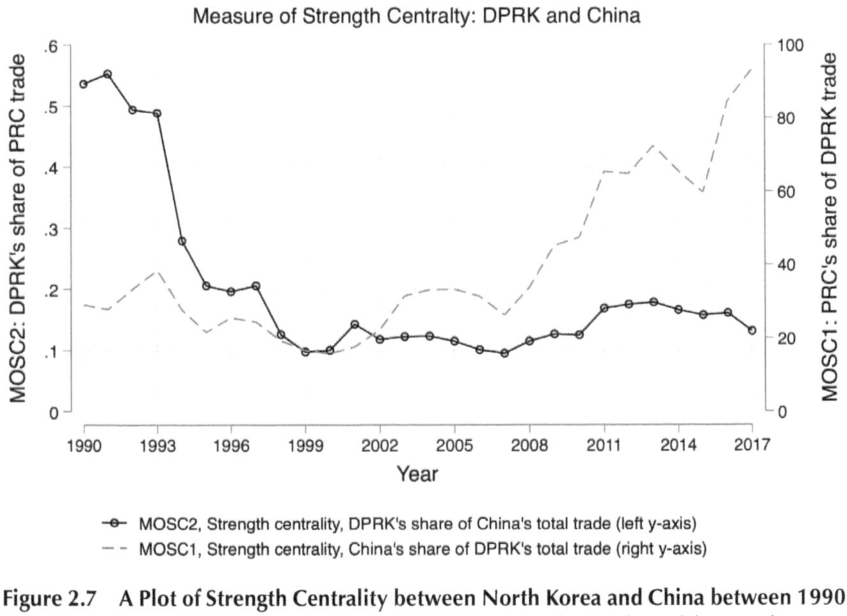

Figure 2.7 A Plot of Strength Centrality between North Korea and China between 1990 and 2017. Both measures are weighted by the total trade conducted by North Korea (MOSC1) and China (MOSC2), respectively. *Source*: Created by Authors.

total annual trade with higher values indicating North Korea's reliance on China. Starting in 2000, this value increased as North Korea became more dependent on China for trade. MOSC2, the connected line, reflects North Korea's share of China's annual trade, which reflects the centrality of North Korea to China's annual trade. MOSC1 and MOSC2 are expressed as percentages, ranging from 0 percent to 100 percent. North Korea's strength centrality vis-à-vis other countries is quite small, and, as a measure on its own, is not very telling. However, when juxtaposed against the first measure of strength centrality (MOSC1), a relationship emerges.

For most countries engaged with North Korea, these two measures move in tandem and in parallel with each other and support our second hypothesis (H_2), as reflected in the values in Table 2.1 and 2.2. Both Japan and South Korea exemplify this pattern with North Korea in their respective provisions of sanctions busting support to North Korea. Japan's support was, arguably, more driven by economic interests as Japanese businesses had desired greater access to North Korea's market (Okano-Heijmans 2010, 379; Hagström and Söderberg 2006, 3). Furthermore, the *chongryon* (or *chosen soren*) North Korean community in Japan have played a key role in maintaining trade linkages between the two countries since its inception in 1955, ferrying goods and remittances (Blomquist and Wertz 2015; Samuels 2004, 319). South Korean support was also economic-driven and politically driven, as policymakers hoped that joint ventures and economic cooperation (such as the Kaesong Industrial Complex) would eventually translate to greater political cooperation (H.-J. Kim 2021). Once unilateral and UN sanctions are imposed by Japan and South Korea, North Korea's importance to Japan and South Korea vanishes, and Japan and South Korea's importance to North Korea evaporates.

Before 2000, North Korea's importance to China is much larger even if the value is quite small, which is likely due to China's vast trade profile and commercial motivations for international trade. The pattern seen in Figure 2.7 is indicative of what one might expect from a black knight where Chinese trade is not driven by solely commercial imperatives—given North Korea's small market relative to China's overall trade profile—but more likely due to increasing political and economic support as economic sanctions are increasingly imposed on North Korea. The measures of strength centrality provide support for our third hypothesis (H_3): by 2017 China accounts for over 93 percent of North Korea's trade. North Korea's network reflects its dependence on China as it relies on 111 minor trading partners to account for the remaining 7 percent of its annual global trade.

These figures suggest that economic sanctions required North Korea to insulate itself from sanctions pressures, readjusting its relationships to key nodes in the network. The asymmetrical network reacted and responded accordingly to both the imposition of sanctions and the domestic concerns of

North Korea's key trading partners and key nodes (like the United States). The asymmetry in the network increased further as North Korea sought to insulate itself from the effects of economic sanctions by shifting its reliance on trade to China and away from former trading partners now imposing and enforcing sanctions.

The United States may dominate global and, in some cases, regional networks of information, finance, and trade, through its ability to generate panopticon effects and chokepoint effects. In the case of North Korea, however, North Korea's relationships with Japan, South Korea, and, especially, China, were key factors in shaping the structure of its network (Preble and Willis 2024b). As this network structure changed across time, it isolated the United States and key allies through which the United States could exercise influence, such as Japan and South Korea. The isolation of the United States from North Korea's network prevented the United States from utilizing its network connections—that is, its leverage—to undermine North Korea's nuclear and ballistic missile programs.

ILLICIT TRADE CONDUCTED BY NORTH KOREA

Any discussion of North Korea and economic sanctions must take into account the adeptness of North Korea's ability to evade economic sanctions. Using Panel of Expert reports from 2010 to 2022 published by the UNSC, we have created a data set of DPRK sanctions evasion efforts globally identified in the reports. While the events captured in the Panel of Expert reports is likely incomplete and unlikely to capture every illicit activity conducted by North Korea (Figure 2.8), the Panel of Expert reports provide critical insights into how the DPRK is able to resist the US, EU, and UN sanctions onslaught that seeks to limit the Kim regime's ability to fundraise and acquire strategic goods for its WMD and ballistic missile programs.

The map (Figure 2.8) offers some key insights into North Korea's sanctions evasion. First, there is a clear connection between North Korean licit and illicit trade through China. While China is North Korea's largest licit trading partner, it also serves as a conduit for North Korean sanctions evasion where many North Korean front companies operate in support of the regime. These front companies generate revenue for the regime through the sale of missile parts, rocket fuses, and host of other military related goods destined for jurisdictions, such as Syria, Myanmar, and Egypt. The procurement of luxury goods also uses China as a re-exporter. For example, in 2016, luxury vehicles traced to Europe that had been customized in the United States were shipped to North Korea via China (Panel of Experts 2016). Besides China, both Russia and India, DPRK's next two largest trading partners, have also

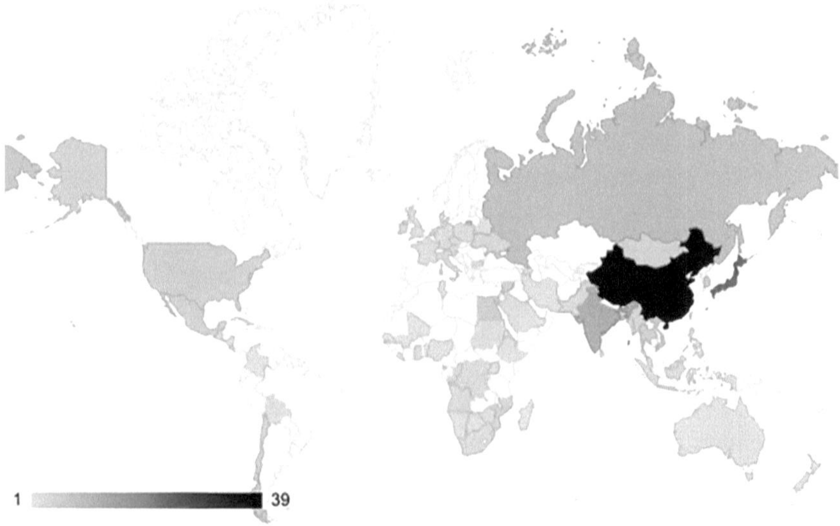

Figure 2.8 Map Showing Illicit Trade Conducted by DPRK. Events were coded using UN Panel of Expert reports (2012–2022). *Source*: Created by Authors.

participated in or have supported DPRK illicit activities. In 2017, India imported iron and steel and associated products totaling over $300k from North Korea in clear violation of UN sanctions. Russia, too, has violated UN sanctions by purchasing iron and steel and associated goods from North Korea in 2018 totaling nearly $350k (Panel of Experts 2017a, 2018). US adversaries are not the only countries engaging in sanctions violations. Japan, too, also serves as a conduit for illicit trade entering North Korea. After China, Japan is the second most likely transit point for illicit trade destined for North Korea, mainly luxury goods, such as wine and vermouth, tobacco, sake, and passenger vehicles (Panel of Experts 2012).

There is a vast global reach to North Korea's illicit activities for which the Panel of Expert reports are likely only capturing only a small portion of overall illicit trade passing through UN member states. Powerful and less powerful jurisdictions have willingly or unwittingly taken part in providing goods or facilitating trade with North Korea, and the reach of North Korea's sanctions evasion is global in scale as it seeks to generate revenue in support of its WMD programs. Even the United States is sometimes ensnared in these activities. Vehicles with armor customization, which was completed in the United States, ultimately ended up in North Korea via China, and Dennis Rodman, along with the Irish company Paddy Power, provided gifts to North Korea that violated both US and UN economic sanctions (Panel of Experts 2015, 2016).

Figure 2.9 shows the distribution of outcome of the 208 illicit activities we coded using the Panel of Expert reports. While a fair number of illicit activities are thwarted or interdicted by UN member states, a significant number nearly 76 percent of illicit activities tracked by the Panel of Experts were completed and made their way to North Korea or to one of North Korea's illicit trading partners. Two problematic factors emerge from this data. First, sanctions are having only a minor impact on North Korean illicit activities, especially if only one quarter of such activities have been stopped since 2012. Second, a significant number of member states are willingly (and sometimes unknowingly) contributing to the DPRK regime's efforts to fundraise and generate revenue in support of its WMD programs, reflecting uneven efforts at sanctions enforcement by UN member states. Efforts by senders to impose more sanctions when North Korea tests a missile or explodes a nuclear device might be imprudent given that the larger issue is the lack of adherence by UN member states to the enforcement of UNSC resolutions, resolutions to which all states must comply, rather than a weakness in the design of the sanctions.

Illicit trade and its growth undermine the ability of sender states to weaponize interdependence. If such trade cannot be tracked and monitored, there is no ability for states to gather the information until such efforts are thwarted or interdicted. By the time such activities are uncovered, it is likely that North Korea will simply shut down a front company, change its name, and reopen the newly renamed front company, thus avoiding the reach of authorities around the world. Economic sanctions do little to inhibit illicit trade and

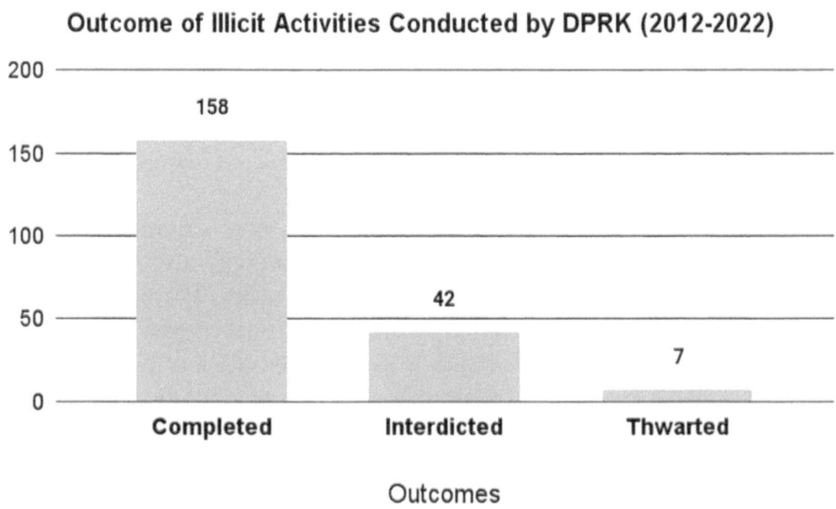

Figure 2.9 Bar Graph Showing the Distribution of Outcomes for Illicit Trade Activities Involving North Korea Coded Using UN Panel of Expert Reports. *Source*: Created by Authors.

more likely help to cultivate it while also stimulating growth in such activities (Early and Peksen 2019).

CONCLUSION

Our analysis has sought to illustrate why the North Korea economic sanctions failed: the lack of interdependence between North Korea and key senders (United States and other US allies), the inability or unwillingness of others to enforce (China), and North Korean agency in pursuing third-party states willing to maintain trade and commerce with it. As the US-North Korea economic relationship was never fully realized due to the implementation of sanctions beginning in the 1950s, the United States's own sanctions have had seemingly little coercive power as there is marginal direct interdependence between the two states for the United States to weaponize. At the same time, as depicted in the network analysis, North Korea has found other trading partners who have been unwilling to implement or enforce sanctions, thereby allowing North Korea to evade sanctions pressures. Despite its weak connection to North Korea's network due to its own sanctions, the United States may have been able to influence North Korea vis-à-vis two key allies—Japan and South Korea—in East Asia that played key roles in the region. Both countries have been key nodes in North Korea's trading network.

We contend that North Korea has been able to survive and adapt to economic and financial sanctions because it finds a new benefactor when others begin implementing and enforcing sanctions, which reflects its agency in mitigating the impact of economic sanctions by seeking out trade partners willing to engage. In the case of North Korea's relationship with Japan, Japan's share of North Korean trade went from one of the largest in the 1990s to almost non-existent from the mid-2000s onward as Japan began imposing sanctions. As a result of unilateral and multilateral sanctions, North Korea sought other support from a wide array of trading partners but relied singularly on China. This development is especially problematic from the US perspective as not only can North Korea evade the United States's sanctions pressures, but sanctions pressures from the US allies such as Japan and South Korea as well.

North Korea's trading partners have not only diversified, but its share of trade has moved from being distributed across the remaining members of the Six-Party Talks (minus the United States) to one, in which China accounts for the lion's share of North Korea's trade and South Korea and Japan no longer provide nearly any share of North Korea's total trade. The "walks" through the asymmetrical network in which the United States can potentially impact North Korea now pass through key nodes in the network dominated by China or Russia, countries whose interests often fail to align with those of the United States.

The United States' ability to weaponize interdependence is a lost cause with North Korea as North Korea by 2017 relies almost solely on China as well as Russia, India, and other minor trading partners. As with any criminal syndicate (Sanger 2020), North Korea has also created a dense network through which it can pursue illicit activities to finance the developments of its nuclear and ballistic missile programs. Future research should work to map North Korea's illicit trade and financial activity, data that is partially captured through media investigations and UN Panel of Expert reports. The United States' ability to exert chokepoint or panopticon effects is further limited as, for example, North Korea continues to develop sophisticated cyberoperations to generate hard currency for itself (Inskit Group and Recorded Future 2020; Izenman and Norton-Williams 2020; Panel of Experts 2019; Sanger 2020). Given North Korea's reliance on illicit networks and its dependence on rents in the form of foreign aid and humanitarian assistance. Future studies should also consider different types of networks, specifically the network of overseas development assistance or foreign aid, which also helps to explain North Korea's resilience against economic sanctions.

From the perspective of policymakers looking for solutions to the North Korea dilemma, current approaches are unlikely to bring about a change in the status quo (Brewer and Terry 2021). As the United States continues to isolate North Korea from the global financial system and maintain blistering unilateral coupled with multilateral sanctions through the UN, North Korea's licit and illicit networks will further limit the United States' ability to coerce North Korea into changing its behavior. The United States' efforts to isolate North Korea has only pushed the two sides farther apart, and a solution to the diplomatic impasse that leads to the denuclearization of the Korean peninsula remains elusive. The overuse of economic sanctions is instead allowing North Korea to develop more sophisticated methods of sanctions evasion, methods that could be reproduced and exported to other states facing similar situations with the United States and the UN (Inskit Group and Recorded Future 2020). Continued economic and financial sanctions are undermining US power (Arnold 2016) and generating anti-dollar bias (McDowell 2023), and North Korea's recent shift to mining cryptocurrencies may be the first sign that US dollar dominance in the global financial system is unable to hinder North Korean efforts to grow and develop its nuclear arsenal and means of WMD delivery. While sanctions may have slowed DPRK progress in growing its WMD arsenal and programs, slow progress is still progress.

Chapter 3

Traders with Pariahs

An In-Depth Examination of North Korea's Key Trading Relationships

Chapter 2 profiled North Korea's licit and illicit trade networks and showed how the DPRK's networks have shifted dramatically from isolated to a black knight network, especially after the UN began levying sanctions in 2006. In this chapter, we provide an in-depth discussion of the trajectory of North Korea's key trading relationships to better understand why a state would trade with a "pariah" or why it would abstain, paying special attention to trading partners' policies that led to the generation of chokepoint or panopticon effects. Figure 3.1 provides a summary of the economic trajectories of North Korea's trade relationships with key partners. As the figure shows, several individual countries have been integral to North Korean trade from 1990 to 2017, namely China, Japan, and South Korea. We thus profile North Korea's relationships with its neighbors in the sections to follow. We also examine the DPRK's relationship with both Russia and the United States, despite their low levels of North Korea's trade share. While Russia's trade with North Korea was minuscule during this period (albeit with a peak in the early 2000s), the Soviet Union was a major DPRK trading partner prior to 1990 and, as we showed in chapter 2, Russia has become an important trading partner once again as sanctions inhibit North Korea's trade with many other states. As we show later, this is no accident: Russian policymakers have sought to strengthen Russia-DPRK ties since the late 1990s. Thus, we examine this increasingly important trading relationship. And while the DPRK-US relationship is virtually non-existent throughout this period (and for most of the relationship), we discuss the United States as it is a major sender of sanctions against the North. While Figure 3.1 shows that there is little economic exchange between the United States and North Korea, an in-depth analysis shows that there have been several moments for the relationship to potentially change. However, these moments typically have not panned out due to

American domestic politics and US interests, North Korea's "adventurism" and weapons tests, and the inability of both countries to see eye-to-eye at the bargaining table.

We begin the chapter by discussing the Sino-North Korean relationship, one that has been important to the DPRK for its entire existence but especially after losing its other key benefactor, the Soviet Union, at the beginning of the 1990s and in the face of blistering sanctions. The Sino-North Korean relationship is one that is classic in both the sanctions and pariah state literature: a black knight (China) who is willing to bust sanctions and a pariah (North Korea) who has little choice but to find a powerful ally in a hostile international environment. We then discuss inter-Korean relations, another one that is significant to North Korea politically and economically. While inter-Korean relations were generally hostile until South Korea's democratization in 1987, South Korea's foreign policy toward the DPRK has vacillated between policies that generate panopticon effects and those that spawn chokepoint effects depending on which political party is in power. Also, UN sanctions have made economic exchange riskier and thus, even the ROK's engagement strategies are limited.

Next, we profile the North Korea-Japan relationship, one that is complicated by Japan's imperial past. We find that DPRK-Japan economic relations are largely driven by the North Korean diaspora living in Japan, the

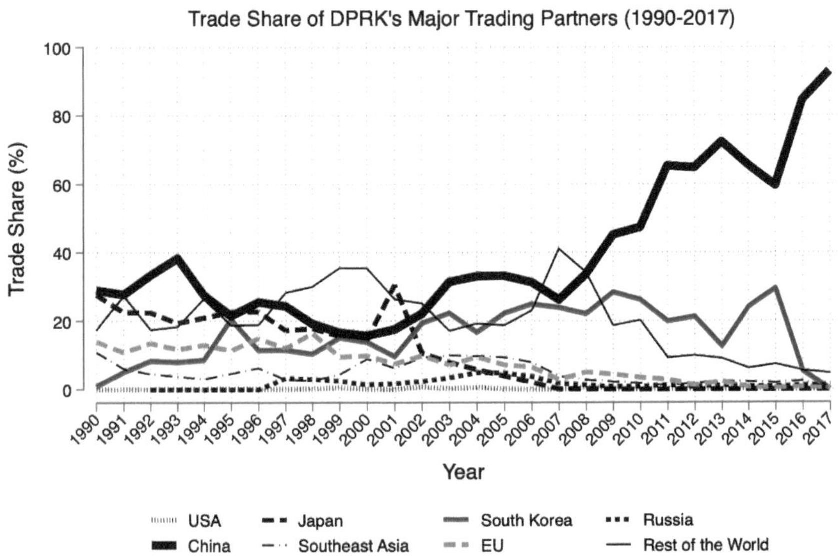

Figure 3.1 Share of Trade (%) with North Korea. Thicker lines are the countries profiled here (all participants of the Six-Party Talks); dashed lines indicate trade from other key regions and the rest of the world. *Source*: Created by Authors.

chongryon or *chosen soren.* Although Japan was one of North Korea's top trading partners in the early 2000s, the relationship quickly soured as Kim Jong-Il revealed that North Koreans had kidnapped Japanese citizens and the DPRK began its nuclear tests. The fourth relationship examined in this chapter is the Russian-North Korean relationship. The Soviet Union was, along with China, one of North Korea's patrons during the Cold War, providing it with aid, technical expertise, and large volumes of economic exchange. However, the relationship changed dramatically when the USSR collapsed in the early 1990s and Russia began to democratize, leaving its "younger brother" behind. Russia quickly realized, however, that its key to regional influence was having a close relationship with the DPRK and thus, mostly under Vladimir Putin's leadership, Russia has tried to restore its relationship. Finally, we profile the US-DPRK relationship, which has never really developed economically or politically. We argue that the US sanctions have largely failed to change North Korean behavior because the two countries engage in virtually no commerce with each other. The United States, like South Korea and Japan, has also been constrained in creating foreign policy toward North Korea due to infighting between Congress and the president and within the president's own cabinet. As such, besides a preference for sanctions, there has been little inconsistency in US foreign policy toward North Korea.

LIMITED LEVERAGE THROUGH ECONOMIC TIES: CHINA-NORTH KOREA RELATIONS

While the development of North Korea's nuclear weapons program has complicated the Sino-North Korean relationship, China has remained a key ally of North Korea since the beginning of their relationship. Economically, North Korea has been highly dependent on China, not only as its top trading partner but also as a receiver of economic aid (Haggard and Noland 2007; Snyder 2009b). That dependence has largely not translated to Chinese leverage over North Korea as many policymakers believe: the North Korean government perceives Chinese aid as penance for its betrayal when it normalized relations with South Korea. Additionally, the Chinese government had hoped that North Korea would use China as a model for economic development and make similar liberalizing reforms as Deng had in China. Despite some minimal reforms in 2002, North Korea has not followed China's model and the Kim regime remains "resistant to suggestions of Chinese-style economic reforms" (Snyder 2009b, 122). While its leverage over North Korea is debatable, China has arguably the most leverage out of any other member of the international community due to the strength of its economic and political ties with the country.

However, the Sino-North Korean relationship changed significantly under Deng's regime, which began in the mid-1970s and lasted into the late 1980s (though his influence on Chinese politics carried into the 1990s). Deng, recognizing that economic prosperity was crucial to regime survival and legitimacy, prioritized economic development over political considerations and thus was willing to do business with states who were ideologically different from China such as South Korea and the United States. By instituting economic reforms that allowed China to attract foreign direct investment (FDI) and foreign technology, Deng was able to significantly spur China's economic growth: China's national income grew from 242.7 billion yuan in 1976 to 2488.2 billion yuan in 1993 (Zhao 1996, 62). Additionally, the collapse of several Eastern European states and the Soviet Union in the late 1980s and early 1990s meant that North Korea lost major political allies and economic partners, thus making it even more dependent on China for support. This development also gave China more leverage over North Korea, especially as China established an economic relationship with South Korea in 1992. Therefore, China indisputably became North Korea's biggest trading partner in the early 1990s, as shown in Figure 3.1.

The nuclear crises involving North Korea, starting with the first crisis in 1994, have complicated the Sino-North Korean relationship. From 1994 to 2006, China regularly used its veto power on the UN Security Council (UNSC) to impede multilateral sanctions against North Korea, due to its concerns about North Korean regime collapse. For China, maintaining the status quo is crucial to allowing it to focus on its own economic development. Economic sanctions may upset the status quo in ways that may hinder China's economic development. First, economic sanctions that facilitate North Korean regime collapse may lead to an influx of Korean refugees into China. Second, even if the North Korean regime does not collapse, sanctions may provoke North Korea, potentially leading to armed conflict that could destabilize the region. At the same time however, China has used the threat of abstaining from UNSC resolutions as leverage to bring North Korea to the negotiation table, as it did during the First Nuclear Crisis in 1994 (Funabashi 2007, 323). Between China's frustration at North Korea's instigation of the crisis, the death of North Korean leader Kim Il-Sung, and the emergence of China's new trading relationship with ascendant South Korea, Sino-North Korean trade plummeted between 1993 and 1995, as depicted in Figure 3.1 (Snyder 2009b, 111–8).

The Sino-North Korean relationship, politically and economically, improved somewhat in 1996 and 1997. North Korea hesitantly agreed to the South Korea-US proposal for four-party talks on peace in the Korean Peninsula, of which China was both a participant and a host (Snyder 2009b, 119). From the Chinese perspective, this boded well in terms of providing the regional stability necessary for economic development. Second, China was the first country to provide humanitarian assistance to North Korea during the latter's food crisis (Snyder 2009b, 111–20). However, China decreased its humanitarian aid to North Korea in subsequent years as other countries and international organizations increased their aid to the country (Snyder 2009b, 111). This pattern of a modest increase in China's share of North Korean trade in 1996–1997 and a slight decrease in its share from 1998 to 2000 is reflected in Figure 3.1.

While the 2000s started with a decline in the Sino-North Korean economic relationship, it ended with China as an indispensable ally of North Korea, as reflected by the trajectory of their trading relationship in Figure 3.1. Although there was relatively little interaction between the two countries in the year 2000, trade jumped notably in 2001 as both countries sought to reinvigorate their bilateral relationship via high-level visits and negotiations (Snyder 2009b, 122–3). Between Kim Jong-Il's visit to Beijing and President Jiang's visit to Pyongyang, the two countries agreed to consult on regional issues, economic cooperation, increasing high-level exchanges, and increased Chinese aid and economic assistance to North Korea (Snyder 2009b, 123). Such engagement policies, especially consultation, exchanges, and economic cooperation, generated panopticon effects and allowed each country to get information about the other.

China also played a major role in facilitating North Korean participation in the Six-Party Talks, which began in 2003 (Funabashi 2007). In its role as host and mediator, China has continuously urged North Korea to discontinue its nuclear program and to return to the talks when it has abandoned them. China also discouraged the United States and others from using military force against the North, as well. Additionally, China "sought to enhance its political influence on North Korea" by increasing its share of economic trade with North Korea; as depicted in Figure 3.1, China's share of North Korean trade has increased significantly since 2002 (Snyder 2009b, 111). In the context of the Six-Party Talks, China also used economic incentives to specifically induce North Korean participation in the talks. Two examples illustrate these economic incentives. First, in 2004, China promised North Korea an additional $50 million if it would rejoin the talks (Funabashi 2007, 321; Snyder 2009b, 125). Second, in 2005, China further tightened its economic relationship with North Korea by increasing investment in projects near the countries' shared border (such as the Rason Economic Special Zone) and economic assistance (Snyder 2009b, 125–6).

The Sino-North Korean relationship had a setback in 2006, following North Korea's first nuclear test. For the first time, China abstained from voting on economic sanctions against North Korea in the UNSC, which enabled the passage of UNSCR 1718. Accordingly, Figure 3.1 shows a downturn in China's share of North Korea's trade from 2006 to 2007. China notably voted in favor of UNSCR 1874 following North Korea's second nuclear test in 2009; it has consistently voted in favor of UN economic sanctions since 1874.

China's preference for multilateral sanctions vs. unilateral ones generated chokepoint effects that served as leverage in its dealings with North Korea. However, China's economic relationship with North Korea has continued to grow, especially as other countries have ceased or significantly curtailed trade with North Korea due to the implementation of multilateral sanctions, supported by Figure 3.1 (Haggard and Noland 2017, 228).

One of the major debates around the effectiveness of multilateral sanctions against North Korea is the extent to which China has complied with the UNSC resolutions. China, arguably, has a tendency to comply with the resolutions in name but not in spirit. For example, as Jun (2013) states, China does not view economic sanctions as mutually exclusive to other forms of economic cooperation and continues to contribute to joint projects such as the Rason Special Economic Zone. Additionally, when China has complied with Security Council sanctions regarding one economic sector, it compensates by increasing trade with North Korea in another area, leading to sustained or even increased trading revenues between the two states (Haggard and Noland 2010). China has also insisted on the inclusion of a "livelihood exemption" in the UNSC resolutions where UN member states could continue to import North Korean coal if "cutting it off might affect the livelihood of the exporter, so long as the revenue doesn't go to North Korea's nuclear program" (Hu 2016, 20). China often invoked this loophole for importing North Korean goods such as coal and has thus remained mostly in compliance with the UNSC resolutions. More problematically, trade has continued vis-à-vis private entities while the Chinese government has typically turned a blind eye (Early 2015, 25–8).

As this discussion highlights, the Sino-North Korean relationship is a complicated one. North Korea's continued nuclear provocations and ailing economy have devalued North Korea as a partner in the eyes of the Chinese government. While China is clearly committed to preventing regime collapse, it has been increasingly vocal about its dissatisfaction with North Korean behavior. At the same time, however, China's policy toward North Korea is driven by its concerns about North Korean regime collapse, and it is willing to exert economic pressure on North Korea only to a point. As stated by one Chinese official: "the fact is that a collapsing country in chaos and turmoil won't serve Chinese interests. So from that perspective, we won't reduce our assistance to the DPRK" (Snyder 2009b, 128).

TO ENGAGE OR NOT TO ENGAGE? INTER-KOREAN RELATIONS

The inter-Korean relationship is, arguably, one of North Korea's most important albeit complicated ones. Unlike most of the other countries profiled in this chapter, South Korea democratized in the years leading up to the timespan of our study. South Korea's democratization created a profound shift in the inter-Korean relationship, going from a foreign policy that largely treated North Korea as an enemy to a more unstable relationship where North Korea policy vacillates depending on who is in the Blue House. The progressive presidents (Kim Dae Jung, Roh Moo Hyun, and Moon Jae-In) opted for policies of unconditional economic engagement with the North (generating panopticon effects) while the conservative administrations of Lee Myung Bak and Park Geun Hye sought greater reciprocity from the relationship. However, both the Roh and Moon's administrations were somewhat constrained in economic engagement with the DPRK due to the UN sanctions that started in 2006. In this sense, it is unsurprising that the line representing inter-Korean trade in Figure 3.1 has many peaks and valleys over the course of our study. However, neither approach has been effective to date in inducing North Korea to abandon its nuclear and ballistic weapons programs. South Korea's relationship with the United States also impacts the former's *nordpolitik.* Taken together, this section shows how domestic politics and international alliances impact foreign policy decisions, at times limiting states' ability to establish and weaponize interdependence over others through chokepoint and panopticon effects.

Between the Korean War and 1987, the inter-Korean relationship was mostly "characterized by mutual antagonism, without compromise or dialogue," with few exceptions (K. A. Park and Lee 1992, 429). In the decades after the Korean War, both sides conceived different ideas of how the country might reunify. The high point in the inter-Korean relationship during this period occurred in the early 1970s with the North-South Joint Communique, which included "three basic principles for reunification: independence from foreign interference, unification through peaceful means, and promotion of 'grand national unity'" (K. A. Park and Lee 1992, 432). However, both Koreas ultimately failed to meet the goals of this agreement as the United States maintained its military bases in the South and neither side made further tangible steps to "peaceful reunification." While there were several meetings between the two countries in the subsequent decade, they made little progress toward reunification or even ameliorating inter-Korean relations (K. A. Park and Lee 1992, 433–35). In fact, several events during the 1980s hurt the relationship including North Korea's 1983 attempted assassination of South Korean president Chun Doo Hwan in Myanmar and the North Korean bombing of a Korean Air Lines plane in 1987 (K. A. Park and Lee 1992, 435).

However, a major critical juncture in the inter-Korean relationship occurred in 1987 when South Korea began to democratize. The relationship has generally improved since South Korea's democratization for several reasons (Chung 2003, 32). First, democratization led to new freedoms of expression and other civil rights. As in other authoritarian regimes, the

South Korean government repressed civil rights, such as the freedom of expression, between the end of the Korean War to 1987. Debates about topics such as the US-South Korean security alliance and South Korea's North Korea policy were taboo (S. A. Smith 2006, 17). However, after democratization, such topics became open to discussion. Furthermore, leftist civil society organizations and activists began advocating for a more conciliatory stance toward North Korea (Chung 2003, 15). Second, democratically elected leaders are more responsive than their authoritarian counterparts, at least if they want to win re-election. As democratization facilitated open public debate about inter-Korean relations, South Korean leaders have since taken a variety of stances on North Korea in the hopes of appealing to the public. Progressive presidents Kim Dae Jung, Roh Moo Hyun, and Moon Jae-In have taken a more conciliatory approach to dealing with North Korea while conservative presidents Lee Myung Bak and Park Geun Hye have taken a harder line. Although inter-Korean relations have improved since democratization, "they have become more erratic, depending on who is in charge of democratized South Korea and its relations with the North at the moment" (Chung 2003, 11).

Thus, South Korean engagement with North Korea during our study is in part a function of Korean domestic politics. The first years of our study, the early 1990s, represented a high point in inter-Korean relations, in part because of South Korea's democratization and interest in improving relations with the North. For its part, the North also had the incentive to improve its relationship with South Korea due to the collapse of the Soviet Union, one of its key economic benefactors, and the general decline of the North Korean economy. North Korean trade decreased steadily in the late 1980s while its foreign debt increased (K. A. Park and Lee 1992, 444). In this context, "it needed to reduce its excessive military expenditures, which would be difficult without an agreement on arms reduction with the South" (K. A. Park and Lee 1992, 444). These favorable conditions for inter-Korean relations manifested in a series of high-level talks in the early 1990s (generating panopticon effects) and eventually two significant agreements, the Agreement on Reconciliation, Nonaggression, Exchanges and Cooperation between the North and the South and the Joint Declaration for a Non-Nuclear Korean Peninsula in 1991 (K. A. Park and Lee 1992, 436). As Figure 3.1 depicts, inter-Korean trade began to pick up in the 1990s as South Korea encompassed a larger share of North Korea's total trade.

Unfortunately, the détente between the two Koreas did not last as North Korea refused International Atomic Energy Agency (IAEA) inspections of its nuclear development program and threatened to withdraw from the Non-Proliferation Treaty (NPT) (Mazarr 1995, 95–6). As mentioned, the IAEA inspections can generate important panopticon effects by obtaining information about states' nuclear programs, including if they are using them for weapons instead of energy, a violation of the NPT. For their part, the United States and South Korea also hindered inter-Korean reconciliation as they resumed their annual Team Spirit joint military exercises, which they had paused per North Korea's request (Mazarr 1995, 95). Inter-Korean relations eventually improved following the signing of the Agreed Framework in 1994.

South Korea's North Korean policy went through a dramatic change in 1998 with the election of President Kim Dae Jung. Kim is perhaps known best for his "Sunshine Policy" toward North Korea. Named for one of Aesop's fables, the policy emphasized various forms of engagement with the North. The idea, stemming from liberalism in international relations, is that cooperation and trust-building in areas like economics and culture will spill over into security cooperation and lessen conflict between the two Koreas (Insoo Kim and Lee 2011, 57). Accordingly, Kim promoted various forms of inter-Korean engagement. First, the early 2000s saw several high-level summits between the two countries, including a rare summit between the countries' two leaders in 2000 (Chung 2003, 29). These diplomatic exchanges generated panopticon effects through data gathering by diplomats and other officials. Second, through inter-Korean meetings, Kim was able to create a variety of people-to-people exchanges such as family reunions and cultural exchanges (Chung 2003, 28; Son 2006, 84). For example, after the 2002 inter-Korean ministerial summit, North Korea agreed to participate in the Asian Games in Busan (Chung 2003, 30).

The area of inter-Korean engagement under the Sunshine Policy most germane to our study was the economic exchanges. One of the key developments in this area took place shortly after Kim took office: lifting the ceiling on South Korean investment in North Korea and making it easier for South Koreans to travel North (Chung 2003, 29; Son 2006, 83). One consequence of this policy was the establishment of the Mt. Kumgang tourist resort in North Korea in 1998, which the chaebol (South Korean business conglomerate) Hyundai and the North Korean Asia-Pacific Peace Committee (KAPPC) founded (Son 2006, 84). Another was the discussion of the Kaesong industrial project involving South Korean companies and North Korean workers in Kaesong, North Korea (Chung 2003, 30). The project, now known as the Kaesong Industrial Complex (KIC), was launched under the Roh Moo Hyun administration in 2004. Roh, like his predecessor, believed that engagement and cooperation with the North would foster "peaceful coexistence" (Bae and Moon 2014, 15). Thus, it is unsurprising that inter-Korean trade rose to its highest level in the early 2000s, as shown in Figure 3.1 (Chung 2003, 29).

While both the Kim and Roh administrations opted for engagement with North Korea, the inter-Korean relationship changed dramatically with Lee Myung Bak's election in 2009 (Snyder 2009a, 92). Lee's "Denuclearization and Opening, 3000" policy toward North Korea reflected the South Korean public's dissatisfaction with his predecessor's conciliatory approach to the North (Snyder 2009a, 93). Despite increased political, cultural, and economic exchanges as well as unconditional foreign aid, North Korea continued to develop its nuclear weapons program. Under Roh's administration, North Korea tested its first nuclear weapon. Thus, it is unsurprising that Lee's more hardline approach appealed to the Korean electorate. However, North Korea noticed this policy shift, leading to "frustration and irritation with South Korea" (Snyder 2009a, 93). One result was North Korea's *tongmi bongnam* policy, "through which the North focused on negotiations with the United States while marginalizing South Korea" (Snyder 2009a, 93). As the inter-Korean relationship deteriorated, North Korea began using its joint ventures with South Korea, Mt. Kumgang and KIC, as bargaining chips and threatened to close off South Korea's access to these projects over numerous issues, namely South Korean civilians' propaganda leaflets (Snyder 2009a, 94–6). Inter-Korean relations continued to nosedive in 2010 after the Republic of Korea (ROK) naval vessel, the Cheonan, sank near Baengnyeong Island. The cause of the ship's sinking was inconclusive, but some evidence suggests that North Korea was the culprit (Cha 2010). Inter-Korean relations took another hit later that year after the two sides exchanged artillery fire near South Korea's Yeonpyeong Island (*BBC News* 2010). Unsurprisingly, inter-Korean trade steadily declined from 2009 to 2013, as Figure 3.1 depicts.

Inter-Korean relations continued to cool under Park Geun Hye's truncated regime, who was Lee's successor. Although Park had initially proposed incremental engagement (albeit not the unconditional aid policies of Lee's predecessors), she eventually severed inter-Korean economic cooperation in response to North Korea's various ballistic missile tests and fourth nuclear test in 2016, generating chokepoint effects (Klinger 2016, 2017, 165). As Figure 3.1 shows, inter-Korean trade improved at the beginning of Park's tenure but sharply declined in 2016, the same year as the fourth nuclear test. However, the relationship took another turn in 2017 with the election of the progressive Moon Jae-In. Moon, like Kim Dae Jung and Roh Moo Hyun, emphasized engagement and unconditional aid in his North Korea policy, generating panopticon effects. During his presidential campaign, Moon stated that "I would consider visiting Pyongyang first before Washington" and criticized the United States' deployment of the Terminal High Altitude Area Defense (THAAD) system in South Korea (Inhan Kim 2017, 165). Perhaps most notably, Moon's diplomacy played a key role in diffusing the Third North Korean Nuclear Crisis in 2017. Moon met his North Korean counterpart, Kim Jung-Un, in Panmunjom, the first inter-Korean summit between the countries' leaders in eleven years and the first time since the end of the Korean War that a North Korean leader has been in the South (Roegiers and Almond 2018).

South Korea's foreign policy toward North Korea has changed a lot since the division of the Korean Peninsula and the Korean War. Authoritarian regimes from the end of the Korean War until South Korea's democratization in 1987 largely opted not to engage with North Korea. After 1987, South Korean leaders' North Korea policies have vacillated from unconditional engagement to severing ties depending on the president's political affiliation. However, it appears that none of these approaches have been successful in stemming North Korea's nuclear weapons and missile development programs. One complicating factor is South Korea's relationship with the United States. Given the US-ROK security alliance, it is imperative for both countries to consult one another and take each other's stances into consideration when interacting with North Korea. However, the United States and South Korea have often taken different approaches to deal with North Korea, at times contradicting the other's approach (Bae 2010, 335). A key example occurred in 2002 during the Kim Dae Jung administration. While Kim Dae Jung was advocating for unconditional engagement with North Korea through his Sunshine Policy, the Bush administration declared that North Korea was part of the "Axis of Evil" (Chung 2003, 30). Naturally, this complicated Kim's efforts to dissuade North Korea from developing its weapons programs; as the opening quote suggests, he partially blamed US-DPRK relations for the Sunshine Policy's failure.

However, the disjuncture between South Korean and US policy toward the North does not appear to necessarily be about different political affiliations. The Lee and Bush administrations (both conservative), for example, also struggled to get on the same page while Moon and Trump (one progressive, one conservative) both opted for engagement with the North after the crisis in 2017. With a series of UN sanctions imposed on North Korea since 2006 as well as the United States' own sanctions, South Korean economic engagement with North Korea is more difficult now than ever before (Inhan Kim 2017, 176–7). This case shows that it is important for allies to adopt the same sorts of policies (those generating panopticon or chokepoint effects) for them to have a chance at being effective in weaponizing leverage. Otherwise, divergent policies may undermine each other.

WHEN DOMESTIC POLITICS WEAKENS ECONOMIC LEVERAGE: JAPAN-NORTH KOREA RELATIONS

The Japan-North Korea relationship has been a turbulent one since its inception, characterized by periods of estrangement and rapprochement. A review of the Japan-North Korean economic relationship reveals two crucial elements: the extent to which economic relations are driven by political developments and the North Korean diasporic community in Japan (*chongryon* or *chosen soren*). Notably, no formal diplomatic relations have existed between the two countries since North Korea's formation, in contrast to the normalization of the Japan-South Korean relationship in 1965 (H. N. Kim 1991, 164). However, the *chongryon*, established in 1955, have served as a de facto North Korean embassy in Japan and a link to North Korean trade (Samuels 2004, 319; Blomquist and Wertz 2015). However, without formal relations or formalizing the *chongryon*'s role in Japan's North Korea policy, the emergence of panopticon effects is unlikely. Instead, Japan has largely opted for policies like sanctions that generate chokepoint effects.

There were few positive interactions between Japan and North Korea in the decades following the Korean War, particularly in the political realm. Despite an atmosphere of reconciliation in East Asia in the 1970s, there was limited change in the political relationship between the two countries. However, economic linkages between the two largely developed in that decade, driven by small- and medium-sized businesses associated with the *chongryon* community (Okano-Heijmans 2010, 379). The relationship took a turn for the worse in the 1980s after North Korea's attack on South Korean cabinet members in Burma in 1983 (Hagström and Söderberg 2006, 2; H. N. Kim 1991, 164).

The 1990s, where the current study begins, were arguably the pinnacle of Japan-North Korean relations. Japan was one of North Korea's top trading partners during the decade, behind China (Figure 3.1). There were several reasons for Japan-North Korea rapprochement at the beginning of the 1990s for both countries. For Japan, normalization would provide Japanese businesses with greater access to the North Korean market and other business opportunities (Hagström and Söderberg 2006, 3; Okano-Heijmans 2010, 379). Negotiations were also politically important because they could help procure the release of the crew of the *Fujisanmaru,* a Japanese fishing vessel whose crew had been captured in North Korean waters in the 1980s (Hagström and Söderberg 2006, 2–3). For its part, North Korea had several pressing reasons for ameliorating its relationship with Japan. First, North Korea's traditional "patrons" (China and the Soviet Union) had begun opening relations with North Korea's foes, namely South Korea (H. N. Kim 1991, 165; Okano-Heijmans 2010, 374). Furthermore, and perhaps more importantly, several Eastern European states and the Soviet Union collapsed around the beginning of the decade, depriving North Korea of significant trade partners and political allies. These developments encouraged North Korea to diversify its economic relations, especially as North Korea's economy was rapidly deteriorating and its traditional allies experienced economic difficulties of their own (H. N. Kim 1991, 165).

In 1990, a Japanese delegation led by a Liberal Democratic Party (LDP) official, Shin Kanemaru, met with Korean Workers Party (KWP) representatives in Pyongyang. The negotiations, at first, appeared to signal an improvement in Japan-North Korean relations in several respects. First, North Korea agreed to release the crewmembers of the *Fujisanmaru*. Second, both delegations issued a Joint Statement in which the Japanese side agreed to apologize for Japanese atrocities during its colonial rule of Korea and compensate North Korea accordingly (it had already made a similar agreement with South Korea) (Blomquist and Wertz 2015; Hagström and Söderberg 2006, 3; H. N. Kim 1991, 166). Additionally, both countries pledged to move toward normalization (Blomquist and Wertz 2015; Hagström and Söderberg 2006, 3; H. N. Kim 1991, 166). Prospects of improved relations between Japan and North Korea corresponded with a relatively stable level of Japan's share of North Korea's trade between 1991 and 1992 (Figure 3.1).

Eight rounds of normalization negotiations took place between Japan and North Korea from the beginning of 1991 to the end of 1992 (Hagström and Söderberg 2006, 3). Normalization between the two countries ultimately failed to manifest for several reasons. First, the Japanese and North Korean governments could not agree on terms regarding wartime reparations (Hagström and Söderberg 2006, 3). Second, the two countries could not agree on how to address the case of Lee Eun-hye, a Japanese citizen whom a North Korean soldier had admitted to kidnapping; the issue of Japanese abductees would play an even larger role in bilateral relations a decade later (Blomquist and Wertz 2015; Hagström and Söderberg 2006, 3; Okano-Heijmans 2010, 373). The straw that broke the proverbial camel's back in this attempt at Japan-North Korean normalization was North Korea's 1993 declaration that it would withdraw from the NPT and its successful Nodong-1 missile test (Blomquist and Wertz 2015; Hagström and Söderberg 2006, 3; Okano-Heijmans 2010, 373). One of the implications of these developments on the Japan-North Korea economic relationship was that Japanese officials were becoming increasingly wary of engaging with North Korea. As Okano-Heijmans (2010) states, "organizations with a friendly attitude towards North Korea became marginalized and replaced by groups considering ways to contain Pyongyang" (372). However, the *chongryon* continued to facilitate economic relations between Japan and North Korea; from 1992 to 2006, they ferried goods and remittances between the countries using large commercial vessels, such as the Mangyongbong-92 (Blomquist and Wertz 2015).

The Japan-North Korea relationship improved somewhat in the mid-1990s with the signing of the 1994 Agreed Framework between North Korea and the United States, a major Japanese ally (Blomquist and Wertz 2015). As a member of KEDO, Japan agreed to contribute funding to develop light-water nuclear reactors for North Korean energy usage per the Agreed Framework (Hagström and Söderberg 2006, 3; Okano-Heijmans 2010, 372). It also started providing humanitarian assistance to North Korea in 1995 during the latter's widespread famine and attempting to restart normalization talks in the same year (Blomquist and Wertz 2015; Hagström and Söderberg 2006, 3; Okano-Heijmans 2010, 372). However, any progress toward normalization came to a halt in 1998 when North Korea test-fired its Taepodong-1 missile over the Sea of Japan (Blomquist and Wertz 2015; Hagström and Söderberg 2006, 3; Okano-Heijmans 2010, 373). In response, Japan ceased its contributions to KEDO, its humanitarian aid, and its normalization negotiations (Blomquist and Wertz 2015; Hagström and Söderberg 2006, 3; Okano-Heijmans 2010, 373). The missile test also dampened Japan-North Korea economic relations as Japanese politicians prepared to stop remittances from the *chongryon* community to North Korea (Hagström and Söderberg 2006, 3). Furthermore, the Japanese government began to closely scrutinize and crack down on illicit economic activities associated with *chongryon*, such as making false loans (Funabashi 2007; Blomquist and Wertz 2015). This decline in the Japan-North Korea relationship corresponds with a slow but steady decline in Japan's share of North Korean trade from the mid-to late-1990s.

The turn of the century saw another attempt at Japan-North Korea rapprochement, following the summit between the two Koreas in 2000 (Okano-Heijmans 2010, 373). Japan agreed to restart its contributions to KEDO and resume humanitarian aid to North Korea (Blomquist and Wertz 2015; Hagström and Söderberg 2006, 4; Okano-Heijmans 2010, 383). The two countries also resumed normalization talks in the same year (Blomquist and Wertz 2015; Hagström and Söderberg 2006, 4; Okano-Heijmans 2010, 373). The relative stability in the relationship and promising outlook corresponded with an increase in Japan's share of North Korea's trade in 2000, as demonstrated in Figure 3.1. However, normalization negotiations came to an impasse as the two countries could not agree on the terms of either wartime reparations or Japanese abductees (Blomquist and Wertz 2015; Hagström and Söderberg 2006, 4).

Following two years of informal contact, Japanese and North Korean leadership embarked on another round of normalization talks in 2002. This round was especially notable because it was the first time in history that the leaders of both countries, Koizumi Junichiro and Kim Jong-Il, met (Blomquist and Wertz 2015; Hagström and Söderberg 2006, 4). The negotiations yielded the Japan-North Korea Pyongyang Declaration in September 2002. Initially, the declaration appeared to issue a new era of positive relations between the two countries as North Korea agreed to Japan's terms for war compensation, Japan issued an official apology for its occupation of Korea during WWII and pledged economic assistance after normalization, North Korea admitted to and apologized for the abduction of Japanese citizens, and both parties committed to further normalization talks (Blomquist and Wertz 2015; Hagström and Söderberg 2006, 4; Okano-Heijmans 2010, 369). However, North Korea's admission of abducting Japanese citizens proved to be a domestic bombshell in Japan, especially as North Korea reported that more than half the abductees had previously died (Blomquist and Wertz 2015; Hagström and Söderberg 2006, 4). North Korea agreed to allow five abductees to visit their families in Japan; however, Japan-North Korea relations deteriorated quickly when Japan refused to return the abductees to North Korea as agreed (Hagström and Söderberg 2006, 4).

The rupture over the abduction issue had significant implications for the economic relationship between Japan and North Korea, largely driven by Japanese domestic politics. The LDP, Japan's largest party, had adopted a more conservative stance toward North Korea in 2003, favoring chokepoint generating policies, such as sanctions and economic "sticks" over engagement and "carrots." For example, several LDP Diet members proposed to revise the Foreign Exchange and Foreign Trade Control Law to allow Japan to stop *chongryon* remittances to North Korea (Samuels 2004, 322). Furthermore, the LDP prioritized resolving the abductions issue and cracking down on North Korea through economic sanctions in its 2003 election manifesto (Samuels 2004, 322). This strategy paid off for the LDP when the Japanese electorate went to the polls in November, as LDP candidates outperformed those from the Democratic Party of Japan (DPJ) and the Social Democratic Party (SDP), parties who have held more conciliatory positions on North Korea (Samuels 2004, 322–4).

Meanwhile, the Japanese government cracked down on other *chongryon*-linked economic activity, such as conducting more vigorous inspections of cargo ships to North Korea such as the Mangyongbong-92 due to "the suspicion that it was transporting narcotics, illegal remittances of cash, and missile parts" (Samuels 2004, 328). The Japanese government also began cracking down on *chongryon's pachinko* operations (gambling parlors), believed to have funneled money into North Korea, in the following year (Okano-Heijmans 2010, 381). While these policies were not economic sanctions, per se, they too generated chokepoint effects, further diminishing DPRK-Japan economic ties. Therefore, it is unsurprising that after the abductee issue became front-page news in Tokyo in 2002, Japan's share of North Korean trade declined steadily as shown (Figure 3.1).

Japanese and North Korean leadership held another round of high-level talks in 2004, despite the creation of a legal framework for unilateral Japanese sanctions (Okano-Heijmans 2010, 381; Samuels 2004, 328). During negotiations, Japanese leadership pledged to resume humanitarian aid to North Korea (Hagström and Söderberg 2006, 5; Okano-Heijmans 2010, 383). Subsequently, however, progress toward normalization came to a halt in 2004 over the abductee issue. In December of that year, DNA tests reportedly showed that the supposed remains of one of the deceased abductees, Yokota Megumi, belonged to several other people (Hagström and Söderberg 2006, 5). Again, the abductee issue came to the fore of the Japan-North Korea relationship, especially in the minds of the Japanese public. It also played a key role in the Six-Party Talks in the 2000s, as Japan brought the issue to the multilateral bargaining table in the hopes of resolving it as part of a comprehensive agreement along with encouraging North Korea to pledge to stop its nuclear weapons development program (Hiraiwa 2020, 10).

Japan-North Korea relations, both politically and economically, went from bad to worse in 2006 when North Korea tested its first nuclear weapon. Japan began imposing unilateral economic sanctions on North Korea starting in 2006. The sanctions, which went beyond what was required by UN Security Council Resolution 1718, included a ban on "all North Korean imports and prohibit[ed] the Mangyongbong-92 ferry from entering the country" (Blomquist and Wertz 2015; Okano-Heijmans 2010, 381). Relations between the two countries continued to deteriorate in the following years, as the Japanese government refused to provide humanitarian assistance to North Korea or cooperate with KEDO unless the abduction issue was resolved (Okano-Heijmans 2010, 383–4). The continued deterioration of the Japan-North Korea relationship is reflected in Figure 3.1, as Japan's share of North Korean trade dropped to almost $0 around 2007, mirroring the US-North Korea economic relationship.

At the beginning of the 1990s, Japan-North Korea rapprochement appeared possible and even likely as both countries looked to diversify their economic relationships. However, by the 2010s, there were few political and economic connections between the two countries as they had reached an impasse over the abduction issue and the Japanese government imposed economic sanctions and cracked down on *chongryon*-linked economic activities, an important source of North Korean revenue. While sanctions were not the only reason for the decline in economic relations between Japan and North Korea, they had a significant impact on trade: total trade declined from $120 million in 2006 (itself only one-third of the 2002 level) to $9 million in 2007 (Okano-Heijmans 2010, 380). The decline in the economic relationship not only signifies fewer economic opportunities for Japan but also undermines the effectiveness of Japan's sanctions. Instead of bringing North Korea to the bargaining table, sanctions have forced North Korea to find other countries willing to do business, such as China and South Korea (Hiraiwa 2020, 14; Okano-Heijmans 2010, 380). North Korea is thus less economically dependent on Japan, and Japan has little of its own leverage over North Korea (Hiraiwa 2020, 14; Okano-Heijmans 2010, 384).

IN SEARCH OF LEVERAGE: RUSSIA-NORTH KOREA RELATIONS

Like North Korea's relationship with China, its relationship with the Soviet Union and later Russia is more complicated than is conventionally believed. The relationship has gone through both cold snaps and warm periods, with little interaction between the two at times and high levels of exchange at others. The USSR was one of two of North Korea's patrons, along with China (Haggard and Noland 2007, 27). However, the relationship fundamentally changed with the collapse of the Soviet Union and Russia's democratization during the early 1990s. Russia lost interest in maintaining a close relationship with the DPRK in favor of normalization with South Korea and stronger relations with the US and other Western powers. However, it soon found that its value in East Asia was predicated on its relationship with the North. In the late 1990s and since Vladimir Putin's election in 2000, Russia prioritized a strong relationship with the DPRK to bolster its regional influence and fashion itself as an "honest broker" on the increasingly tense Korean Peninsula, opting for engagement policies that generate panopticon effects. For its part, North Korea has welcomed another ally that can help it survive in the face of escalating sanctions and to lessen its dependence on China.

The USSR and the United States agreed on the design and the terms of the division of the Korean Peninsula at the end of WWII, with a US-backed state in the southern part (now South Korea) and a USSR-backed state in the North (North Korea). The USSR's support was largely ideological, driven by its policy of supporting socialist states and opposing "imperialists" (Zhebin 1995, 726). Accordingly, it supported the North in its war of reunification (the Korean War) and until the 1990s recognized the DPRK as the "only legitimate representative of the Korean people" (Zhebin 1995, 726; T.-H. Kim 2019). At the same time, however, there were several conflicts and disagreements in the Soviet-DPRK relationship. One root cause of the discord was North Korean "adventurism," which has continued in the contemporary Russia-North Korea relationship. For example, North Korea did "not consult and sometimes misinformed" the USSR about the *USS Pueblo* crisis in 1968, during which it attacked and captured a US naval vessel (Zhebin 1995, 733–4). Another cause was the divergent views on the nature of their relationship, namely whether North Korea had a special status within the USSR's bilateral relationships. For example, the North Koreans were "indignant" in 1962 "when Krushchev demanded payment in rubles for weaponry supplied to the DPRK" (Zhebin 1995, 727).

Ironically, the USSR-DPRK relationship was arguably at its height in the years leading up to the former's collapse. The 1980s were marked by several high-level meetings, the expansion of military ties, and increasing economic cooperation (Zhebin 1995, 728–30). It was also during this period that the two countries convened agreements on techno-economic cooperation, including an agreement whereby the USSR assisted the DPRK in building nuclear power plants on the condition that the latter join the nuclear NPT (Zhebin 1995, 729–30). The Soviet Union and North Korea also signed a long-term trade agreement in 1986 which likely facilitated the increase in bilateral trade between the two. During the late 1980s, "the USSR again became North Korea's largest trade and economic partner, reaching as much as 60% of the DPRK's foreign trade volume" (Zhebin 1995, 730). However, North Korea had racked up a lot of debt with the Soviets by that time, and, "facing economic constraints of its own and perhaps frustrated by North Korean unwillingness to repay accumulated debts, the Soviet Union began to cut aid and reduce its support beginning in 1987" (Haggard and Noland 2007, 27). North Korea's debt to the USSR is important to note as it overshadowed the relationship until it was resolved during Vladimir Putin's presidency.

The first critical juncture of the Soviet Union-DPRK relationship during the period of our study was the collapse of the Soviet Union in the early 1990s, which, unsurprisingly, had a profound impact on the relationship and North Korea in general. Prior to the collapse of the USSR, the Gorbachev administration had begun a Westward shift in its foreign policy. The most significant manifestation of that shift was Moscow's decision to recognize South Korea and establish diplomatic and economic relations (Funabashi 2007, 178; T.-H. Kim 2019). This pro-Western stance continued after democratization and the election of Boris Yeltsin in 1991 (Funabashi 2007, 178; Buszynski 2009, 810). Russia was willing to drop North Korea from its "sphere of attention" strategically, economically, and ideologically" and vice-versa (Funabashi 2007, 178). Economically, the collapse of the USSR "instantly deprived Pyongyang of its main economic and security benefactor" (T.-H. Kim 2019). While the beginning of the pro-Western shift under Gorbachev signaled a decline in the USSR-DPRK economic relationship, the relationship hit a brick wall after the collapse as the Soviet Union's "political and diplomatic support and economic and military assistance" of the North was absent entirely (Zhebin 1995, 737). Unsurprisingly, trade with Russia was minuscule in the early 1990s, as shown in figure 3.1.

Although Russia began turning toward the West, it ironically lost its value to the West (namely the United States and South Korea) because it lost its interdependence with North Korea and no longer had leverage to weaponize. This decline in value was acutely visible during the First North Korean Nuclear Crisis of 1994 and the resulting Agreed Framework. Not only was Russia left out of negotiations, it was also excluded from the Agreed Framework as well (Zhebin 1995, 739; Funabashi 2007, 178; Buszynski 2009,

811–2). It was the United States that had bilateral talks with North Korea when the latter threatened to pull out of the NPT (Buszynski 2009, 811). When North Korea and the United States signed the Agreed Framework as a resolution to the crisis, the United States only involved its regional allies, South Korea and Japan, in forming KEDO to provide the DPRK with light-water reactors (LWRs) per the agreement (Zhebin 1995, 739; Buszynski 2009, 811–2). Furthermore, Russia's proposal for eight-party talks with North during the crisis was rebuffed, and it was excluded from the Four-Party Talks in the late 1990s, which only included North Korea, the United States, South Korea, and China (Buszynski 2009, 811–2). For its part, North Korea also refused to allow Russia to participate in KEDO or post-crisis talks, likely a result of Russia's increasing indifference toward the DPRK (Funabashi 2007, 178).

Wanting to strengthen its influence in the region, Russian policymakers began to realize that maintaining a relationship with North Korea was crucial, a clear preference for foreign policies that generate panopticon effects (Zhebin 1995, 739; T.-H. Kim 2019). Furthermore, its economic relationship with the South did not take off as hoped (T.-H. Kim 2019). As a result, Russian policymakers tried to improve their relationship with the DPRK in the late 1990s. Accordingly, trade between the two increased (Figure 3.1). However, another critical juncture in the relationship occurred when Vladimir Putin was elected as Prime Minister in 2000. Putin also realized the value of the Russia-DPRK relationship to Russia's status and influence in the region, "the Korean Peninsula is integral to Russia's national interest, both historically and geopolitically" (Funabashi 2007, 178). Thus, Putin continued the efforts from the late 1990s to strengthen the relationship. Most notably, the two countries convened the DPRK-Russia Treaty of Friendship, Good Neighborliness, and Cooperation early into Putin's tenure, an update of the DPRK-USSR Treaty of Friendship, Cooperation, and Mutual Assistance convened during the Cold War (Funabashi 2007, 178; Buszynski 2009, 814). Additionally, Putin visited Pyongyang in mid-2000, the first such visit of a Soviet or Russian leader (Funabashi 2007, 178; Buszynski 2009, 814).

Another development that facilitated increasing relations between the two countries was the election of US president George W. Bush in 2000. Even prior to President Bush including North Korea as a member of the "axis of evil," Kim Jong-Il worried that the United States' neoconservatives would "target" North Korea (Buszynski 2009, 815). He stated that "...the new American administration was 'out to isolate' the North, and that the US plan for ballistic missile defenses "brought [North Korea and Russia] together'" (Buszynski 2009, 815). Taken together, these developments signaled growth in the Russia-North Korea relationship. Unsurprisingly, the early 2000s marked the pinnacle of Russia's share of North Korean trade over the course of our study as highlighted in Figure 3.1.

Since Putin came to power, Russia's approach to its relationship with North Korea has been multifaceted. As mentioned, Russian policymakers believed that a close relationship with North Korea was important to maintaining regional influence and balancing the United States and China, a lesson it had learned in the 1990s (Buszynski 2009, 830). As such, Russia fashioned itself as an "honest broker" capable of ameliorating regional tensions, given its ascendant relationship with North Korea (Funabashi 2007, 185). This stance featured prominently in Russia's position in the Six-Party Talks and the aftermath of North Korea's various weapons tests in the 2000s. Russia consistently called for multilateral dialogue with the North, even when the Six-Party Talks faltered (Buszynski 2009, 825; Toloraya 2011). It has also tried to broker a stronger inter-Korean relationship, including trilateral economic projects to connect railways and oil pipelines on the Korean Peninsula to Russia (Funabashi 2007, 179–80; Toloraya 2011; Zakharova 2016, 157). North Korea's continued "adventurism" vis-à-vis its weapons tests put Russia in a difficult position, however (Zakharova 2016, 153). In order to maintain the image of an "honest broker" in terms of tensions in East Asia, Russia could not condone the tests, especially as North Korea conducted them without notifying or consulting with Russia (Buszynski 2009, 822). On the other hand, Russia also wanted regional stability and did not want the North Korean regime to collapse or military escalation involving the United States (Zakharova 2016, 153). Thus, Russia agreed with the United States's calls for UN sanctions within the Security Council in the wake of North Korea's nuclear tests beginning in 2006. However, like China, it was also resistant to the stringent sanctions that the United States proposed, often allowing UN "member states to decide how the [sanctions] would be enforced" (Buszynski 2009, 822).

Following the 2009 nuclear test and the sinking of the *Cheonan* in 2010, DPRK-Russia relations again declined under President Medvedev (Toloraya 2011). However, the 2010s, the final years of our study, proved to be a strong decade for Russia-North Korea relations and may prove to be a solid foundation for future cooperation. "Russian-North Korean economic transactions are mostly pragmatic, driven by market demand and supply," and Moscow will not "return to the Soviet pattern of being a major donor for the DPRK" and give preferential terms to the DPRK out of ideological alignment (Lukin and Zakharova 2018, 260). However, during this period, "they resolved the debt problem, intensified economic contacts, facilitated bank transactions, created new bodies, and favourable conditions were provided to Russian businessmen in North Korea" (Zakharova 2016, 155). The specter of North Korea's debt to Russia was an issue that had hung over the relationship for decades. However, the two countries reached an agreement in 2012 where Russia agreed to forgive 90 percent of North Korean debt ($9.91 billion) while the remaining 10 percent was to be paid in installments into a Russian bank account, which could be used to fund joint projects (Zakharova 2016, 153). Russia has also continued to provide humanitarian aid, such as food, which was particularly notable as neither the United States nor South Korea had provided any (Toloraya 2011; Zakharova 2016, 154). Additionally, both countries worked toward making it easier for Russian companies to invest and conduct business in North Korea (Zakharova 2016, 155; Lukin and Zakharova 2018, 246).

It is perhaps unsurprising that Russia has reemerged as one of North Korea's top trading partners. However, its contributions are marginal compared to China's share of North Korean trade, which clocks in at around 90 percent (Lukin and Zakharova 2018, 245). Comprehensive economic sanctions against North Korea have stymied the development of DPRK-Russia economic exchange, as they have in most of the North's other bilateral relationships (Zakharova 2016, 154; Lukin and Zakharova 2018, 260). The centrality of the United States in the international financial system makes sanctions evasion difficult as doing business with North Korea has become increasingly risky with each round of sanctions (Lukin and Zakharova 2018, 260–1). However, the two countries have found ways to mitigate the obstacles sanctions pose to DPRK-Russian trade. For example,

> The Russian Federation and the DPRK agreed to account settlements in rubles in all trade transactions between the two countries. The first contracts on opening of North Korean accounts at Russian banks were signed in June 2014 between Russian AKB "Regional Development Bank" and "Foreign Trade Bank of the DPRK" and "Korean Bank of Unification and Development." The first settlements in rubles between the assigned banks were conducted in October 2014. (Zakharova 2016, 154)

Although risky and at times difficult, both countries have incentives to continue strengthening their relationship, at least in the realm of economic cooperation. For North Korea, Russia represents another economic "lifeline" that is willing to continue doing business with the DPRK despite the sanctions regime. A robust relationship with Russia lessens North Korea's dependence on China and leaves it less vulnerable to any leverage China may try to exercise (Funabashi 2007, 181; Buszynski 2009, 816; Toloraya 2011; Zakharova 2016, 153). At the same time, a strong relationship with North Korea helps maintain Russia's influence in East Asia, balance the United States and China, and project its status as an "honest broker" in tensions around the Korean Peninsula, as it can gather information and monitor North Korea in a way that few other countries can. A robust DPRK-Russia relationship also helps Russia build economic leverage over the former, although whether and to what extent Russia will exercise that leverage remains to be seen.

WHEN SANCTIONS UNDERMINE LEVERAGE: US-NORTH KOREA RELATIONS

The United States's trade with North Korea has never amounted to significant levels. The subject of economic sanctions in the form of trade embargoes since 1950, the United States has banned most exports to and imports from North Korea, financial transactions, along with a travel ban (Wertz 2020, 1–2). Therefore, the trade relationship between the two countries has never had time to develop into a strong one, meaning that sanctions have had little coercive power. US foreign policy toward North Korea has tended to favor sanctions over engagement. One major exception to this, as discussed in the sections below, was the Agreed Framework, an agreement negotiated between the DPRK and the United States during the Clinton administration. As that episode showed, however, the United States's political will to engage with or to even relax sanctions against the DPRK is limited. Over time, the two countries have arrived at an impasse where North Korea will return to the negotiating table only in exchange for the United States lifting economic sanctions and the United States is generally only willing to offer concessions (such as relaxing sanctions) if the DPRK commits to "Complete, Verifiable, Irreversible Disarmament" (CVID). In this case, policies that generate choke-point and panopticon effects have become inexorably intertwined, making it difficult for DPRK-US relations to grow. Also, because neither state engages in any significant forms of diplomacy with the other, the asymmetry in the perception of issue salience may in fact undermine the success and effectiveness of US economic sanctions (Ang and Peksen 2007).

Tensions between the DPRK and the United States remained high during the Cold War, as it did between the United States and most of its adversaries. The US cast its enemies "in a mold of military and economic containment" (Martin 2002, 54). It has maintained a large troop presence in both South Korea and Japan since the end of the Korean War, its largest in the Pacific, with the explicit purpose of deterring or defending against attacks from North Korea (C. J. Kim 2023, 13). After the Korean War, animosity between North Korea and the United States reached a crisis point in 1968 when the former captured the USS Pueblo and subsequently tortured its crew (Houghton 2017). The United States claimed that the vessel was in international waters while the DPRK argued that it had crossed into North Korean territory (Houghton 2017). The crisis abated in late 1968 as US officials signed an apology in exchange for the release of the USS Pueblo's crew, though US-DPRK relations remained tense (Lerner 2023). However, this episode along with "memories of war, murderous confrontations in the Demilitarized Zone, [. . .] and support for international terrorism" continued to drive American perceptions of and policy toward the North (Martin 2002, 54).

By the 1980s, some of the sanctions imposed due to the Korean War were relaxed with small exchanges of trade. However, US-North Korea relations reached yet another crisis point in the 1990s during the First North Korean Nuclear Crisis. As mentioned in previous sections, the crisis began when North Korea stated that it would withdraw from the NPT after refusing IAEA special inspections of its nuclear (energy) development program. IAEA inspections generate panopticon effects whereby the organization gathers data about and monitors states' nuclear energy programs. The United States played a key role in resolving the crisis through bilateral negotiations, which included meetings between former US president Jimmy Carter and North Korean leader Kim Il-Sung (Mazarr 1995, 96). The two countries eventually signed the Agreed Framework in late 1994, which was an "incentives-based strategy" on the part of the United States to dissuade North Korea from developing nuclear weapons (Martin 2002, 51). The agreement involved three phases of reciprocal moves by each party over the course of ten years (Mazarr 1995, 97–8). Over the three phases, North Korea was to stop the development of its nuclear energy program, permit inspections of its nuclear facilities (per the NPT), and, eventually, dismantle several reactors including its thirty-megawatt Yongbyon reactor. In exchange, the United States promised not to use nuclear weapons against North Korea, to compensate for the DPRK's energy shortfall (by providing oil shipments and light-water reactors), and "to begin removing barriers to political and economic contacts between the two countries within three months" (Mazarr 1995, 97–8). The US and South Korea also paused their joint military exercises, *Team Spirit*, from 1994 to 1996, a constant irritant in both DPRK-US and inter-Korean relations (Willis 2018). Not only did the United States stop pushing for new sanctions, but it also relaxed the trade embargo in 1995. The United States and North Korea engaged in low levels of trade after the signing of the Agreed Framework. Between 1999 and 2001, for example, the United States permitted the import of transformers, printed matter, works of art, and miscellaneous electrical machinery and equipment (Harvard Growth Lab 2021).

However, US-North Korean trade never took off as progress toward fulfilling the terms of the agreement stalled shortly after signing. There were several obstacles to the success of the Agreed Framework. First, negotiations between North Korea and KEDO (composed of the United States, South Korea, and Japan) took "years" to "arrange details, resolve disputes, and clear bottlenecks"

(Wit 1999, 60). Second, South Korea had reservations about the Agreed Framework. The Kim Young Sam administration was unhappy that the United States pledged that South Korea would build the light-water reactors without consulting it first. The ROK "felt betrayed that their old ally, the Americans, dealt with their arch-enemy without their direct involvement" and believed that the United States' engagement may facilitate the survival of a country on the "verge of collapse" amid a devastating famine (Chung 2003, 25).

Finally, developments in American domestic politics inhibited the United States's ability to fulfill the original terms of the agreement, namely "the rise of congressional assertiveness in foreign policy, Republican control of Congress after 1994, and eroding support for all forms of foreign aid" (Martin 2002, 55). Accordingly, Congress began pushing for conditions on US assistance to the DPRK and new issue linkages beyond North Korea's nuclear development (Martin 2002, 55–8). One result was that the United States eventually linked lifting economic sanctions to "both the termination of the North's nuclear program and 'the complete and verifiable cessation of testing, production and deployment of missiles exceeding the parameters of the Missile Technology Control Regime [MTCR]'" (Martin 2002, 59). The issue with US conditional assistance was that one of the terms of the Agreed Framework stated that the United States and North Korea were to reduce barriers to trade within three months of signing the agreement (Mazarr 1995; Martin 2002). North Korea interpreted that provision to mean that the United States would drop its sanctions within three months (Martin 2002; Laney 2011). While the United States lifted some of its sanctions, it did not lift others (Laney 2011). Unsurprisingly, the continuity and conditionality of many of the US sanctions outraged the North Korean government.

An analysis of statements issued through North Korea's primary state media outlet, KCNA, in the late 1990s reveals the DPRK's frustration with the United States' refusal to lift all its sanctions as well as its belief that the total lifting of sanctions is a provision of the Agreed Framework. One 1997 article from KCNA stated that "the U.S. position concerning the economic sanctions is a wanton violation of the DPRK-U.S. framework agreement" and that by not lifting all of them, "the U.S. has dared transgress the agreement, a legal document" (*KCNA* 1997). An article a year later stated that,

> The U.S. must abandon all its anachronistic policy of "sanctions." In particular, it must at once lift "sanctions" it has stubbornly imposed upon the DPRK, the bulwark of socialism, for scores of years with a view to isolating and stifling it. The lifting of the "sanctions" is also an obligation of the United States under the DPRK-U.S. framework agreement. If it persists in "sanctions," turning a blind eye to this stark reality, it will be held wholly responsible for all consequences arising there from. (*KCNA* 1998a)

A KCNA article later that year recognized that the United States removed some sanctions, which the article stated were a "mere symbol" and admonished the United States for not removing all of the sanctions, stating that "the sanctions which may bring a practical stop to the hostile policy have not been lifted at all" (*KCNA* 1998c). Taken together, these statements confirm that North Korea was adamant about the United States lifting all its economic sanctions as a condition of the Agreed Framework, or else there would be consequences.

The United States further relaxed sanctions in 2000, which allowed some bilateral trade to flow (Wertz 2020, 2). North Korea acknowledged the development, praising it as a "good development" and "a step taken by the U.S. to fulfil its commitments under the DPRK-U.S. agreed framework signed in 1994" (*KCNA* 1999). However, even the relaxation of sanctions "had little, if any, impact on North Korea's trade with the United States, because North Korea's exports to the United States are still subject to higher tariffs in the United States" (Chang 2006a, 45). Any progress that the United States and North Korea made toward fulfilling the Agreed Framework and normalizing relations ceased during the George W. Bush administration in the 2000s. A key reason from the US side was that the Bush administration believed that the Agreed Framework was a "failure," too generous toward the DPRK, and generally had a "near allergic reaction" to the Clinton administration's strategy of engagement (Martin 2007, 113, 130).

The 9/11 attacks in 2001 and the 2002 revelation of North Korea's highly enriched uranium (HEU) processing program solidified the Bush administration's disdain for the agreement and engagement toward North Korea in general. The 9/11 attacks spawned the United States' "War on Terror" (U.S. Department of State 2002). The result was that the United States defined "all aspects of U.S. security policy in terms of a war on terror" and "ensured that security in Northeast Asia and Korea would be perceived through the lens of homeland security" (Martin 2007, 128). Accordingly, Bush included North Korea in the "Axis of Evil" during his 2002 State of the Union Address ("President Bush's 2002 State of the Union Address" 2002). He stated that one of the administration's goals was "to prevent regimes that sponsor terror from threatening America or our friends and allies with weapons of mass destruction" and that North Korea is one such regime, "arming [itself] with missiles and weapons of mass destruction, while starving its citizens" ("President Bush's 2002 State of the Union Address" 2002). From the neoconservative perspective, it is unsurprising that the United States would only agree to engage or aid North Korea if the latter took significant steps to be a "good citizen" of the international community. However, as we argue, diplomatic engagement or other exchanges that generate panopticon effects may be necessary for changing the behavior of a pariah state like North Korea.

Additionally, Bush's inclusion of the DPRK in the "Axis of Evil" angered both the DPRK and South Korea, which, as mentioned, had opted to pursue engagement with the DPRK at that time.

The DPRK's relationships with several players in the region, especially the United States, deteriorated after a North Korean diplomat revealed to a US counterpart that the DPRK had been developing its HEU processing program clandestinely, a key component of nuclear weapons (Funabashi 2007, 153). The Agreed Framework collapsed as North Korea again threatened to withdraw from the NPT, which it did in 2003, and openly began developing its nuclear weapons program (Davenport 2022b). For their part, the United States and South Korea failed to deliver on the pledge of light-water reactors and the former never lifted the totality of its sanctions against the DPRK (Funabashi 2007, 153). Following North Korea's withdrawal from the NPT and brazen development of its nuclear weapons program, the United States pursued both policies of pressure and multilateral engagement to encourage the DPRK to stop and dismantle its nuclear weapons program (Martin 2007, 113). The Bush administration's overarching goal for North Korea was "Complete, Verifiable, Irreversible Disarmament" (CVID), a buzzword that has remained in discussions of US foreign policy toward North Korea in the years since (C. N. Willis 2018). As a result,

> the U.S. was guided by four principles (1) refusal to engage in direct bilateral talks, (2) refusal to offer rewards for bad behavior, and (3) backloading benefits until after CVID was assured, and (4) delaying full diplomatic relations until after the North addressed additional security and human rights concerns. (Martin 2007, 113)

Ultimately, the United States and North Korea, along with China, South Korea, Japan, and Russia, took to the negotiation table through the Six-Party Talks, which began in August 2003 (Davenport 2022a). The Talks were a classic example of a foreign policy that generated panopticon effects, arguably for each party at the table. Each party expressed its country's position regarding how to address North Korea's nuclear program and could gather information about each other.

The DPRK-US relationship during Bush's second term could be characterized as "one step forward, two steps back" as developments that could have facilitated the normalization of ties were often offset by major events that caused them to deteriorate further. The United States softened its stance slightly at the beginning of Bush's second term and "began to exhibit greater flexibility at the Six-Party Talks" (Martin 2007, 114). Perhaps the most significant breakthrough in the Talks came about during the first year of Bush's second term when the six countries issued the 2005 Joint Statement (Martin

2007, 114). This statement, albeit nonbinding, appeared to signal a growth in North Korea's political and economic relationships with the other parties. Among the various points in the agreement, North Korea notably "committed to abandoning all nuclear weapons and existing nuclear programs and returning at an early date to the treaty on the nonproliferation of nuclear weapons (NPT) and to IAEA (International Atomic Energy Agency) safeguards" (*The New York Times* 2005). Additionally, "the DPRK and the United States undertook to respect each other's sovereignty, exist peacefully together and take steps to normalize their relations subject to their respective bilateral policies" (*The New York Times* 2005). However, the DPRK-US relationship did not change much after the Joint Statement. One reason was that the United States not only maintained its economic sanctions but also issued new financial sanctions against the DPRK around the same time (Martin 2007, 130). As a result, North Korea refused to return to the Six-Party Talks as outlined in the Joint Statement "until [US] financial sanctions were lifted" (Martin 2007, 114).

The following year also presented opportunities to enhance US-DPRK relations. One of the major developments was the departure of hawks like Donald Rumsfeld, John Bolton, and Robert Joseph from the Bush administration (Martin 2007, 130–2). Another was "the stunning Democratic election victory in 2006" which could have brought a return to "Clinton-style engagement" (Martin 2007, 126). At the same time, 2006 marked North Korea's first nuclear test and the first time a sanctions resolution made it through the UNSC without getting vetoed by either China or Russia, North Korea's longtime patrons. Following the DPRK's missile test in July 2006, the UNSC passed Resolution 1695, which prohibited member states from selling fissile material to North Korea as it sought to develop a nuclear weapon (United Nations Security Council 2006b). The UNSC levied further sanctions against the DPRK after its nuclear test in October 2006. Resolution 1718 and subsequent resolutions related to North Korea since 2006 have also sought to ban the export of dual-use and military goods to North Korea as well as prohibit trade in luxury goods and impose quotas or bans on key North Korean commodities (United Nations Security Council 2006a). Domestically, North Korea's test also prompted Congress to pass the "North Korea Non-Proliferation Act," which "urged all governments to comply" with UNSCR 1695 (Martin 2007, 126).

The DPRK-US relationship appeared to be on an upswing in 2007 when the two, along with the other members of the Six-Party Talks, issued another Joint Statement that essentially pledged to implement the stipulations of the 2005 agreement (Davenport 2022b). The 2007 statement was notable as it appeared to mark a further shift in Bush's policy toward the DPRK. Specifically, the United States "forsook its former refusal to engage in direct bilateral negotiations, accepted the DPRK's formula of sequenced actions for actions, and expressed willingness to front-load limited economic and political rewards" (Martin 2007). The United States began making other concessions that were seemingly impossible during Bush's first term such as taking "North Korea off the U.S. list of terrorist-sponsoring nations" and unfreezing "bank accounts controlled by the Kim family" (Spetalnick and Yukhananov 2013).

Initially, the Obama administration appeared to be willing to engage with North Korea, although not unconditionally (Spetalnick and Yukhananov 2013). However, the DPRK-US relationship became increasingly complicated in 2009 after North Korea conducted a test of its TaepoDong-2 rocket, which eventually led to further UN sanctions and North Korea declared its exit from the Six-Party Talks (Davenport 2022a). The DPRK's departure from the Talks was important in terms of panopticon effects, cutting off another source of information about the Hermit Kingdom from the other five members of the Talks. The North Korea-US relationship deteriorated further as North Korea conducted its second nuclear test in 2009 and, as discussed earlier, was involved in several high-profile conflicts with a major US ally, South Korea, in 2010 (Spetalnick and Yukhananov 2013). The Obama administration's North Korea policy became characterized by "strategic patience," "a diplomatic waiting game in which Washington focused on sanctions and condemnation while leaving the door open to easing North Korea's isolation if it behaved better" (Spetalnick and Yukhananov 2013). DPRK-US relations were tense through the 2010s as the former conducted various missile and nuclear tests and was the subject of increasingly harsh US and UN sanctions. In 2016, along with UNSCR 2270, the United States passed the North Korea Sanctions and Policy Enhancement Act (NKSPEA) that expanded US secondary sanctions and targeted third-party states facilitating North Korea's nuclear and WMD programs (Wertz 2020, 4).

North Korea's burgeoning nuclear program and attempts to finance the development of nuclear and ballistic missile technology have scuttled the development of further trade between the two countries. North Korea has made use of illicit trade networks, cyberheists, and cryptocurrency to finance its nuclear and ballistic missile programs. The United States has significantly begun to rely more on financial sanctions by cutting off access to the financial networks of North Korean banks and banks in other parts of the world that continue to do business with North Korea. Banco Delta Asia, a bank in Macau, had been accused of helping North Korea launder funds from its illicit activities, which US financial sanctions successfully scuttled (Zarate 2013). Without any significant movement toward North Korea's denuclearization and political rapprochement between it and the United States, it is unlikely that there will be any significant economic exchange between the two countries.

CONCLUSION

This chapter uncovered a variety of motives for states' engagement with (or disengagement from) North Korea. For many states, the decision to engage is based on a view that it will (somewhat) pacify the DPRK and foster regional stability. For Russia and China, engagement with North Korea is also driven by a desire to exert regional influence and forestall a potential increase in United States involvement in the region. As discussed, Russian foreign policy toward the DPRK in the Putin era is explicitly driven by the idea that creating a strong relationship with North Korea will create interdependence and give Russia the potential to weaponize it. For Japan, engagement with North Korea has come primarily through its North Korean diaspora, the *chongryon*, and its ties to the DPRK. And even though the United States has a preference for sanctions toward the DPRK, it has also engaged with North Korea, often diplomatically and in times of crisis.

Economic engagement with North Korea has taken many forms, both licit and illicit. Legal economic exchange with the DPRK has occurred through trade, investment, remittances, and, perhaps most notably, joint projects. South Korea, Russia, and China have all undertaken joint projects with North Korea at various times. These projects naturally generate panopticon effects where partners can glean information about the Hermit Kingdom and monitor it. The UN sanctions (a policy generating chokepoint effects) which began in 2006, however, have also made economic engagement difficult and risky, especially for US allies Japan and South Korea. That said, Japan and the United States, at times attempting to normalize relations, have shown a preference for sanctioning North Korea and have both levied sanctions beyond what UN resolutions have called for. In addition, Japan has also engaged in other policies, such as cracking down on exchanges between the *chongryon* and North Korea (such as remittances), which generate chokepoint effects.

Examining the trajectory of North Korea's relationships with China, South Korea, Japan, Russia, and the United States yields several important insights about sanctions and foreign policy in general. First, as Putnam (1988) argued, domestic politics influence international politics, and policymakers must balance the two constituencies. As these cases show, domestic impacts on foreign policymaking sometimes cause incohesive policies and unexpected outcomes. This is especially true in democracies, but domestic politics impact authoritarian regimes, as well. Politicians in democracies must take public opinion into consideration, at least to some extent, if they want to remain in office. Thus, it is unsurprising that, although Japan-DPRK relations appeared to be improving, Japan ultimately turned away from normalizing relations because of the abductee issue and strong Japanese public opinion against North Korea. However, the public may also hold contradictory views that complicate foreign policymaking. In the US, for example, "a large majority of U.S. public opinion consistently has viewed the DPRK as a threat to the United States [. . .] yet the public continued, even after the DPRK's nuclear test, to oppose using military means to end the threat and to favor a diplomatic solution" (Martin 2007, 128–9). South Koreans, similarly "wearied of unconditional assistance to North Korea with relatively little return on investment" but "continued to value stability in inter-Korean relations and did not want to see the relationship undermined to the extent that North Korea might pose a renewed danger, either from internal instability or from North Korea's capacity to make external threats" (Snyder 2009a, 93). Additionally, conflicts within a state's government can lead to incohesive foreign policy, sometimes with contradictory goals and tactics, which was the case for the US's North Korea policy during the George W. Bush administration.

The second key insight is that international relationships also constrain foreign policymaking toward other states, whether they are rivals or allies. American, Chinese, and Russian foreign policy toward North Korea often failed to take the interests of others into account and instead sought to counter each others' influence in the region by adopting different strategies to deal with North Korean provocations. While conflicting policies may be expected among rivals, they are perhaps more alarming among allies, who at times pursued foreign policies that generated panopticon effects while other allies pursued policies that generated chokepoint effects. The continual conflict between South Korea's and the United States' foreign policy toward the DPRK stymied the effectiveness of each other's policies. When the Clinton administration opted to negotiate with North Korea during the First Nuclear Crisis, the Kim Young Sam administration was frustrated that the United States would "reward" its enemy. Conversely, when Kim Dae Jung adopted the Sunshine Policy to engage North Korea, George W. Bush included North Korea in his "Axis of Evil." Thus, the myriad of policies that spawned panopticon and chokepoint effects often worked against each other. For either of these effects to create change in the target's behavior, states need to coordinate their foreign policies. Otherwise, with friends like these, who needs enemies?

Chapter 4

Opting for Panopticon?

The Myanmar Sanctions Regime

In 1988, the United States and Canada imposed economic sanctions on Myanmar (Burma) after nationwide protests led to a coup, the first Western countries to impose sanctions in response to Myanmar's return to autocratic rule. These events set the stage for further US and Western sanctions with the goals of bringing about a return to democracy and a collapse of the military regime that had taken hold (Jones 2015). As the Global Sanctions Data Base indicates, economic sanctions imposed on Myanmar addressed concerns of Myanmar's deteriorating human rights situation. Seventeen countries and the European Union (EU) (and EEC) imposed an array of sanctions to address these human rights failures (Felbermayr et al. 2020). Sanctions senders increasingly had imposed strict and successive rounds of economic sanctions against Myanmar since 1988 (Giumelli 2013a, 29–31; Giumelli and Ivan 2013; Anguelov and Bryant 2015). The Myanmar sanctions regime appeared to be a success story for many observers when the junta began making reforms in the 2010s, including holding competitive elections in 2012. In 2012, Daw Aung San Suu Kyi, the iconic leading figure of the opposing National League for Democracy (NLD), long under house arrest, and her party won a majority of seats in Parliament (Fuller 2012). Their ascendance into Burmese political power sparked headlines in Western newspapers like "From Prisoner to Parliament in Myanmar," "'People's triumph' heralds new age of democracy, claims exultant Suu Kyi," and "Myanmar on cusp of new era: Suu Kyi; Veteran activist's election to political office marks key democratic step forward" (Fuller 2012; Buncombe and Allchin 2012; MacNamara 2012). Several news stories cited getting senders to lift sanctions as one reason why the junta allowed competitive elections, with one article stating that "there is no doubt sanctions against Burma appear to have encouraged many of the reforms of the past year" (*The Australian* 2012). Both Western leaders and even members of the Burmese political opposition, most notably Aung San Suu Kyi herself, attributed the elections to Western sanctions pressures (Jones 2015, 94). After two strong NLD performances at the voting booth in 2015 and 2020 however, the military seized power back in 2021, resulting in a new round of sanctions.

In this chapter, we explore the impact of sanctions from 1980 to 2017 on Myanmar. We concur with several other scholars who view the sanctions against Myanmar as having done little to undermine the military regime (Anguelov and Bryant 2015; Early 2016; Jones 2015; Pedersen 2013; Seekins 2005; Steinberg 2007). We find that the sanctions regime, imposed mostly by Western countries, had little impact. As we have argued, we attribute the inability of chokepoint effects generated by sender states to have their desired effects the results of Myanmar's regional isolation and its regionally focused network of trade. Unlike Western sanctioning states, "Myanmar's regional neighbors moved to normalize relations with the former hermit state, arguing that international trade and investment provide the best path to a more stable, prosperous and ultimately freer and rights-abiding country (business as usual)" (Pedersen 2013, 191). After sanctions are imposed, Myanmar's trade network sees only minor shifts to South, East, and Southeast Asia, although we are careful to note that South, East, and Southeast Asia dominated Myanmar's trade profile even *before* the imposition of economic sanctions, as Seekins (2005) also notes. Additionally, we find that while economic sanctions reduced trade with the United States, Canada, and Western Europe, these trade ties did not disappear entirely. Within our typology of network configurations, Myanmar's network is isolated (see Table 1.1).

We note that while the statistical frequency of international sanctions against Myanmar (as depicted in Figure 1.1 in the introduction) is greater than toward North Korea, the sanctions are less impactful because Myanmar conducted only a modest amount of trade (and economic engagement) with the sending states prior to the implementation of sanctions. Unlike North Korea, where sanctions led North Korea to depend largely on "black knight" support from China, Myanmar's trading partner distribution is markedly more diverse as it continued to trade even with those states that had imposed sanctions on it, such as the United States, Canada, and Western Europe. Furthermore, while North Korea and Iran have had substantial multilateral sanctions levied on them by myriad sender states, the only international organization to sanction Myanmar is the EU, a group of states with whom Myanmar did not trade as much. Because the sanctions imposed on Myanmar are less impactful, the ability of economic sanctions to both change the course of Myanmar's domestic politics and the structure of its network are minimal. We attribute this lack of change primarily to the lack of extensive trade and economic linkages of sender states. The very states that could bring about changes in the structure of the network through the imposition of economic sanctions, namely other Association of

Southeast Asian Nations (ASEAN) member states and China, never do. Thus, we see few changes to Myanmar's network of trade, which remains largely stable from 1988 through the relaxation of Western sanctions in 2013.

Furthermore, we contend that the Western sanctions against Myanmar are better understood as signaling devices in line with previous studies (Pedersen 2007, 225). Using primary and secondary sources, we find evidence that both parties used sanctions more as a signal to convey to the junta and the international community Myanmar's "pariah" status rather than to cause reform or regime change. Thus, as in this case, sanctions "success" may also include sending a message to the target state's government and the international community that the target state is flouting international norms. The sanctions against Myanmar *were successful* in meeting their symbolic goal of highlighting Myanmar's violations of democratic norms (such as the coup in 1988, the repression of pro-democracy protests, and the lack of "free and fair" elections) and human rights norms such as the oppression of various historically marginalized ethnic minority groups. For example, they worked to draw attention to the plight of Aung San Suu Kyi, the lack of political freedoms, and a multitude of human rights abuses. However, some observers believed that the junta wanted Aung San Suu Kyi to win a parliamentary seat in the 2012 elections to persuade the international community of the legitimacy of its reform process and to ease the economic sanctions, due to the West's fixation on Aung San Suu Kyi (McDonald 2012; Teo 2012).

We situate our analysis within the framework of weaponized interdependence (Farrell and Newman 2019). Within this framework, the policies that lead to the creation of economic sanctions generate chokepoint effects, which isolate the sanctioned (or target) state from being able to interact with key nodes within the asymmetrical network represented by the international system. In this case, the EU and US sanctions were chokepoint effects. Weaponized interdependence posits that key nodes that act as hubs within this network can also create policies that generate panopticon effects. Panopticon effects allow key nodes within the asymmetrical network to monitor the activity of other nodes in the network and gather information. In the case of Myanmar, ASEAN members' choice to grant Myanmar membership despite the civil and human rights issues generated panopticon effects that allowed the regional organization to maintain its economic engagement with Myanmar while also allowing member states to monitor and collect information about developments in Myanmar. For a country like Myanmar, its ability to resist the intensity of economic sanctions imposed by the West is largely due to its reliance on non-sanctioning regional powers for trade and investment, such as China and its fellow ASEAN member states.

This case shows the limits of Western power and Western control over key nodes in compelling Myanmar to make policy adjustments and resolve the issues that led to the imposition of economic sanctions. Sanctions against Myanmar were ineffective (beyond signaling Myanmar's "bad behavior") because of its regionally focused economy and its limited connection to nodes generating chokepoint effects. The few economic interests held by the West that could have been weaponized were too meager or poorly placed to impact the military junta in Myanmar (Win 2007; Nyun 2008; Pedersen 2007, 2013; Jones 2015). Meanwhile, the states that were arguably in the best position to impose sanctions, notably China, India, and other ASEAN members refused to do so. Perhaps more problematically from a US perspective, key regional allies such as Japan and South Korea chose not to sanction Myanmar and instead, like Myanmar's neighbors in the region, chose to engage with Myanmar economically. In essence, Myanmar's regional trading partners preferred policies of engagement, because they brought economic benefits while the act of engagement also generated panopticon effects by allowing states like Japan, South Korea, and ASEAN members to capture information about the regime through channels of diplomacy, trade, and other forms of economic engagement. We explore the rationale for ASEAN and ASEAN member states' economic engagement with Myanmar and in doing so, contribute to the literature on the Myanmar sanctions regime by highlighting why states decided to sanction Myanmar or not.

IMPOSITION OF SANCTIONS AGAINST MYANMAR

Sanctions against Myanmar were first implemented in 1988 when the United States and Canada enacted arms embargoes against the country (Jones 2015, 105). The United States also refused to appoint a new ambassador to Burma (a new one was not appointed until after the democratic reforms of the 2010s) and "threatened to reduce its funding to any United Nations agencies found to be conducting programs in Burma" in the early 1990s (Maung Thawnghmung and Sarno 2006, 43–4). More stringent US sanctions against Myanmar began in 1997—the same year ASEAN admitted Myanmar as a member—through Executive Order 13047, signed by President Clinton, which prohibited US companies from making new investments in Myanmar but did not impact existing operations (Anguelov and Bryant 2015, 33). The year 2003 marked the next round of US sanctions against Myanmar, largely in response to an "attack on Aung San Suu Kyi's motorcade and her later arrest" by the military junta (Maung Thawnghmung and Sarno 2006, 43). Congress then passed the Burmese Freedom and Democracy Act, which further limited US-Myanmar trade by prohibiting any firm from importing Burmese goods into the United States (Maung Thawnghmung and Sarno 2006, 43; Anguelov and Bryant 2015, 33). The legislation also addressed asset freezes of Burmese officials and denying officials' entry into the United States, among other additional provisions (Maung Thawnghmung and Sarno 2006, 43; Anguelov and Bryant 2015, 33).

The final round of new US sanctions against Myanmar in our study (which ends in 2017) started in 2007 in response to the military junta forcibly repressing protests against the increase in fuel prices (Anguelov and Bryant 2015, 34). Executive Order 13448, signed by President George W. Bush, increased the severity of the US sanctions against Myanmar by granting "the Treasury Department the authority to impose specific targeted sanctions on persons responsible for human rights abuses or public corruption within Myanmar—a broad classification under which arguably all government officials fell" (Anguelov and Bryant 2015, 35). US sanctions eased minimally after the Burmese government began implementing democratic reforms in 2010s as the US government was unconvinced that the Burmese government was taking significant steps to democratization (Anguelov and Bryant 2015, 53). Unsurprisingly, after the 2021 coup, the United States has imposed increasingly severe sanctions on the junta on top of the sanctions in place prior to the coup (Lewis and Psaledakis 2023).

The EU and Australia also began implementing their own sanctions against the military junta in Myanmar in the early 1990s (Jones 2015, 105; Bünte and Portela 2012; Steinberg 2007, 226; Giumelli 2013a, 29–30; Giumelli and Ivan 2013, 27–28). The EU began sanctioning Myanmar after the junta refused to acknowledge the NLD's victories in the 1990 elections (Giumelli 2013a, 29–30; Giumelli and Ivan 2013, 27–28). This initial round of sanctions included an arms embargo in addition to stopping non-humanitarian aid (Giumelli 2013a, 29–31; Giumelli and Ivan 2013, 27). In the mid-1990s, the EU adopted its first common position on the issue, which included travel bans and asset freezes on several groups of Burmese officials (Giumelli 2013a, 29–31; Giumelli and Ivan 2013, 29–30; Maung Thawnghmung and Sarno 2006, 44). The second round of EU sanctions began in 2007 with a ban on trade in lumber, precious metals such as gold, and other resources (Giumelli 2013a, 29–30; Giumelli and Ivan 2013, 27). After the 2012 elections, the EU suspended all sanctions except for the arms embargo (Giumelli 2013a, 29–30; Giumelli and Ivan 2013, 27–28). However, like the United States and other countries, it has levied increasingly severe sanctions against Myanmar since the 2021 coup (Council of the European Union 2023).

The Myanmar sanctions regime ostensibly had two goals during the period of our study. Sanctions' main goal was for political change and curbing human rights abuses, either directly targeting elites or through public pressure (Seekins 2005, 441; Steinberg 2007, 228). Part of the US sanctions implemented in 2003, for example, "were designed to hit hard at the military regime's economic foundation in order to persuade it to release [opposition leader] Aung San Suu Kyi and make genuine progress toward democracy"

(Seekins 2005, 440). As Nyun (2008) notes, however, the US sanctions goals as encapsulated in the 2003 Burmese Freedom and Democracy Act are somewhat ambiguous, aiming simply "to sanction" the junta, "to strengthen Myanmar's democratic forces," and to recognize Aung San Suu Kyu's NLD as the legitimate Burmese governing party (484). The sanctions' second goal, at least from the perspectives of the United States and the EU, was largely a symbolic gesture to draw international condemnation to the military junta's[1] repression of political opposition (most notably Aung San Suu Kyi and the NLD) and express support for the said opposition (Seekins 2005, 440; Steinberg 2007, 230). As Early and Preble (2021) note, economic sanctions often serve to send signals and highlight norm violations and are frequently employed in this way. While US sanctions against Myanmar appear to have pursued these related but distinct goals simultaneously, Giumelli (2013a) argues that the EU's sanctions goals have shifted over time from signaling members' concerns with the junta's policies to addressing human rights issues and actually undermining the junta's grip on power (29).

THE IMPACT OF THE MYANMAR SANCTIONS REGIME

Despite international condemnation, loss of aid and trade, the brutal regime in Myanmar has had immense "staying power" (Callahan 2005, 2). Indeed, since the beginning of the Western-led sanctions imposed on Myanmar, scholars have been skeptical of the prospects for sanctions success (Seekins 2005; Pedersen 2007; Steinberg 2007; Win 2007; Nyun 2008; Jones 2015; Early 2016). As discussed, it is unclear what role the sanctions played in Myanmar's democratizing reforms in the 2010s, especially, as we show, little changed in Myanmar's trading network under the sanctions regime. Jones (2015) argues that sanctions delayed the country's planned transition to civilian rule: "constraints on economic development did hamper the regime's transition strategy, by limiting growth, intensifying predatory resource extraction, and thereby undermining the regime's legitimacy" (123). They further undermined political opposition, perhaps most notably by inhibiting "the emergence of an organized working class" (Jones 2015, 125). Others contend that the combination of engagement helped facilitate the reforms. Early (2016), for example, argues that the combination of sanctions and engagement used during the early years of the Obama administration facilitated the transition to democracy. The use of engagement and the prospects of lifting sanctions "helped to assuage the regime's security concerns and allowed its leaders to feel more confident about relaxing the draconian policies it had adopted during the previous two decades" (Early 2016) while also allowing the military to retain their control over Myanmar's governing institutions.

Several studies indicate that the military junta in Myanmar was largely unaffected by sanctions, though they were concerned to some degree about their "pariah" status. For example, Pedersen (2007) details how international censure compelled the junta to deal with Aung San Suu Kyi and the NLD, use the language of "human rights" and "democracy," release some political prisoners, and even hire a public relations firm in Washington, DC, to improve its image (Pedersen 2007, 218–20). However, like other authoritarian regimes, such as North Korea, the political elite under the military junta was largely able to insulate themselves from sanctions pressures. This is in part because the sanctions had a negligible impact on the economic sectors dominated by state-owned companies such as oil and natural gas (Pedersen 2007, 226–7; Jones 2015, 116). The sanctions also created some unintended consequences that worked to the regime's advantage. Similar to the North Korea case, the junta publicly cited the sanctions and their senders as the reason Myanmar's economic underdevelopment (Nyun 2008, 484–5; Pedersen 2013, 192). Additionally, "international interference in what [leaders] perceived as Myanmar's sovereign affairs caused a nationalistic backlash, heightening the resistance to change, undercutting potential reformers and further discrediting Myanmar democracy groups" (Pedersen 2013, 192). Thus, far from encouraging the junta to reform, scholars generally believe that the sanctions strengthened the regime's position to some extent.

Conversely, scholars have found that the economic sanctions have impacted Burmese citizens in a variety of ways. First, sanctions *did* impact the Burmese economy, but the pain was largely borne by small business owners and private citizens (Seekins 2005, 444; Win 2007, 283). Perhaps most notable was the impact of US sanctions on Myanmar's garment industry. As Jones (2015) details, the United States and the EU were the two largest importers of Burmese garments from 1990 to 2000, together making up 90 percent of Myanmar's garment exports (107). However, in 2003 the United States banned Burmese garment imports and the EU followed in 2005 with a measure that restricted its imports of garments from Myanmar (Jones 2015, 107). Smaller, privately owned businesses felt the "sting" of these measures most acutely:

> After deducting the cost of imported parts, manufacturers received only 6 to 10 percent of the final retail price. After sanctions were imposed, this share was further cut. Coupled with fierce competition for the remaining market share, this bankrupted many small firms, while larger ones—often subsidiaries of foreign companies—survived. This concentrated the industry in the area where state-linked enterprises were most dominant: joint ventures with foreign partners. (Jones 2015, 107)

Sanctions more severely impacted smaller and privately owned businesses than large state-owned companies in several other areas as well, such as tourism (Nyun 2008, 490; Jones 2015, 108–12). Accordingly, Burmese citizens experienced massive layoffs in the garment and other industries (Maung Thawnghmung and Sarno 2006, 47; Pedersen 2013, 192–3).

Sanctions negatively impacted the general Burmese population in other ways. The sanctions, largely through their symbolic use to identify Myanmar as a global pariah, impacted a variety of foreign aid to Myanmar, including funds for counternarcotics operations and public health programs (Win 2007, 283; Nyun 2008, 508–9; Pedersen 2013, 193). Sanctions may also have weakened the opposition to the junta. As Nyun (2008) notes, the US Burmese Freedom and Democracy Act of 2003 recognizes the NLD as "the legitimate representative of the Myanmar people," alienating moderates in the junta who may have been more willing to encourage reform policies (484–5). Additionally, the West's fixation on Aung San Suu Kyi may have "impeded the development of a broader, more diverse democracy movement within the country by disadvantaging other potential opposition leaders and groups" (Pedersen 2007, 228). Finally, in contrast with the engagement policies of many Asian countries to address civil and human rights issues in Myanmar, the chokepoint effects that the Western sanctions generated "deprive[d] the Burmese civilian population of Western political ideas about freedom, human rights, democracy, and the rule of law that normally accompany trade with the United States and other Western countries" (Nyun 2008, 496).

EXPLAINING THE FAILURE OF THE MYANMAR SANCTIONS REGIME

There are several reasons why the sanctions against Myanmar largely missed their mark. One of the major reasons that Western-led sanctions have been largely ineffective is that several states in Myanmar's network engaged in extensive sanctions busting trade. Outside of "Western" states, sanctions against Myanmar went largely ignored or were non-existent. Several scholars have argued that the Burmese economy is and has been largely focused on South, East, and Southeast Asia (Seekins 2005; Maung Thawnghmung and Sarno 2006; Jones 2015). For some of these countries, this was partially for economic reasons and partially a strategy of engagement to encourage change in Myanmar from within, as discussed later in the chapter. Some states in the region such as Thailand and India have long been major trading partners (Anguelov and Bryant 2015, 37). However, others such as China increased their share of Burmese trade as Western states like the United States levied increasingly strict sanctions (Anguelov and Bryant 2015, 37–9; Maung Thawnghmung and Sarno 2006, 44–9). In line with our findings, the result was that Myanmar's economy *grew* in spite of or perhaps because of the Western sanctions (Steinberg 2007,

220–1; Anguelov and Bryant 2015, 51–2; Jones 2015, 106) due to the nature of its isolated network. Similar to North Korea's reaction to sanctions (discussed in chapters 2 and 3), the military junta in Myanmar

> found that their mitigation policies—reaching out to America's regional adversaries (e.g., China and North Korea) and economic competitors (India, Thailand, China again, Malaysia, Singapore, and Japan) and offering them preferential trade conditions—resulted in much more wealth generation for the Burmese economy than when trade with the United States was legal. (Anguelov and Bryant 2015, 54)

Thus, discussed in more detail below, Asian states continued and, in some cases, increased trade with Myanmar undermined Western-led sanctions. As Steinberg (2007) relays, "former Secretary of State Madeleine Albright in her Georgetown academic role stated in one of her classes [that] the ineffectiveness of sanctions applied to Myanmar is traceable to the lack of cohesion among all powers concerned" (230).

Perhaps most concerning for the United States was the sanctions busting of regional allies such as South Korea and Japan. Both states imposed some sanctions policies against Myanmar, but they also continued to trade with or provide aid to Myanmar. Japan and South Korea both imposed arms embargoes against Myanmar (Pedersen 2007, 227), yet both countries continued to provide foreign aid to Myanmar (Seekins 2005, 447; Maung Thawnghmung and Sarno 2006, 49–51). Several former US State Department officials and ambassadors have reported on Japan's unwillingness to stop providing aid and to fully cut economic ties, much to the United States's chagrin (Brown 1998; Lord 1998; Plaisted 2001). Like other countries in the region, Japan favored engagement with Myanmar to try to address the same issues that the United States and other Western countries did with more comprehensive sanctions: "[Japan] believed in keeping up business relationships with Burma and, in their own way, trying to moderate the attitudes of the Burmese regime through these relationships, rather than the heavy stick which is favored by certain people in Washington" (Brown 1998, 858). Thus, not only was the United States unable to pressure other countries in Asia to sanction Myanmar, it was unable to persuade its own allies to do so.

In addition to continued economic engagement between many countries in Asia and Myanmar, the sanctions regime largely failed to facilitate change in its target because of the lack of credible commitments of the sanctions' senders and largely due to the nature of the sanctions themselves. As mentioned, some of the goals of the US sanctions "are ubiquitous and, in some cases, conflicting," requiring ambiguous benchmarks for improvement in Myanmar's human rights situation in exchange for sanctions relief (Nyun

2008, 484). Additionally, the first rounds of US and EU sanctions focused on arms embargoes, travel bans, and asset freezes, but did not prohibit trade with Myanmar. Until at least the early 2000s, prominent EU members such as the UK and France continued to invest in Myanmar businesses (especially its oil companies) and, along with Germany, imported Burmese goods (Maung Thawnghmung and Sarno 2006, 48–9). Even the asset freezes and travel bans likely had little impact on the junta as they rarely traveled to Western countries and had few assets there (Pedersen 2007, 225; Win 2007, 283). When the United States began banning trade with Myanmar in its second round of sanctions in 1997, it "grandfathered in" US firms who had already been doing business in Myanmar (Anguelov and Bryant 2015, 36). Anguelov and Bryant note that "total net exports to the United States grew between 1992 and 2001 with the largest increases coinciding with the implementation of sanctions in 1997," suggesting that the 1997 sanctions achieved the opposite of the desired outcome if harming the Burmese economy was what the United States and other policymakers intended (36).

Unsurprisingly, several scholars have cited the flaws in the sanctions regime as evidence that the sanctions, at least in some instances, were merely symbolic. Pedersen (2007) and Nyun (2008) both contend that the US sanctions, at least in the first few rounds, were mostly symbolic, with the latter noting that "the often repeated rhetoric of promoting democracy and protecting human rights in Myanmar was intended only to appease domestic pressures to take action" (2008, 484). The EU's sanctions were also to some degree symbolic. Giumelli (2013a) contend that that at least initially, the sanctions were intended to send a message to the junta of its condemnation of the government's policies and to the NLD of its support: "if sanctions were intended to change the behavior of targets according to the degree of direct material impact, then the first fifteen years of EU sanctions on Burma would be difficult to explain" (30–1). Indeed, some anecdotal evidence confirms that at least the United States intended for the sanctions to send a message. Steinberg (2007) states that former Secretary of State Madeline Albright noted that the imposition and the goals of sanctions against Myanmar were meant to communicate a "moral posture" (230). As we discuss in more detail later in the chapter, other State Department officials have expressed similar sentiments.

THEORY

Building on our previous chapters on North Korea, we make two claims. First, in line with Anguelov and Bryant (2015), economic sanctions can potentially alter the structure of a target state's trading network by shifting ties from one set of trading partners to others or creating new trade linkages to compensate for lost trade. These structural changes make economic sanctions less effective because they limit the ability of powerful states to weaponize interdependence. In other words, by generating chokepoint effects, economic sanctions can alter the trading relationships that exist within a target state's trading network, acting as a stimulus to the target's economy in finding new markets for imports and exports. Economic sanctions that induce changes in the network isolate not only the target state but also key hubs from interacting with the target. This isolation limits the impact that economic sanctions could potentially have. As the target state shifts its trade portfolio away from key hubs, the ability of these hubs to coerce diminishes. Economic sanctions, in some cases, force states to create new walks in the network to new trading partners, of which North Korea (profiled in chapters 2 and 3) provides an example as it generates new trade linkages to mitigate the economic pain of US economic sanctions. In this case, we expect that when the United States began imposing sanctions on Myanmar (more so the 1997 and 2003 sanctions), other countries will fill in the void.

Second, economic sanctions are less likely to achieve their goals when trade relations before sanctions imposed are minimal. Sanctions imposed against targets where the sender has few economic interests may be counterproductive. In the case of Myanmar, for example, US and European interests in the country involved sectors that had little impact on the junta's economic activities. Arms embargoes had little effect on the junta since a significant portion of the junta's arms came from China and Russia, countries that were unlikely to support UN sanctions and never imposed their own bilateral sanctions. Most of Myanmar's neighbors also had economic interests in the country, which made sanctions unattractive tools for ASEAN members with sanctions being incompatible with the ASEAN Way. As we discuss later, ASEAN members indeed opted for engagement policies, generating panopticon effects, to monitor and try to persuade the military government to address some of the civil and human rights issues.

We present two hypotheses. First (H_1), economic sanctions from a major trading partner force target states to adjust their trade network and create new trade linkages. Second (H_2), economic sanctions, even from powerful states, have little impact on network shifts when sending states are minor trading partners with the target state. Myanmar represents an excellent case where the United States and Europe, minor trading partners in the aggregate, lacked the necessary economic influence to make sanctions work effectively.

Myanmar serves as a critical case for showing how pre-existing trade relationships via the structure of the target state's network impact sanctions' success and effectiveness. In this case, economic sanctions have little impact on Myanmar's trade network, which remains largely intact during the decades in which economic sanctions were imposed due to its isolation from sanctions senders. The ability of states that matter to Myanmar's economic interest to weaponize their interdependence remained; however, no ASEAN member state saw economic sanctions as a viable policy option.

The weaponization of interdependence is not automatic and requires states to apply it through a variety of policies. We argue that ASEAN and other Asian states worked to weaponize interdependence not through the use of chokepoint effects emanating from the imposition of economic sanctions but instead through the use of panopticon effects created by policy choices that brought Myanmar into the regional organization in 1997. As an ASEAN member, Myanmar's actions and activities could be monitored. ASEAN membership and the policies developed to support that membership generated a panopticon effect by providing ASEAN members with information and monitoring capabilities that other states outside of ASEAN might be unable or unwilling to utilize, especially Western governments critical of the Myanmar regime. This is consistent with the "ASEAN Way" and the organization's norms of "consensus decision-making, informal diplomacy, [and] noninterference and respect for sovereignty" (Loh 2018). The organization touts itself as "providing a practical framework for confidence-building and meaningful regional cooperation" (Chalermpalanupap 1999). In this sense, the organization's preference for engagement with Myanmar and exchanging information (panopticon effects) over economic sanctions is unsurprising.

DATA AND METHODOLOGY

Our study uses UN Comtrade data (United Nations 2021) cleaned by the Growth Lab at Harvard University (2021) from 1980 to 2017 in exploring trends in trade between Myanmar and its key trading partners. Using the trade data from these two sources, we then constructed several *trade share* variables that capture each state's percentage of Myanmar's total trade in each given year. For our analysis, trade share serves as a means of measuring changes in the structure of Myanmar's trade network, our dependent variable. We then merged geospatial locations (Google 2012) for all the countries in the dataset for use in the creation of the geospatial network visualizations. Using the trade data collected from the sources indicated, we generated several geospatial network visualizations (Knapp 2017). To understand the effect of economic sanctions on Myanmar, analyses of the social networks based on trade linkages provide a look at how these relationships have changed across time as economic sanctions from not just the United States but other states and international organizations in the international system have influenced trade flows and trade linkages.

Social network analysis (SNA) relies on three key assumptions. We introduced these assumptions in chapter 1, but we revisit them here and connect these assumptions to the empirical realities of the Myanmar sanctions regime. First, structural relations—in this case, between states—are key to understanding what "observed behaviors" occur between actors in the network (Knoke and Yang 2020, 8). In our case, Myanmar's trade network helps to explain not only how and why Myanmar behaves the way it does toward its trading partners but also helps to explain those "observed behaviors" of other states connected to Myanmar within the network.

Second, the direct contacts within these social networks are the result of social interaction (Knoke and Yang 2020, 8–9); it is through social interactions that Myanmar can influence and be influenced by its trading partners. For example, the multitude of trade linkages between Myanmar and its trading partners, which demonstrates an isolated network, would indicate that many countries in Myanmar's region could potentially have influence and leverage over Myanmar's foreign and domestic politics. Lastly, the networks in which these countries trade, behave, and interact are dynamic and are changing, forming, and reforming as social relations between these states change (Knoke and Yang 2020, 9–10). As we argue in our paper, the intensity of economic sanctions should play a role in the structure that the network assumes.

From the trade data collected, we created several network visualizations that show Myanmar's trade linkages with states in the international system for the years between 1980 and 2017. We then used SNA to descriptively show countries' share of Myanmar's trade (indicated by the size of each node) but also the geographic distribution of that trade both regionally and across the international system by mapping the network geospatially. The geospatial network visualizations help us to show that while Myanmar's trading network does not concentrate on only two or three trading partners, the distribution of trade across a number of trading partners can be visualized to provide a useful tool for understanding how the structure of this network has—in the case of Myanmar—failed to shift dramatically across time.

SOCIAL NETWORK ANALYSIS

We utilize three measures that are common in SNA: degree centrality and strength centrality. Our measure of degree centrality (Figure 4.1) reflects the importance of third-party states to the target state and vice versa. It captures the target state's connectedness to all potential trading partners in any given year. Myanmar's degree centrality declines in the early 1990s and then rises through the 1990s until sanctions begin to be relaxed by 2015.

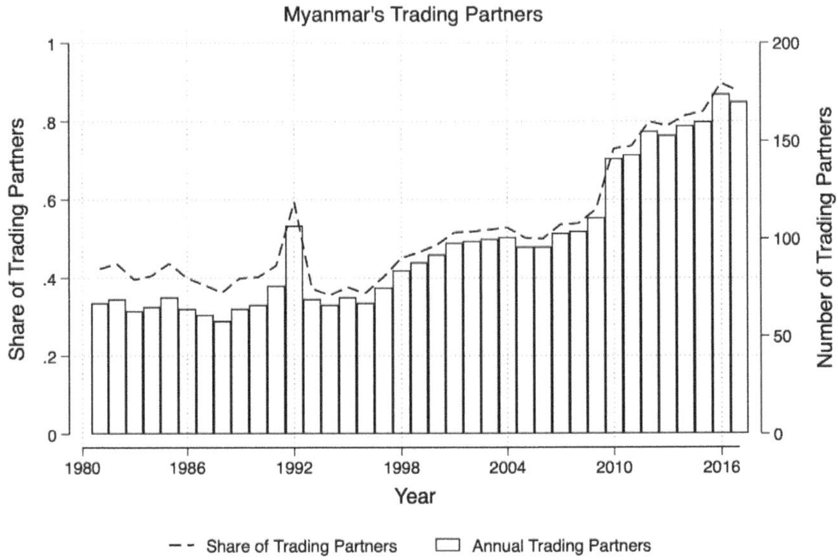

Figure 4.1 Myanmar's Trading Partners from 1980 to 2017 Using UN Comtrade Data. The figure shows Iran's degree centrality (left y-axis) while the bars represent the total trading partners in each year. *Source*: Created by Authors.

Our first strength centrality measure, MOSC1, represents the trading partner's commercial dependence on Myanmar or its annual bilateral trade (imports and exports) with Myanmar relative to the target's total annual trade. When this value is high, it indicates that Myanmar is a key market for trading partners, which helps identify sanctions busters. Variation in MOSC1 can be seen in Figures 4.2–4.5. MOSC2, on the other hand, represents the target's state's (in this case, Myanmar) bilateral trade (imports and exports) relative to a given trading partner, which reflects the importance of the trading partner to Myanmar's overall trade. When this value is high, it indicates that the trading partner in question is an important market for the target as it seeks to avoid the economic pain generated by the economic sanctions. When sanctions busting is rampant, both of these values, when charted together, should increase in tandem. When sanctions are effective, these two strength centrality measures should decline in tandem.

Table 4.1 below shows Myanmar's major trading partners via MOSC2. We categorize major trading partners as the top twenty states whose total aggregate trade since 1962 is the highest. As the table depicts, more than half of Myanmar's top twenty trading partners are in the Indo-Pacific, many of them also within Southeast Asia. The United States is one of Myanmar's top trading partners, but it is not central to Myanmar's network. As Table 4.1 also shows, Myanmar's network is diverse within the region and relatively evenly distributed, with only China making up greater than 3 percent of Myanmar's trade

Table 4.1 Measures of Strength Centrality (MOSC2)

	Measure of Strength Centrality (MOSC2): Third-Party Importance to Myanmar's Trade				
Major Trading Partner	1980	1990	2000	2010	2017
Australia	0.01	0.01	0.01	0.02	0.04
Bangladesh	0.01	0.00	0.01	0.02	0.04
China	-	0.08	0.17	1.20	3.65
France	0.00	0.01	0.02	0.01	0.11
Germany	0.02	0.01	0.03	0.03	0.20
India	0.00	0.02	0.06	0.38	0.49
Indonesia	0.01	0.00	0.02	0.09	0.26
Italy	0.01	0.00	0.01	0.01	0.06
Japan	0.08	0.04	0.08	0.17	0.51
Malaysia	0.01	0.02	0.08	0.16	0.32
Netherlands	0.01	0.01	0.01	0.00	0.05
Russia	-	-	0.00	0.02	0.03
Singapore	0.04	0.08	0.15	0.39	0.91
South Korea	0.00	0.01	0.08	0.17	0.28
Taiwan	-	0.00	0.06	0.05	0.08
Thailand	0.00	0.05	0.21	1.34	1.32
United Arab Emirates	0.00	0.00	0.00	0.02	0.06
United Kingdom	0.02	0.01	0.04	0.02	0.09
United States	0.01	0.01	0.13	0.00	0.16
Vietnam	-	-	0.00	0.04	0.21

Source: Created by Authors.

in 2017. Of its fellow ASEAN members, Thailand makes up the second highest amount of trade in 2017 (over 1 percent) followed by Singapore. Overall, Table 4.1 shows Myanmar's preference for trading partners in the Indo-Pacific, particularly neighboring China and Thailand. As discussed previously, this is partially due to states within the Indo-Pacific opting to engage with Myanmar (economically and otherwise) instead of isolating it through sanctions. Figure 4.1 shows that as the sanctions regime against Myanmar ages, the number of trading partners increases. These increases in trading partners from year to year may reflect both the inadequacies of the economic sanctions imposed as well as the commercial opportunities that the weak sanctions that were imposed had created, drawing new trading partners to Myanmar.

This measure captures the importance of each trading partner to Myanmar trade in the five years profiled above. Lower values indicate countries that are less central to Myanmar's trade. Myanmar's major trading partners are located in the Indo-Pacific; notice how for many of them their share of trade with Myanmar increases.

Myanmar's trade partner distribution remains relatively stable as trade share remains distributed among several trading partners. Before sanctions were imposed in 1988, Myanmar's key trading partners were Japan, Taiwan, Malaysia, Indonesia, Singapore, Sri Lanka, Australia, Western Europe, and the United States (Figure 4.2).

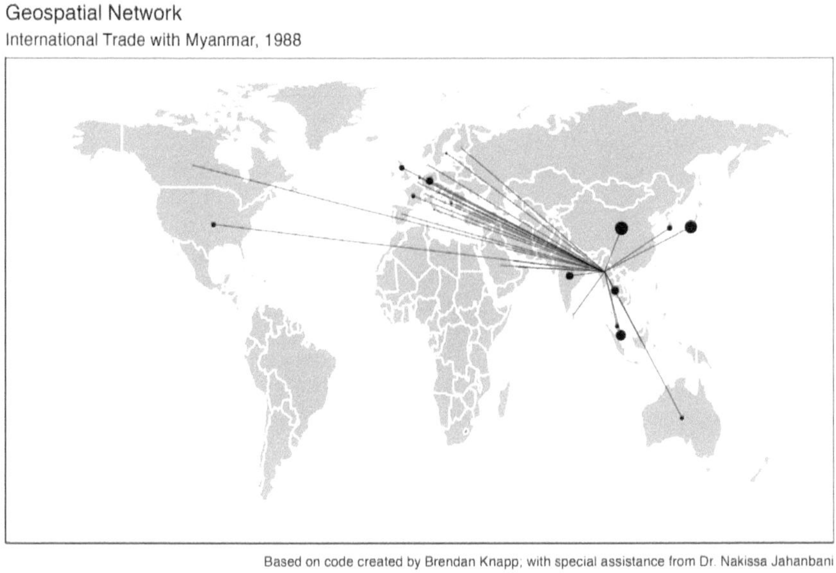

Figure 4.2 Trading Partner Distribution. Ties between Myanmar and trading partners capture all trading partners in 1988. The ties between Myanmar and its trading partners are indicated with solid black lines. We only consider Myanmar's trading relationships when total aggregate trade exchanged is greater than or equal to $1 million current USD, which we argue are more significant trading ties. Filled black circles are nodes or states in the international system. The size of the node increases as that country's trade share with Myanmar increases. *Source*: Created by Authors.

By 1992 (Figure 4.3), economic sanctions had been imposed for four years. As is typical when economic sanctions are imposed, there is a slight adjustment in a country's network of trading partners, especially as sender states and their allies potentially reduce economic relations. Many countries in Western Europe ceased or reduced their trade with Myanmar (although, as mentioned, EU trade sanctions were not officially in place), and China became a key trading partner. Southeast Asian countries remained engaged, as their "roaring economies . . . were prompt to secure trade and investment opportunities" with the regime (Egreteau 2020, 90). The regime likely welcomed these developments given that Myanmar pursued a policy of non-interference with its neighbors to lessen potential meddling in Myanmar's internal affairs while promoting a climate of economic cooperation to assist with development (Haacke 2006). Even countries like Japan that had suspended aid and economic engagement restarted development cooperation. Two approaches dominated: one group of countries that preferred to remain engaged with the regime and a second group within the international community that had come to rally around democracy icon Aung San Suu Kyi, leading "Myanmar

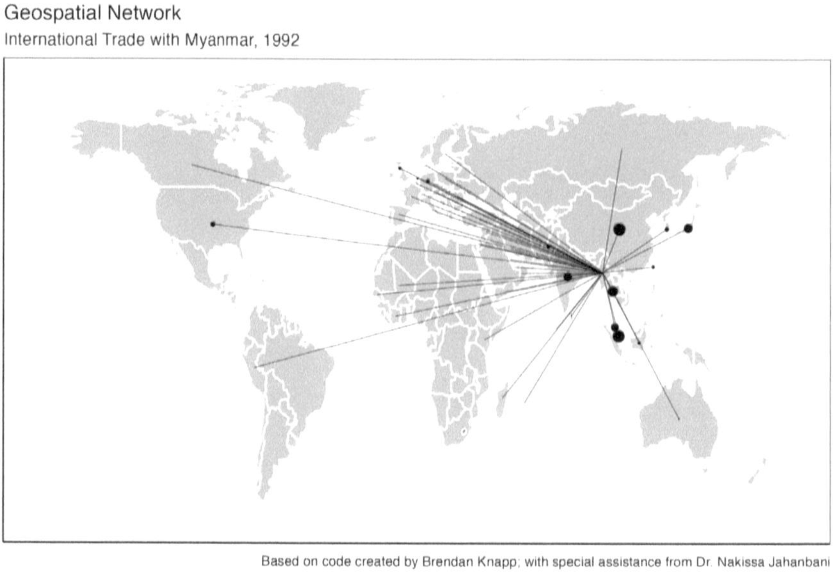

Figure 4.3 Trading Partner Distribution. Ties between Myanmar and trading partners capture all trading partners in 1992. The ties between Myanmar and its trading partners are indicated with solid black lines. We only consider Myanmar's trading relationships when total aggregate trade exchanged is greater than or equal to $1 million current USD, which we argue are more significant trading ties. Filled black circles are nodes or states in the international system. The size of the node increases as that country's trade share with Myanmar increases. *Source*: Created by Authors.

to become a pariah state" (Egreteau 2020, 91). As previously discussed, this dichotomy tended to have a regional orientation, with Asian countries preferring engagement and Western countries like the United States and many in Europe opting for isolation (Maung Thawnghmung and Sarno 2006, 54).

Figure 4.4 shows the distribution of Myanmar's trading partners in 2008 after new rounds of sanctions levied by the EU, the United States, and other predominantly Western countries. As discussed previously, although the sanctions imposed by the EU and the United States initially focused on travel bans and asset freezes targeting Burmese officials, the sanctions eventually prohibited trade. The EU's sanctions focused on the trade of specific goods (such as minerals and timber) while the United States's banned firms from importing Burmese goods (Maung Thawnghmung and Sarno 2006, 43; Giumelli 2013a, 30–31; Anguelov and Bryant 2015, 33). As Table 4.1 and Figure 4.5 show, US-Myanmar trade declined significantly between the 1990s to the late 2000s as did much of EU members" trade with Myanmar. However, as table 4.1, Figure 4.4, and Figure 4.5 also demonstrate, Myanmar became more economically dependent on its trade with other countries in the

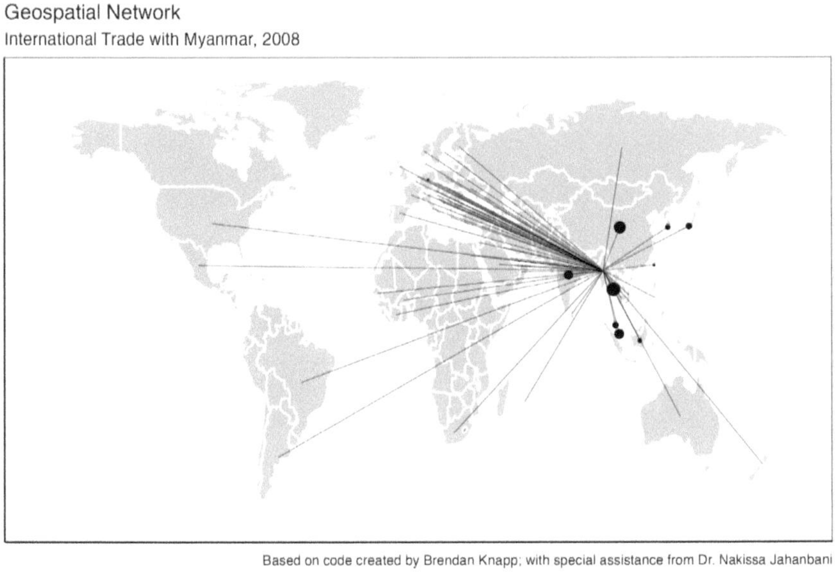

Figure 4.4 Trading Partner Distribution. Ties between Myanmar and trading partners capture all trading partners in 2008. The ties between Myanmar and its trading partners are indicated with solid black lines. We only consider Myanmar's trading relationships when total aggregate trade exchanged is greater than or equal to $1 million current USD, which we argue are more significant trading ties. Filled black circles are nodes or states in the international system. The size of the node increases as that country's trade share with Myanmar increases. *Source*: Created by Authors.

Indo-Pacific, especially China and trade partners in Southeast Asia. The trade shares of many of Myanmar's Asian trading partners increased significantly, some twofold or more. For example, China's share of Myanmar's trade increased from 0.08 percent in 1990 to 1.20 percent by 2010 and India similarly from 0.02 percent to 0.38 percent. Within Southeast Asia, Thailand and Singapore most notably jumped from making up 0.05 percent of Myanmar's trade share in 1990 to 1.34 percent by 2010 and 0.08 percent to 0.39 percent, respectively. And as discussed previously, two of the United States's key allies in the Indo-Pacific, Japan and South Korea, chose economic engagement over isolation as well, despite pressure from the United States. Accordingly, Japan's share of Myanmar's trade increased from 0.04 percent in 1990 to 0.17 percent by 2010 and South Korea's share jumped from 0.01 percent to 0.17 percent. In terms of weaponized interdependence, the United States and to some extent the EU relinquished any minor leverage they may have had over Myanmar (given their relatively smaller trade shares to begin with compared to other states in the Indo-Pacific) when they levied the trade sanctions. Several former US officials from the Department of State expressed

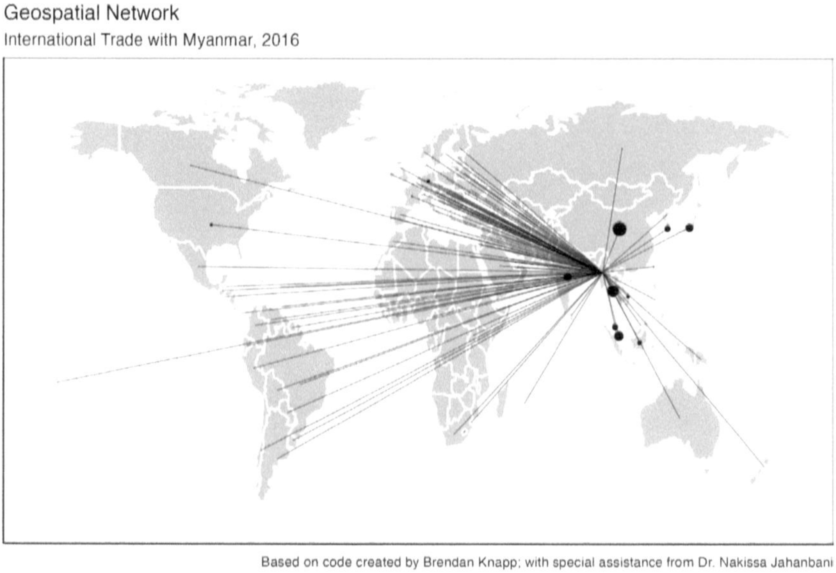

Figure 4.5 Trading Partner Distribution. Ties between Myanmar and trading partners captures all trading partners in 2016. The ties between Myanmar and its trading partners are indicated with solid black lines. We only consider Myanmar's trading relationships when total aggregate trade exchanged is greater than or equal to $1 million current USD, which we argue are more significant trading ties. Filled black circles are nodes or states in the international system. The size of the node increases as that country's trade share with Myanmar increases. *Source*: Created by Authors.

their concerns with the sanctions in terms of the United States' leverage (Brown 1998; Huhtala 2005). Former Ambassador Huhtala, for example, expressed skepticism toward the US sanctions levied in 1997 (which prohibited US firms from making new investments in Myanmar), stating that "the problem with [the sanctions] was that once we'd imposed sanctions we'd used up one of our few remaining tools of diplomatic leverage with a regime that was very impervious to our concerns" (Huhtala 2005, 128). In terms of the impact of sanctions on the United States' and the EU's influence on Myanmar (especially relative to that of Indo-Pacific trade partners), "Western countries are marginalizing themselves" (Win 2007, 282).

Figure 4.5 shows the final year of economic sanctions imposed on Myanmar. This distribution of trading partners displays what we term an isolated network (Table 1.1): more than three significant trading partners concentrated in Southeast and East Asia along with India, Germany, UK, and even the United States. Myanmar had largely preserved its regional trade and investment while also maintaining trade and investment linkages with countries employing sanctions as signals to highlight Myanmar's pariah status. What

Figure 4.6 Third-Party State's Share of Trade with Myanmar (MOSC1). Higher shares indicate greater commercial dependence on Myanmar. *Source*: Created by Authors.

we fail to see in this case is a single "black knight" coming to the rescue of the military regime with trade concentrated in one or two key trading partners. As others have noted (Nyun 2008; Jones 2015; Early 2016), economic sanctions against Myanmar were hardly comprehensive, and Myanmar remained economically engaged both regionally and internationally. The lack of comprehensive multilateral and biting unilateral sanctions created political and commercial opportunities that are known to undermine the effectiveness of economic sanctions (Early 2011).

STRENGTH CENTRALITY

Figures 4.6–4.8 show the major trading partners and their strength centrality to Myanmar. Figure 4.6 shows Myanmar's trading partners' commercial dependence on Myanmar. As this value increases, it reflects the importance of Myanmar as a trading partner to the third-party state. This value is calculated by dividing the total bilateral trade between any trading partner with Myanmar by the total annual trade conducted by the third-party state. China, followed by Thailand and Singapore have the highest values of commercial dependence with Myanmar.

Figure 4.7 depicts Myanmar's second measure of strength centrality (MOSC2) from 1980 to 2000. What is striking about Figure 4.7 is that while

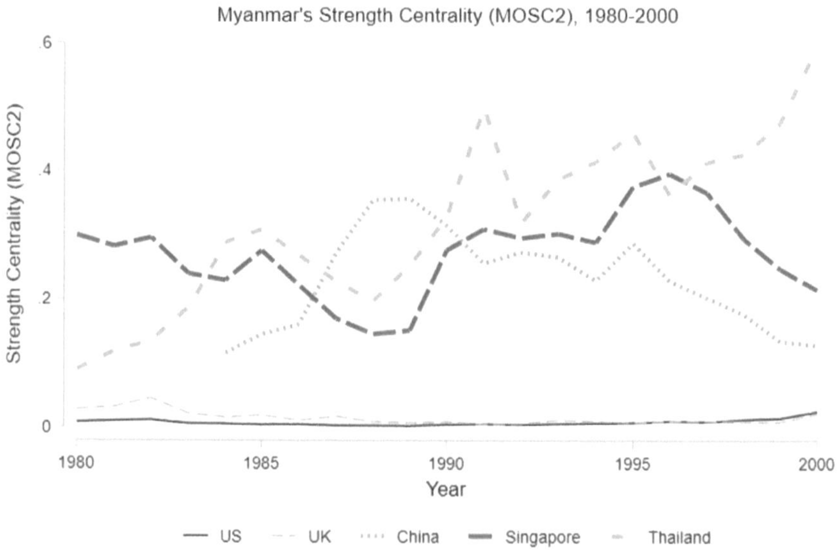

Figure 4.7 Strength Centrality (MOSC2) of Myanmar from 1980 to 2000. *Source*: Created by Authors.

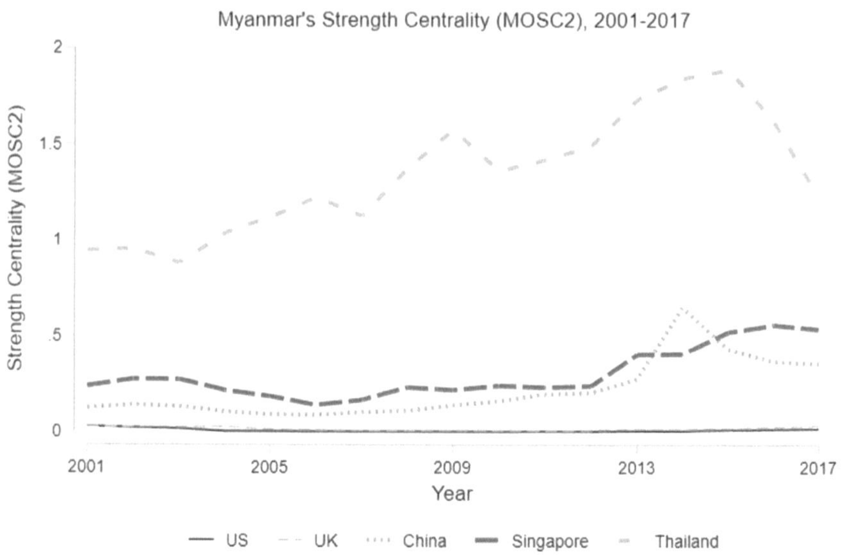

Figure 4.8 Strength Centrality (MOSC2) of Myanmar from 2001 to 2017. *Source*: Created by Authors.

Myanmar's trade with China, Singapore, and Thailand play a more central role than trade with Western countries. MOSC2 highlights the relative isolation of Myanmar's trading partners with a preference for the Indo-Pacific over sanctioning Western states. Figure 4.8 shows the continued commercial isolation of Myanmar with its preferred trade partners of Thailand, Singapore, and China. Figure 4.8 further indicates that the strength centrality of trade with the United States and the UK, remains relatively stagnant from 2001 to 2017, indicating an avoidance by the junta of Western markets.

This value captures the importance of the third-party state's market to Myanmar. Higher values indicate greater importance of Myanmar to third-party state's annual trade in any given year. Profiled here are the main sanctions busters from 1980 to 2000.

These figures (4.7–4.8) capture the importance of the third-party state's market to Myanmar reflecting preferred markets for Burmese trade. Higher values of MOSC2 for non-sanctioning trading partners and lower values for sanctioning trading partners (i.e. senders) reflects Myanmar's efforts to isolate their economy from the impacts of economic sanctions.

SANCTIONS AS SIGNALS AND ECONOMIC ENGAGEMENT

While economic sanctions hardly caused Myanmar to democratize, economic sanctions likely played a secondary role in imposing some pressure on the regime through signaling. Economic sanctions are not simply tools of coercion, which failed to move the military regime, but can also serve as potent signaling devices by drawing attention to regimes that violate international norms (Early and Preble 2021, 380) and may have also created the conditions for more bargaining in the future (381). As a signaling device, economic sanctions helped to draw attention to the military regime's human rights violations and kept the issues related to the junta's brutal crackdown on the international community's agenda. The sanctions also served as a signal to the Burmese opposition including the NLD that the international community supported them, "[keeping] the NLD on life support" (Pedersen 2007, 227). As mentioned, several scholars have contended that indeed, the Western sanctions against Myanmar were symbolic, at least in the sanction regime's initial rounds (Nyun 2008; Pedersen 2007, 2013). In the United States's case, former state department officials have suggested that the use of sanctions against Myanmar as a signal was indeed one of the United States' policy goals. Perhaps most suggestive of the United States' intention of using the sanctions as a signal to the SLORC to cease its human and civil rights violations, at least initially, is a statement from Senator Dianne Feinstein. Senator

Feinstein co-sponsored an amendment, the Cohen-Feinstein Amendment, that called for sanctions against Myanmar if its human rights record did not improve (Huhtala 2005, 129–30). The amendment was passed in 1996 and in 1997, President Clinton issued an executive order imposing sanctions on Myanmar. However, in a later conversation with the then Director of the Office of Burma, Cambodia, Laos, Thailand and Vietnam Affairs, Marie T. Huhtala, Senator Feinstein stated that, "Well why did you impose sanctions? We never intended for them to be imposed. We just intended to send a warning" (Huhtala 2005, 130). Part of the reason that Congress opted to push for sanctions and embargoes against Myanmar, despite the relatively low level of US-Myanmar trade, was lobbying by human rights organizations in Washington, DC and subsequent domestic pressure (Brown 1998, 856–7).

Conversely, through the lens of weaponized interdependence, countries in Asia (specifically Southeast, East, and South Asian states) may have retained greater influence from their policies of engagement, which generated panopticon effects. Even before ASEAN granted membership to Myanmar, it pursued a policy of "constructive engagement" between member states and Myanmar "to encourage domestic economic-social development that in return will have an influence toward political liberalization and democratization in Myanmar" (Aryani 2019, 3). Perhaps most emblematic of ASEAN member states' policy of engagement was the decision in 1997 to admit Myanmar as a member despite concerns with the situation with the NLD and tensions with Thailand over the SLORC's offensive against the Karen National Union's insurgency near the Burmese-Thai border (Callahan 1996, 162–3).

An article from the ASEAN Secretariat in 1999 after Cambodia was given membership (which finally included all Southeast Asian countries at the time in the organization) is instructive as to why ASEAN has opted for engagement with Myanmar. First, the document emphasizes cooperation and prosperity in several places, suggesting the prioritization of economic development for the region (Chalermpalanupap 1999). Second, the document highlights the importance of state sovereignty and non-interference in ASEAN members' internal affairs, consistent with the "ASEAN Way" (Chalermpalanupap 1999). Thus, it is unsurprising that ASEAN would not, for example, make membership contingent on democratic or humanitarian reforms in Myanmar or levy economic sanctions against Myanmar, especially after it had gained membership. The document also specifically discusses Myanmar and the Western-led sanctions regime, highlighting the difficulties the sanctions posed for ASEAN activities with the United States and the EU. For example, "the ASEAN-EU Ministerial Meeting in Berlin in March 1999 had to be cancelled, because Germany would not issue a visa to the Foreign Minister of Myanmar for fear of violating the EU's sanction against

Myanmar" (Chalermpalanupap 1999). The document proceeds to denounce Western pressure on ASEAN to not allow Myanmar's admission to the organization: "those outsiders certainly have no business of trying to stop ASEAN from admitting Myanmar. [. . .] Like it or not, Myanmar is part of our region and now part of the ASEAN family" (Chalermpalanupap 1999). Finally, the document discusses becoming less economically dependent on the West and trading more with the larger economies in East Asia (China, Japan, and South Korea) through the ASEAN+3 grouping, consistent also with Myanmar's increasing trade with China (Chalermpalanupap 1999). The strategy of engagement may have worked to some extent, as scholars have argued that pressure from Southeast Asian states and Myanmar's trading partners in the greater Indo-Pacific (such as Japan) may have influenced the junta's decision to release Aung San Suu Kyi in 1995 and to step down from becoming ASEAN chair in the early 2000s (Callahan 1996, 159; Maung Thawnghmung and Sarno 2006, 55–6).

Individual ASEAN members pursued their own strategies of engagement before and after Myanmar's accession to ASEAN. Malaysia helped to spearhead Myanmar's inclusion into ASEAN in 1997, which Dr. Mahathir Mohamad stated should help to bring Myanmar around to international norms and behaviors at its own pace (Idris and Othman 2008). These political developments coupled with Malaysia's efforts to invest in Myanmar, especially with its promises to develop Myanmar's Yetagun Gas Project, reflected Malaysia's engagement. Malaysia's foreign investment (1988–2000) ranked fourth behind Singapore, the UK, and Thailand (Idris and Othman 2008, 16). These political and economic developments could have potentially provided Malaysia with unrealized leverage, although the efforts of Malaysia and other ASEAN member states to engage politically and economically with Myanmar may also have had much to do with China's growing influence in the region (Idris and Othman 2008, 14). Furthermore, international attention and an increasing focus on the plight of Aung San Suu Kyi coupled with international demands in 2005 may have prompted Dr. Mahathir to call for Myanmar to be expelled from ASEAN until the Nobel Peace Prize winner was released and human rights improved (Idris and Othman 2008, 19).

Indonesia also took a "constructive engagement" approach to Myanmar (Aryani 2019, 3). Aryani (2019) summarizes Indonesia's strategy:

> This approach prioritizes constructive efforts that are built based on solidarity, closeness, brotherhood and partnership in various fields. Constructive engagement is used as a persuasive diplomacy strategy of the Indonesian Government in promoting democratization in Myanmar. Through this strategy, Indonesia seeks to prioritize consensus, avoid confrontation between the two countries and encourage an inclusive spirit for the realization of democracy and strengthening the protection of human rights in Myanmar. [. . .] The implementation of this

> strategy is carried out by holding bilateral cooperation in the fields of economic, socio-culture and followed by a political approach. (3)

Thus, Indonesia adopted both economic and political engagement strategies toward Myanmar (Aryani 2019, 4). In recent years, Indonesia has pledged to increase trade with Myanmar; as we show in table 4.1, Burmese-Indonesian trade has risen significantly since the late 1980s (Aryani 2019, 10). The Indonesian government also engaged with Myanmar through a variety of programs aimed at improving democracy such as the Bali Democracy Forum and the Institute for Peace and Democracy (Aryani 2019, 4–7). Additionally, Indonesia has expressed concern about the situation in Rakhine State with the Rohingya Muslim minority population located there and "is expected to actively participate in responding" to the crisis, something that is rarely mentioned in reference to the goals of the sanctions regime (Aryani 2019, 11–12).

CONCLUSION

Myanmar represents a case of the lost potential of weaponized interdependence by the West. This chapter attempts to explore how panopticon effects generated by Myanmar's membership in ASEAN and efforts by individual states to maintain trade and economic linkages with Myanmar provided those states with the ability to monitor and engage with Myanmar. The ability to monitor and engage was not possible by the West or even the United Nations,whose special rapporteur was denied entry and access at points through the detention of Aung Sung Suu Kyi. Western sanctions largely drew attention to Myanmar's deteriorating human rights situation. As signals, Western economic sanctions, though, failed to bring about much in the way of appreciable changes to Myanmar's domestic policies. We attribute this failure to the West's lack of economic leverage with respect to Myanmar's regional partners. While Myanmar's economy was already oriented toward Asia, it deepened its economic ties to the region as Western sender states like the United States and EU members began imposing sanctions, reflecting the isolated nature of Myanmar's network. Without commercial and economic leverage, economic sanctions and their gradualism did nothing more than create humanitarian consequences for the population (even while many in Myanmar's opposition pushed for more extensive sanctions on the regime).

As a counterfactual, Myanmar may have represented an opportunity for the West to develop a more robust ASEAN-led multilateral sanctions regime through ASEAN or individually with ASEAN members themselves. However, as former US officials have noted, the United States received little cooperation from ASEAN member states on isolating Myanmar through sanctions, as evidenced by Myanmar's accession to ASEAN in 1997 (Brown 1998, 858–64). With Myanmar's regional trade profile largely within Southeast Asia, ASEAN member states avoided policies that could choke Myanmar out of the network and push Myanmar closer to China's orbit. More importantly, the ASEAN Way and Myanmar's membership to ASEAN generated panopticon effects that allowed fellow members to keep tabs on Myanmar's activities. As discussed in the chapter, some ASEAN member states, such as Malaysia and Indonesia, sought to encourage reforms through political and economic engagement. Additionally, some US allies in the Indo-Pacific, such as Japan, also opted for engagement rather than sanctions, despite US pressure to impose them.

Given China's veto in the UN Security Council, multilateral efforts in the UN we observed in North Korea to combat Myanmar's despotic regime would have been unlikely to occur. While the five permanent members of the UN Security Council rallied around denuclearization on the Korean Peninsula (resulting in sanctions against North Korea), no such coalescence of the major powers on the UNSC occurred with Myanmar. The lack of a comprehensive sanctions policy from the UN helped ASEAN member states avoid being forced to enjoin a multilateral sanctions regime. Since Myanmar relied so heavily on its ASEAN neighbors for trade and investment (although the West, too, played a significant investment role (Maung Thawnghmung and Sarno 2006)), greater commitments from the West and targeted sanctions from Myanmar's key trading partners may have led the regime to change course earlier and spared the populace significant pain that economic sanctions caused. Reflecting on the history of the sanctions against Myanmar, it is unlikely that the post-2021 sanctions will pressure the junta to relinquish power (Willis and Preble 2024) given the orientation of Myanmar's economy, the unwillingness of many countries in East, Southeast, and South Asia to isolate Myanmar, and the West's apparent lack credible commitments to sanctions.

NOTE

1. The official title of the junta's ruling apparatus was the State Law and Order Restoration Committee (SLORC), later the State Peace and Development Council (SPDC).

Chapter 5

Making Weaponized Interdependence Work

The Iran Sanctions Regime

The United States has been the most prolific sender of economic sanctions against Iran since it began imposing sanctions against Iran in 1979. While unilateral US efforts to impose sanctions against Iran have not led to significant policy change or regime change on the part of the Iranians, multilateral efforts that joined European Union (EU) and United Nations (UN) economic sanctions to US unilateral sanctions in the 2010s reflected a new level of potency at imposing significant costs to the Iranian economy in response to growing fears that Iran was developing a nuclear weapon. The EU's autonomous economic sanctions on Iran, in particular, were the first created by the EU due to concerns over weapons of mass destruction (Tabrizi and Santini 2012), as previous efforts had largely focused on state sponsorship of terrorism (Syria and Libya in the 1990s) and against human rights violators (Portela 2005).

This level of sanctions cooperation was propelled by international efforts to restrict the proliferation of nuclear weapons globally even if EU efforts in support of US sanctions surprised many but were seen as integral to complementing US efforts (Castle 2010; Tabrizi and Santini 2012; van Bergeijk 2015, 51). Despite differences in how to deal with the Iranian nuclear question (Onderco 2015), EU member states demonstrated marked cohesion around the potential proliferation of nuclear weapons by Iran (Portela and Ruffa 2015; Seeberg 2016). The new sanctions that emerged to counter Iran's efforts to develop nuclear weapons were both comprehensive and targeted. These economic sanctions sought to compel Iran to negotiate on restrictions to its nuclear weapons program. Targeted sanctions specifically targeted sectors critical to generating revenue and preventing strategic trade that would further enhance and support Iran's efforts to develop WMDs while also restricting the ability of individuals connected to Iran's WMD programs from traveling as well as freezing their assets (Salisbury 2017b, 299).

Iran, unlike other heavily sanctioned states such as North Korea or Myanmar, remains highly interconnected within the global economy while also maintaining robust regional economic and trade ties, a network configuration we term *interdependent* (see Table 1.1). In fact, as van Bergeijk notes, pre-sanctions trade linkages were "substantial" and the denial of SWIFT to Iranian banks was not only highly impactful but raised the likelihood of sanctions success (van Bergeijk 2015, 51). In this case, the ability of the West to weaponize Iran's economic interdependence became a potent weapon only when European countries, which had extensive commercial linkages to Iran, worked cooperatively not only with each other but also with the United States in limiting Iran's ability to generate revenue through exports. The EU issued targeted sanctions against Iran in 2010 that imposed restrictions on Iran's energy sector as well as an arms embargo. However, the oil embargo imposed by European countries in 2012 proved to be the critical nail in the coffin that energized negotiations, which likely emerged from the impact of the oil boycott on the Iranian economy (van Bergeijk 2015, 54–6). The imposition of both EU and UN sanctions coupled with comprehensive US sanctions generated tremendous chokepoint effects that cut Iran off not only from Europe's financial system but also from allowing EU member states to engage in significant trade with Iran, especially in oil.

The Iran sanctions regime serves as a textbook case of how interdependence can be weaponized to bring about key policy outcomes, in this case pressuring Iran to negotiate with the West on the Joint Comprehensive Plan of Action (JCPOA), and ultimately sign the agreement in 2015. Ariane Tabatabai (2017, 229) describes the process as a two-level game (Putnam 1988), one taking place at both the national and international levels that reflects the impact of public opinion, Iranian domestic politics, and international factors, such as Iran's isolation, its pariah status, and the impact of economic sanctions. While we agree that economic sanctions are insufficient to explain Iranian willingness to negotiate or the contours of its negotiation, we see economic sanctions and the difficulties they created as being a necessary condition for the eventual success of the JCPOA negotiations. Economic sanctions deprived Iran of crucial trading ties and reintegration into the global economy, and sanctions relief was a critically important issue for Iranian negotiators. Yet, the success of economic sanctions is prefaced by the domestic politics and public opinion in Iran that allowed for negotiations of the JCPOA to take place (Tabatabai 2017, 229; 233).

This case demonstrates how economic sanctions coupled with panopticon effects generated by policies designed to gather information and monitor trade and financial networks can bring about impactful policy change against hard targets like Iran. Chokepoint effects generated by the imposition of economic sanctions and the severing of Iranian banks (especially Iran's Central Bank) from SWIFT would not have been possible without the resources generated by the panopticon effects coming from EU policies. As analysts have noted, the deal gave Iran very little while giving the West significant concessions in exchange for sanctions relief, especially from Europe. The sanctions regime would not have been able to choke the Iranian regime off from Europe's financial and commercial markets without coordination between both the United States and Europe as well as US and EU efforts at convincing both China and Russia in the UNSC to permit the imposition of UN sanctions (Cronberg 2017b; Tarock 2016).

THE TRAJECTORY OF THE IRAN SANCTIONS REGIME

After the Iran hostage crisis in 1979 and the subsequent release of the hostages at the end of the Carter Administration, the United States steadily imposed more severe and widespread sanctions against the Iranian government, briefly lifted sanctions, and then reimposed them after Iran was found to have supported attacks against the US military in Beirut in 1983 (Esfandiary and Fitzpatrick 2011). Post-hostage crisis, the United States had attempted to make efforts to repair its ties with Iran, a country that was a key "pillar" in the United States' foreign policy toward the Middle East (the other being Saudi Arabia) (Alikhani 2000; Murray 2010). However, the United States and the new theocracy running Iran failed to resolve their concerns diplomatically, and sanctions have remained the cornerstone of US foreign policy toward the regime for decades. As Wendy Sherman noted in her testimony before the US Senate Foreign Relations Committee (NPR 2015), there is much distrust between the United States and Iran at official levels given decades of animosity and severed diplomatic relations. Such enmity and distrust have only complicated efforts to resolve a potential nuclear arms race in the Middle East.

Since the Clinton Administration in the 1990s, economic sanctions as a tool for punishing Iran have not only increased in frequency but also in intensity. Executive orders and legislation enacted during the Clinton Administration sought to punish Iran for its potential efforts at developing weapons of mass destruction (Rice 2000) while also seeking to punish Iran for its state sponsorship of terrorism (Office of the Historian 2001). The George W. Bush Administration worked to reset ties with Iran, but this "reset" failed to appear after Iranian dissident groups published evidence of Iran's efforts at developing nuclear weapons when a dissident group revealed Iran's nuclear facilities in Natanz and Arak (Davenport 2023; Gerami and Goldschmidt 2012; Iran Watch 2002).

Revelations that Iran was developing nuclear weapons changed the sanctions landscape considerably as the EU took a lead in seeking to find diplomatic solutions to the emergent crisis (Cronberg 2017b). The United States and the EU divergence over policy toward Iran and the larger Middle East has been a source of disagreement for decades that has strained transatlantic ties, especially given the Middle East's strategic and economic importance to the EU (Aggestam and Hyde-Price 2019, 119; Mousavian 2008, 4). The E3—France, UK, and Germany—sought a different path than the immediate application of economic sanctions preferred by the United States, which quickly imposed new sanctions against Iran in 2005 through Executive Order 13382 that targeted entities supporting Iran's nuclear proliferation and ballistic missile activities and development (Aggestam and Hyde-Price 2019; Nada et al. 2023). While the E3 worked diplomatically to negotiate with Iran, US economic sanctions culminated with the passage of the *Comprehensive Iran Sanctions, Accountability, and Divestment Act (CISADA)* in 2010. This act revised the Iran Sanctions Act of 1996 that first introduced US secondary sanctions on Iran and represented a harsh unilateral response by the United States against Iran. It also introduced troubling secondary sanctions targeting third-party states' commerce with Iran. CISADA further extended sanctions against Iran and introduced secondary sanctions that have been applied extraterritorially, targeting not only oil but also Iran's financial system (Esfandiary and Fitzpatrick 2011, 145).

These developments led not only to an increase in the number of economic sanctions already targeting Iran but also to a change in legislation and regulations governing sanctions enforcement. It also enhanced the United States' ability to significantly levy more substantial fines over those previously levied against companies violating US economic sanctions, sanctions busters that have proved problematic in the eyes of US policymakers (Early and Preble 2020a, 2020b). These new economic enforcement powers coupled with new executive orders and legislation further increased the severity of economic sanctions against Iran.

Despite US efforts to improve the effectiveness and increase the severity of economic sanctions against Iran since the early 1980s, European commercial interests (Mousavian 2008) as well as China's growing interest in Iran's oil and market (Harold and Nader 2012) have all but consigned US economic sanctions, including those under Clinton and Bush, to failure. In fact, the EU's proximity to the region meant that the EU is more susceptible to the negative externalities generated by US policies in the region (Aggestam and Hyde-Price 2019, 119–20). Thus, it is unsurprising that the EU and other European states have traditionally disagreed with the United States on imposing comprehensive sanctions on Iran. Unsurprisingly, EU trade with Iran through the 1980s and 1990s not only helped to undermine the effectiveness of US economic sanctions, despite the United States' use of secondary sanctions to target sanctions busters (Early 2015), but also reflects the importance of Iran and the region more generally to EU commercial interests and the potential for the EU to weaponize such interdependence. While US secondary sanctions have had a chilling effect on commerce in the form of de-risking and overcompliance, particularly from European firms (Iran Watch 2021), these impacts are relatively recent developments, likely owing to more aggressive US sanctions enforcement stemming from the legal and regulatory changes in the United States during the end of George W. Bush administration (Early and Preble 2020b).

The US unilateral economic sanctions regime against Iran, especially leading up to the 2010s, failed to achieve its stated aims. Additionally, Iran serves as a critical case for understanding the humanitarian impacts sanctions have caused in many jurisdictions, especially economic and health outcomes (Brockmann and Preble 2021; Kokabisaghi 2018; Moret 2015). This impact of economic sanctions, which have done more to harm the average Iranian citizen than topple or weaken the regime, has only drawn attention to the failure of sanctions to alter the status quo in Iran's foreign policy. Sanctions against Iran have also not been very successful in weakening Iran's military, although they have been quite effective at inflicting broad economic harm against the Iranian economy (Jacobson 2008). The idea that sanctions will eventually lead to regime change is likely misplaced despite periodic national protests, especially in 2009 when protests erupted over the re-election of Mahmoud Ahmadinejad (Alexanian 2011) and fighting amongst the elite in Iran (Borszik 2016). Regime change, which is often called for by US leadership across US administrations and Congress, appears unlikely. Sanctions have also been imposed by senders in response to Iran's state sponsorship of terrorism in the region as well as to address human rights violations, especially against protesters and activists seeking change in Iran. The Iranian government remains adept at internal repression despite tough economic sanctions. Thus, economic sanctions have arguably done little to advance democracy in Iran.

The trifecta of US, EU, and UN economic sanctions generated chokepoint effects that largely diminished the trade between Iran and some of its key trading partners. While these chokepoint effects have been tremendous, the importance of panopticon effects cannot be discounted. They played a vital role in developing additional policies that sought to isolate Iranian banks, in particular, from accessing critical European financial markets. As discussed previously, panopticon effects are generated by policies or actions that, at their very heart, collect information and monitor the activities and traffic in a particular node. SWIFT, an entity incorporated in Belgium, provides messaging services for banks engaged in wire transfers. SWIFT plays no part in the actual *transfer* of the funds; in other words, SWIFT is not a conduit for wire transfers but instead collects information related to the transfer of funds from one bank and/or jurisdiction to another. Being disconnected from SWIFT *does not* prevent a bank in one jurisdiction from wiring funds to a bank another that has been disconnected from the service. In March 2012, EU Regulation 267/2012 prohibited SWIFT from providing financial messaging services to EU-sanctioned Iranian banks (Council of the European Union 2012; Swift 2022b). However, internal risk and compliance regulations of many banks likely prohibit wire transfers to banks that do not use SWIFT or some other secure service in facilitating wire transfers. Cutting banks off from SWIFT generates chokepoint effects that have a chilling effect on financial systems globally. Banks, as members, exchange and share information, and SWIFT collects and maintains records of financial messaging of all members utilizing the service and provides records to law enforcement in cracking down on terrorist financing under strict guidelines through the Terrorist Finance Tracking Program (Swift 2022a). Beyond SWIFT, other data are collected and accessed through policies meant to capture information and monitor activity in the financial system. Financial institutions operating in the EU must also comply with Direction 2019/1153, which creates rules for financial information sharing for the purposes of combating crime, requiring member states to create "centralised bank account registries" that allow financial intelligence units (FIUs) to access data on "persons holding bank and payments accounts and safe-deposit boxes" in EU member states (European Parliament and Council of the European Union 2019). These data serve as crucial resources that competent authorities can utilize in the development of chokepoint generating policies, such as economic sanctions.

At the start of the Obama Administration, a wave of record-setting economic enforcement actions (Early and Preble 2020b) as well as increased diplomacy and cooperation between the United States and the EU increased pressure on Iran to negotiate a solution to the nuclear problem and provide sanctions relief, which brought potential humanitarian relief to Iran (Brockmann and Preble 2021). The arrival of EU economic sanctions that limited the ability of member states to purchase oil and cut Iranian banks from using SWIFT, as well as a reduction in waivers from the United States to European firms wary of extraterritorial enforcement of secondary sanctions, increased the impact of both US and EU economic sanctions (van Bergeijk 2015).

While economic sanctions have led to increases in inflation (Batmanghelidj and Moret 2022), a multitude of factors directly and indirectly related to the impact of economic sanctions have only increased the potency of economic sanctions imposed on Iran. A rise in the price of household commodities (oil, lentils, sugar, eggs, etc.), and a lack of access to medical supplies are also to blame. Additionally, problematic aspects of governance within Iran and a series of natural disasters that impacted agricultural production played a role in Iran's vulnerability to the impacts of the sanctions. Together, these factors all facilitated the conditions that led to the agreement of the JCPOA, a relaxation of EU and UN economic sanctions, and a reprieve from some US economic sanctions.

GETTING THE AIM RIGHT WITH WEAPONIZED INTERDEPENDENCE

To understand why sanctions imposed on Iran ultimately succeeded with the implementation of the JCPOA, we agree that it is important to look beyond "bilateral interdependencies" and "aggregate market share" (Farrell and Newman 2019, 43). As with the previous cases that explored the inability of economic sanctions to alter behavior, we turn again to the weaponized interdependence framework.

Weaponized interdependence relies on countries' policies that, when implemented, generate two kinds of effects: panopticon and chokepoint. Panopticon effects, as the previous sections highlighted, come from policies that enable information collection and monitoring. Chokepoint effects emanate from policies that sever linkages between the policy-implementing node and a state that the policy-implementing node seeks to isolate.

Economic sanctions are important sources of chokepoint effects but are not the only source. Earlier, we noted how chokepoint effects can emanate from government policies, like economic sanctions, but also from other constituents within the policy-implementing node generating the chokepoint effect. For example, strategic trade management systems and controls imposed by governments place limits on strategic goods firms trade to jurisdictions deemed problematic. Policies that limit or bar investments and joint ventures from firms of certain countries would also qualify as a form of chokepoint effect. Banks, as private entities, may also generate chokepoint effects in response to government policies, through policies they adapt to limit their exposure to or mitigate the impact of particular risk events. For example, US banks often cancel correspondent banking accounts of banks in other jurisdictions that pose risks, especially if furnishing such services could facilitate illegal trade or other illicit financial activities. Several US banks, for example, canceled correspondent banking accounts with Mongolian banks in response to Russian sanctions as well as its diplomatic relations with North Korea and joint ventures between Mongolian and DPRK firms (Financial Information Unit 2018; International Monetary Fund 2022).

While our analysis explores the impact of state policies, such as the implementation of economic sanctions, there are many types of policies that generate chokepoint effects, which limit the movement of information, people, goods, weapons, and finance. Comprehensive US economic sanctions against heavily sanctioned states like Iran limit the ability of Iran to engage in financial transactions, trade, and even travel in some cases. The United States' dominance regionally and globally can be highly impactful in undermining how less powerfully situated nodes connect not just to the United States but others. Our application of weaponized interdependence mainly considers these types of government policies, which we see as playing a greater role in Iran's actions than chokepoint effects that emerge from policies of private firms, although we acknowledge that de-risking and overcompliance have their role to play in the case of Iran (Brockmann and Preble 2021; Iran Watch 2021).

Prior to the E3's diplomatic efforts and imposition of autonomous sanctions (or restrictive measures), the EU had begun negotiations with Iran for a Trade and Co-operation Agreement (TCA), negotiations that were halted in 2003 once the nuclear issue came to light (Portela 2015, 189–90). Despite the halt to the TCA negotiations, the EU worked diplomatically for both a temporary suspension of Iran's nuclear enrichment and a deceleration of its nuclear program more generally. These efforts led to the provision of "much more information about [Iran's] nuclear program [that] obliged Iran to sign and adhere to the IAEA Additional Protocol" (Sauer 2011, 94). Domestic Iranian politics that culminated with the election of Mahmoud Ahmadinejad in 2005 undermined those agreements and set the stage for the EU to weaponize its interdependence with Iran as the EU's restrictive measures generated potent chokepoint effects on Iran. When European countries cut Iranian financial institutions off from SWIFT in 2012 and imposed a near-total embargo on Iran's oil exports to Europe (Giumelli and Ivan 2013, 15–17), Iran lost a key financial and economic lifeline that had previously enabled it to withstand US unilateral economic sanctions (see Table 5.1).

Despite the pressure of unilateral sanctions on Iran since the Iranian Revolution, Iran largely resisted (quite successfully) early US efforts to isolate it internationally. However, once the EU complemented US unilateral sanctions with its own targeted and sectoral measures, Iran's lifeline evaporated given its interdependent network (Table 1.1). While Iran's degree centrality (that is, its share of possible trading partners) declined between 1970 and 1990, Iran's export of crude oil to energy-dependent countries, especially in Europe, provided sanctions busting support through much of the period of unilateral US sanctions. The United Arab Emirates (UAE), a key transshipment point and financial center in the Persian Gulf, has supplied Iran with a multitude of consumer staples and other consumer products. As Early (2015) demonstrates, the UAE presents an interesting sanctions busting case in that "Iran remains both one of the UAE's most important trading partners and its greatest security threat" (137). On one hand, Iran is perceived as a security threat to both the UAE and the United States and, accordingly, the latter two established a defense agreement in the mid-1990s (Early 2015, 89). On the other hand, the UAE has long maintained a trading relationship with Iran, both despite and because of US sanctions against the latter. China also slowly became one of Iran's major trading partners and has provided significant support in mitigating Iran's economic pain from economic sanctions. Regional trading partners with Iran other than the UAE have provided significant economic support as well.

Once Iran's nuclear program was revealed in 2005, the impact of unilateral US sanctions as well as the EU and UN sanctions that followed became immensely problematic for Iran. Between 2012 and 2015, economic sanctions not only further isolated Iran internationally but limited the access of Iranian banks to the global financial network. Sitting down to negotiate the JCPOA was as much about domestic imperatives as it was to seek sanctions relief and greater integration into the global economy (Tabatabai 2017).

Oil embargoes imposed in 2012 by European countries—even those that have historically relied on Iranian crude—drastically reduced their oil imports with the immediate effect of undermining Iran's revenues. Much more targeted UN sanctions further compelled all member states to reduce forms of economic engagement that could potentially contribute to or support Iran's nuclear and ballistic missile programs (even if the full impact of UN sanctions is difficult to enforce). The chokepoint effects that emanated from these sanctions, which cut off Iranian companies from selling oil and limited the access of Iran's domestic banks to the global financial system, had a crippling effect on Iran's economy (Cronberg 2017b; Tarock 2016). However, the sanctions generated negative externalities in the form of creating workarounds to the ban on financial transactions with Iranian banks. Also, some Iranian companies and transactions utilized bartering or were forced to accept less fungible currencies, such as the Indian rupee and Turkish lira, to settle some oil transactions (Giumelli and Ivan 2013, 16). We theorize then that countries, like Iran, which have many connections to key nodes throughout a network of trade or finance, are more likely to be impacted by the effects of economic sanctions but may also benefit from these additional connections in circumventing economic sanctions. In the case of Iran, however, economic sanctions remain impactful because they are able to isolate and limit Iran's connectivity with its trading partners and limit the ability to conduct financial transactions and trade effectively.

We utilize social network analysis to generate two hypotheses. The first hypothesis involves measuring the target state's degree centrality. Degree centrality is a measure of *connectedness* within the network. In other words, as this number increases, Iran's share of trading partners relative to the potential trading partners in any given year increases. One would posit that a country impacted by economic sanctions would see declines in this value as firms and constituents comply with sanctions or de-risk by avoiding trade with Iran. If we fail to reject this hypothesis, then we posit that the ability of states to weaponize interdependence is limited.

> *H_1: The greater the degree centrality, the greater the susceptibility to weaponized interdependence via chokepoint effects.*

The second and third hypotheses we test involve exploring the *depth* or *strength* of Iran's relationships with its trading partners. *Strength centrality* measures the strength of each connection in the network, that is the linkage or "walk" between Iran and each of its trading partners. We operationalize two measures of strength centrality, MOSC1 and MOSC2, which we discussed in chapter 1. MOSC1 represents the commercial dependence (or trade) of the target state's trading partner on the target (in this case, Iran); in other words, it captures the importance of Iran's market to the trading partner. A higher value indicates greater dependence on Iran for trade. MOSC2, on the other hand, captures the importance of a trading partner's market to the target state, reflecting the target state's efforts to avoid the pain of economic sanctions.

Comparing MOSC1 and MOSC2 between Iran and a trading partner via a graph can help to uncover whether economic sanctions are working: is the trading partner complying with or taking part in the sanctioning coalition? When economic sanctions are effective, both MOSC1 and MOSC2 should decline in tandem, essentially mirroring each other and following similar trends. When a trading partner is engaging in sanctions busting, both MOSC1 and MOSC2 should move higher after the imposition of economic sanctions. If a black knight relationship exists, as we observed between North Korea and China, we should see MOSC1 increase and dominate the target's trade profile while MOSC2 remains constant or declines.

We thus argue that the success of economic sanctions is a function of the depth of these connections. If strength centrality between Iran and another trading partner is high, then the effects of chokepoint effects, if that trading partner imposes economic sanctions, are more impactful and are more likely first to generate economic "pain." Second, if such "pain" cannot be mitigated, then there should be a policy change of some kind. We can empirically identify these sanctioning trading partners by examining the strength centrality between those states and Iran *before* and *after* the imposition of economic sanctions. Since we argue that the imposition of economic sanctions by European partners is both *necessary* and *sufficient* for the sanctions to be effective, we should observe declines in strength centrality measures between Iran and these countries once economic sanctions are imposed.

Our second hypothesis is as follows:

> *H_2: The greater the strength centrality between Iran and a sanctioning trading partner (and vice versa), the greater the susceptibility to weaponized interdependence via chokepoint effects.*

If our hypothesis testing fails to reject the null across our two hypotheses, the theory we have developed using the weaponized interdependence framework will be supported. Long-term economic sanctions have been imposed by successive US presidents since the Iranian Revolution in the late 1970s, but these sanctions have not been adopted or accepted by the international community writ large, especially by European partners. Once Europe joins the United States in imposing sanctions on Iran that target Iranian oil exports, the chokepoint effects created by both sets of sanctions should begin to generate pressure on Iran's economy. The loss of the European market would represent a significant loss of export trade, and Iran has been unable to return to pre-sanction levels of trade.

While the United States has largely shunned Iran commercially with the most minimal commercial engagement, European and regional trading partners have far more potential to weaponize interdependence. Sanctions against Iranian oil exports destined for the EU proved to be impactful. The economic sanctions imposed have been more effective because US and EU sanctions have worked in tandem to target Iran's ability to find alternative customers while also severing commercial vital trade linkages with EU member states (El-Katiri and Fattouh 2012). Thus, we posit that Iran's trading network varied only slightly until its nuclear program was revealed in 2005, which subsequently drew UN and EU sanctions. We expect that Iran's trading network shifted significantly after the UN Security Council began formally sanctioning the country for its unwillingness to allow IAEA inspectors into Iran and to support negotiations for the eventual JCPOA.

WEAPONIZING INTERDEPENDENCE AGAINST IRAN

Our study utilizes UN Comtrade data that captures trade flows between states (United Nations 2021) from 1990 to 2017 to explore trends in trade between Iran and its key trading partners. As discussed in chapter 1 and the previous section of this chapter, we employ SNA to test two hypotheses. The first hypothesis relies on degree centrality, which hypothesizes that a greater value of degree centrality means that a target state is more susceptible to weaponized interdependence via chokepoint effects.

First, we use the trade data from the above sources to operationalize H_1 exploring Iran's degree centrality, that is, its share of trading partners as well as its absolute number of trading partners in each year from 1990 to 2017. Figure 5.1 shows Iran's degree centrality and total number of trading partners, while Figure 5.2 shows Iran's total annual trade. To understand the effect of economic sanctions on Iran, an analysis of the social network based on trade linkages provides insights about how these relationships change across time as economic sanctions move from unilateral US sanctions to blistering multilateral sanctions consisting of United States, EU, and UN sanctions. We create three visualizations of Iran's network of trade that, while largely descriptive, reflect important aspects of Iran's network of licit trade. Figures 5.3 and 5.4 are important in showing two effects: Iran's ability to insulate itself from economic sanctions as its network of trade changes very little from 2000 to 2008 through its ability to attract trade and commerce and a change in the concentration of trade as many economic partners reduce their economic engagement. Figure 5.5 shows how Iran's network of trade changes as European trade partners embargo Iranian oil and EU firms de-risk and avoid trade with the pariah state.

Figure 5.1 shows a marked increase in Iran's share of trading partners across time as it seeks to diversify its trading partners. Not only does the number of trading partners increase but Iran's flow of trade between 1990 and 2012 increases, as well. We remind the reader that degree centrality represents the interconnectedness of a node to other nodes in the network. For each of the undirected networks we construct, the target state sits at the center of the network. We posit that the more connections between Iran and its trading partners, which increases over time despite the presence of economic sanctions, the greater the likelihood that weaponized interdependence occurs

Figure 5.1 The Left y-Axis Represents Iran's Degree Centrality or Connectedness within the Network Whereas the Right Axis Measures the Number of Trading Partners in Any Given Year. While Iran is an international pariah, its connectedness to other economies has increased since 1990. *Source*: Created by Authors.

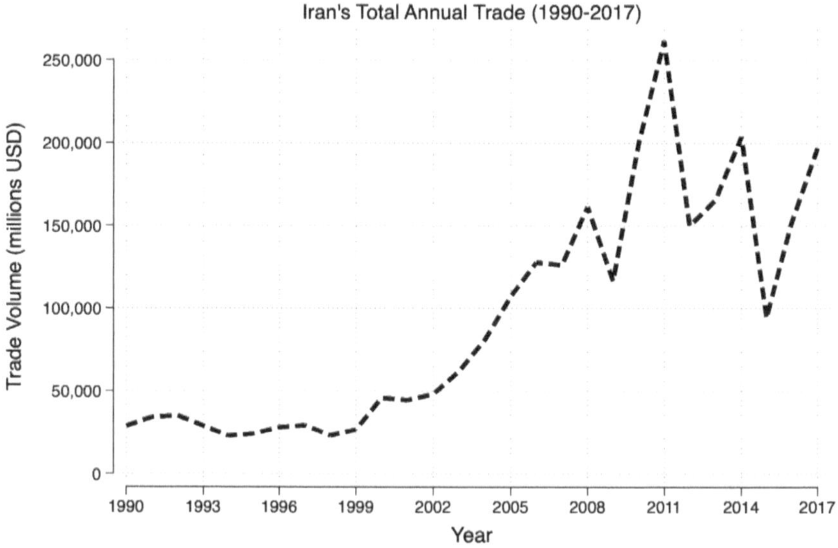

Figure 5.2 Iran's Total Annual Trade from 1990 to 2017 Using UN Comtrade Data from Atlas of Economic Complexity. *Source*: Created by Authors.

via chokepoint effects generated by the imposition of economic sanctions. Beginning in 1995, Iran's trading partners began to increase and surpassed 150 unique countries by 2000. While there are some minor fluctuations, the variation in degree centrality (or share of trading partners) and the absolute number of trading partners between 2010 and 2015 provide evidence that economic sanctions were working to isolate Iran. The year 2015, in particular, represents the lowest degree centrality and lowest number of trading partners, which represents Iran's nadir and culminated with the signing of the JCPOA on July 14.

Degree centrality suggests that Iran has become more central to its trading partners as the number of edges (connections between nodes) has increased. This increase in the number of connections to trading partners indicates an increased ability of actors connected to Iran to weaponize interdependence should they choose to implement policies that generate chokepoint effects, especially as Iran's volume of trade also grows during this period, (Figure 5.2) despite the fact that Iran's major trading partner, the EU, saw its trade with Iran decline substantially after 2011 (Giumelli and Ivan 2013, 17). Iran's degree centrality seems to indicate an increased connectedness to the global trade economy, which increases even in the face of US unilateral sanctions, some of which are secondary and target Iran's key trading partners. The high degree centrality of Iran to its trade partners shows that Iran has been quite adept at resisting the pressures and pain of economic sanctions, but

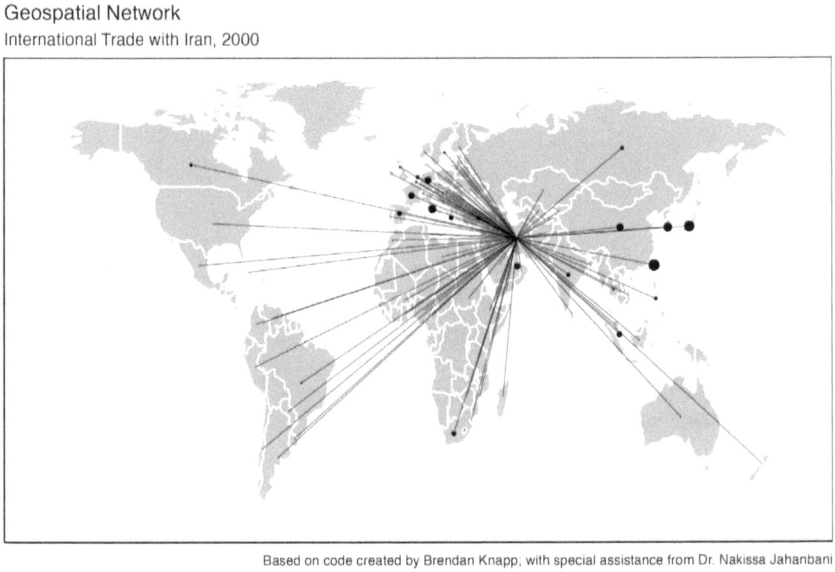

Figure 5.3 Trading Partner Distribution. Ties between Iran and trading partners capture all trading partners in 2000. The ties between Iran and its trading partners are indicated with solid black lines. We only consider Iran's trading relationships when total aggregate trade exchanged is greater than or equal to $1 million current USD, which we argue are more significant trading ties. Filled black circles are nodes or states in the international system. The size of the node increases as that country's trade share with Iran increases. *Source*: Created by Authors.

this adeptness diminishes between 2010 and 2015 as Iran's share of trading partners—its strength centrality—fluctuates. Iran loses trade partners and then replaces them. While instructive, the share of trading partners or degree centrality alone fails to capture the strength of the relationships between Iran and other trading partners in the network.

A discussion of Iranian oil exports provides a clear picture of this nadir. Prior to the imposition of economic sanctions by the EU, it "used to be the most important [trade] partner of Iran" (European Commission 2022). While Iran has one of the more diversified economies in the Middle East (EIA 2022), oil exports represent a significant portion of its trade profile. In 2000, for example, Iran's export profile for crude petroleum (SITC 3330) was significantly more diversified. Using Harvard University's *Atlas of Economic Complexity*, a profile of how Iran's exports have changed shows the impact of economic sanctions. In 2000, $17.2 billion of Iran's exports (approximately 65 percent) involved exports of crude petroleum to 26 countries. Thirty-three percent of Iranian crude oil exports were purchased by European importers with Italy (34 percent), France (17.2 percent), and Greece (15.3 percent)

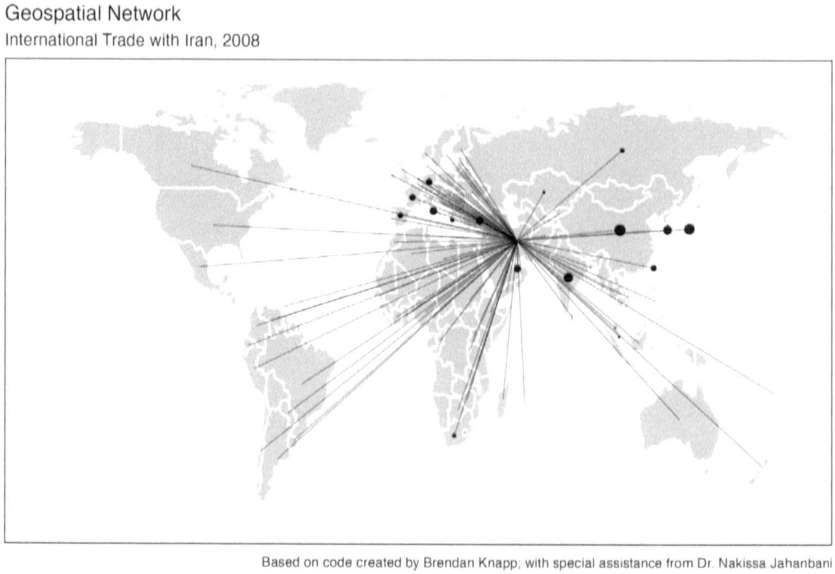

Figure 5.4 Trading Partner Distribution. Ties between Iran and trading partners in 2008. The ties between Iran and its trading partners are indicated with solid black lines. We only consider Iran's trading relationships when total aggregate trade exchanged is greater than or equal to $1 million current USD, which we argue are more significant trading ties. Filled black circles are nodes or states in the international system. The size of the node increases as that country's trade share with Iran increases. *Source*: Created by Authors.

purchasing the most crude. From 2000 to 2012, oil exports to Europe grew considerably from a low of $4.56b in 2001 to a high of $17.5b in 2011. By 2013, as UN sanctions were imposed and EU sanctions increased, Iranian exports to Europe were reduced to only $38.3 million to Greece in 2013 and $215 million to Italy while all other EU member states were no longer prominent importers of Iranian crude oil. After the JCPOA was signed and went into force, EU imports of Iranian oil rebounded somewhat with $3.55b in imports from Iran in 2016 and $8.01b in 2017. Generally, the imposition of economic sanctions impacted Iranian exports to the extent that 2011 had the lowest volume of crude exports by Iran since 1986 (Giumelli and Ivan 2013, 17).

The year 2008 represents a milestone for Iranian crude oil exports with exports totaling nearly $70 billion. After 2008, the number of export partners declined, and the total exports fell to a low of $18.2 billion by 2015. By 2015, only a single European country (Italy) was purchasing a mere fraction of the crude oil the EU had purchased in previous years. The loss of European markets likely resulted in a decline in oil output by Iranian oil producers, which

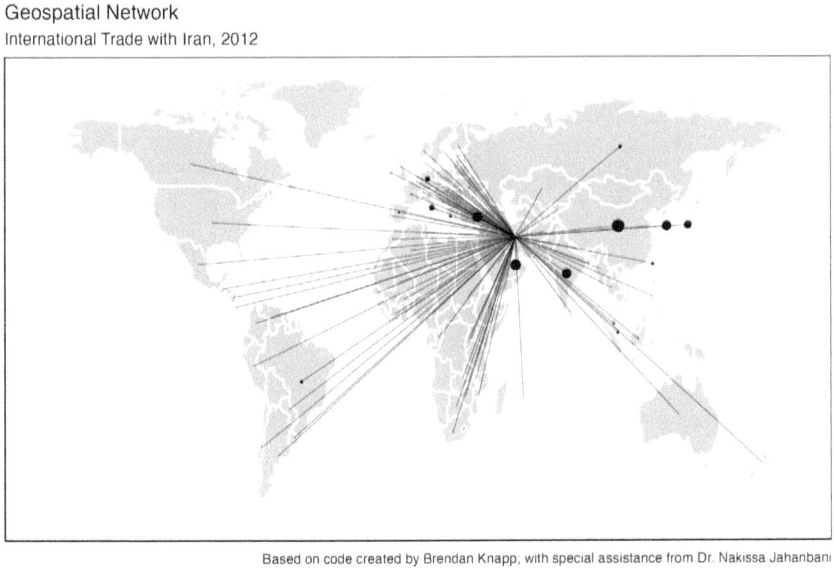

Figure 5.5 Trading Partner Distribution. Ties between Iran and trading partners in 2012. The ties between Iran and its trading partners are indicated with solid black lines. We only consider Iran's trading relationships when total aggregate trade exchanged is greater than or equal to $1 million current USD, which we argue are more significant trading ties. Filled black circles are nodes or states in the international system. The size of the node increases as that country's trade share with Iran increases. *Source*: Created by Authors.

has not completely recovered since the Trump administration scuttled the JCPOA and created greater uncertainty in Iranian oil markets.

Given the preponderance of trade that Iran has conducted in the past with energy-dependent countries in the EU, China, and economic hubs like the UAE, the trade linkages between these states and Iran would indicate that these three major trading partners could potentially have greater influence and leverage over other aspects of Iran's behavior (i.e., its foreign policy) than the United States, which is only loosely connected to Iran through trade. Lastly, the network in which these countries trade, behave, and interact is dynamic in one sense and static in another. It is dynamic in that Iran's connectivity grows by adding new trading partners, firms in countries willing to engage in trade-based sanctions busting, while the relationships it has already cultivated remain fairly constant, leading to a network that makes few adjustments when confronted with US economic sanctions.

We create three network graphs that show the structure of Iran's trade linkages with states in the international system in 2000, 2008, and then 2012 (Figures 5.3–5.5). We selected these "windows" as they show how strength centrality adjusts over time in response to economic sanctions imposed by a multitude of actors. We then use SNA to show descriptively the share of the trade conducted with Iran (indicated by the size of each red node) and the geographic distribution of that trade across the international system by mapping the network geospatially. The geospatial network visualizations demonstrate how Iran's trading network varies only slightly under unilateral US sanctions, yet by 2012, the effects of EU sanctions have now emerged.

We now turn to demonstrating how our strength centrality measures capture weaponized interdependence and sanctions busting trade (H_2). By constructing two measures of strength centrality, both of which are weighted by the total amount of trade conducted by Iran or its trade partner, we study the impact of sanctions on the strength of the ties between the target state and sanctioning trade partners. As noted previously, these measures of strength centrality are similar to trade share measures, which is not unusual when working with trade data (De Benedictus et al. 2013). Strength centrality measures not just the number of connections or the *connectedness* of the target state between nodes in its network (in this case, trade between states), but the depth of the trade relationship.

Table 5.1 shows the strength centrality measures (MOSC1) for key nodes in Iran's network of licit trade that reflect the importance of the trading partner's market for trade, which in turn reflects the importance of the market for Iranian trade. Each value represents the strength or depth of the connection

Table 5.1 Trading Partners' Commercial Dependence on Iran (MOSC1)

Trading Partner	1990	1995	2000	2005	2010	2015
Belgium	4.44	1.30	1.05	0.66	0.69	0.55
Canada	1.12	1.64	1.52	0.24	0.08	0.10
China	0.79	2.04	5.14	9.08	14.20	35.06
France	6.79	7.73	3.75	6.21	1.74	0.74
Germany	11.95	9.99	4.18	5.58	3.09	2.76
Greece	1.32	1.86	2.40	1.70	0.78	0.04
Italy	8.87	9.02	6.31	8.37	4.33	1.93
Japan	16.53	13.80	12.27	17.09	6.35	3.58
Netherlands	4.84	3.96	1.83	1.78	1.05	0.56
Portugal	0.47	1.43	0.75	0.14	0.09	0.05
Russia	-	-	1.67	1.93	1.81	1.34
South Africa	0.00	4.90	2.57	2.11	1.56	0.03
Spain	3.93	3.75	2.56	2.15	2.48	0.47
Sweden	1.56	1.37	1.18	1.12	0.37	0.33
Switzerland	1.24	0.95	0.89	1.11	1.03	0.77
United Kingdom	3.99	2.87	1.09	0.86	0.36	0.19
United States	0.60	1.15	0.54	0.25	0.15	0.31

Source: Created by Authors.

between Iran and a trading partner in any given year. For our undirected network, aggregate trade flows generate a single measure of strength centrality. Higher values of degree centrality and its weighted version, strength centrality, indicate not only the importance of a particular node but also an increased ability to influence or be influenced by others (Yan and Ding 2009, 2108). By 2015, EU member states had significantly reduced their economic engagement with Iran.

Despite these declines in trade with the EU, especially exports of crude petroleum to Europe, Iran was not without agency as it sought to acquire additional markets for its goods. As Table 5.1 indicates, China's importance to Iran's economy rose from 0.79 percent to nearly 35 percent as Iran's trading relationship with China increased significantly (Harold and Nader 2012). By 2011, China was purchasing nearly 11 percent of Iranian crude oil, with overall trade between Iran and China topping $36 billion in 2012 while also providing significant investment in Iran's energy sector (Sun 2014). While China's economic engagement is considerable and replaces much of the lost trade, Iran has a preference for Western European technology. Also, it rarely receives hard currency from China for its exports, and many of the deals that support the regime in the face of economic sanctions are "opaque and subject to corruption" (Slavin 2011, 3). While Iran has been able to replace much of the economic benefits lost due to the imposition of EU sanctions with trade with China, Iranian preferences for Western technology, access to hard currency, and European financial markets further reflect the fallout from Iranian economic interdependence with Europe.

Prior to 2015, the strength of the linkages (or "walks") between Iran and EU member states, in particular, showed not only the importance of such trade but also the extent to which EU member states engaged in trade-based sanctions busting. Other countries also imposed their own unilateral sanctions against Iran, namely Canada and Japan (Esfandiary and Fitzpatrick 2011, 145). By 2011, however, as the UN and the EU's own autonomous sanctions increased, the EU could wield and weaponize its interdependence with Iran. By the signing of the JCPOA in 2015, the EU's importance to Iran dropped significantly as the economic impacts of the layers of economic sanctions from a multitude of senders helped ensure the negotiation and signing of the JCPOA.

What stands out about the EU and Iran is the relationship between MOSC1 and MOSC2 and the construction of strength centrality measures of EU trade as a bloc rather than only bilateral relationships (although these will be discussed). Figure 5.6 shows the trends for both strength centrality measures. The dotted line shows Iranian commercial engagement with the EU, which shows a decline in the importance of EU trade. What explains this decline in the EU's importance to Iran?

We surmise that there are two reasons for this decline. First, between 1994 and 2010, the EU has enlarged several times with the largest increase in members in 2003. As the EU has increased in size, Iranian trade with the EU has not kept pace with the EU's membership increases. The solid black line, which represents the EU's commercial dependence (and interest) in Iran, as a bloc, remains somewhat flat. The lack of growth in the EU's commercial engagement in Iran may also demonstrate the importance of the EU's Single European Market, which has grown to be a substantial market for trade. As the EU has grown in size and this market has become not only politically but economically more expedient, the EU has not only reduced its propensity to engage in trade-based sanctions busting but also engaged in greater intra-EU trade at the expense of extra-EU trade (Preble 2020). Second, as Figure 5.1 shows, Iran's trade profile grows between 1990 and 2017 as its trading partners increase from a low of 82 to 169 trading partners, more than doubling its number of trading partners. Iran has sought to diversify its trade portfolio away from its reliance on the EU, which has likely been helped by increasing trade with China and regionally within the Middle East.

While the EU market has become less important to Iranian trade, the EU still retained significant weaponized interdependence leading up to 2012,

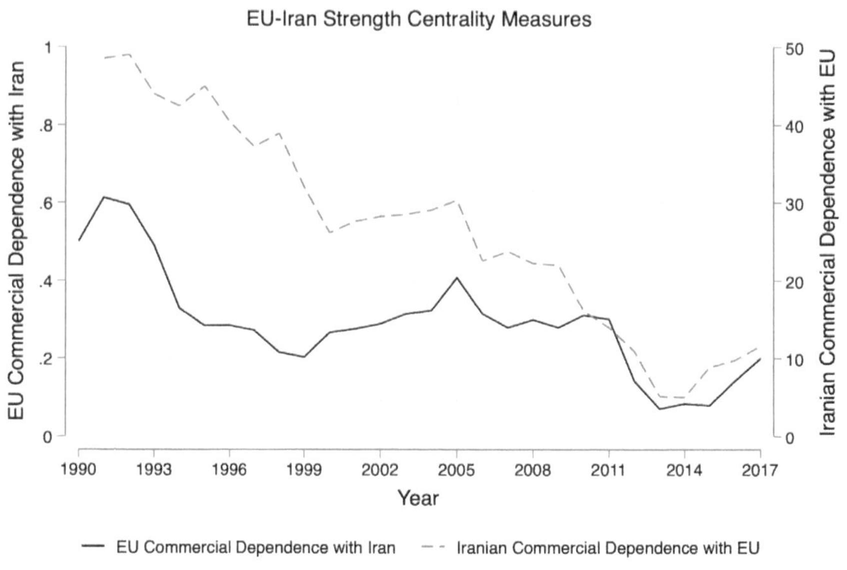

Figure 5.6 Strength Centrality Measures between EU and Iran in Comparison. This figure shows the decline of commercial dependence between the two actors over time. The solid black line shows the EU's commercial engagement dropping significantly in 2011, reflecting EU implementing sanctions in concert with the US and UN on Iran. *Source*: Created by Authors.

which is driven by the economic engagement of individual member states. Figures 5.6–5.8 show the strength centrality measures of the EU and member states Greece and Spain, all of which demonstrate not only growth in the strength of the trade ties but also the effects and impacts of economic sanctions once they come into force in 2011 as strength centrality on both sides declines, which provides strong support for our second hypothesis.

These figures reflect two phenomena of interest to sanctions scholars. First, both of these EU member states engage in trade-based sanctions busting with Iran. As Early (2015) notes in his seminal work on sanctions busting trade, European countries are some of the most likely to engage in trade-based sanctions busting. Both EU member states increase and decrease their commercial dependence on Iran, especially since they have historically purchased significant quantities of crude oil from Iran. Second, once the EU imposes economic sanctions in 2011 against Iran in concert with the United States to propel the JCPOA negotiations, EU member states largely comply as nearly all EU member states between 2012 and 2015 reduced their purchases of Iranian crude (although a handful of EU member states had exemptions to the sanctions carved out).

Once economic sanctions are imposed, the chokepoint effects generated by the combination of United States, EU, and UN sanctions become untenable for Iran. As Tarock (2016) has noted, the easing of some sanctions and

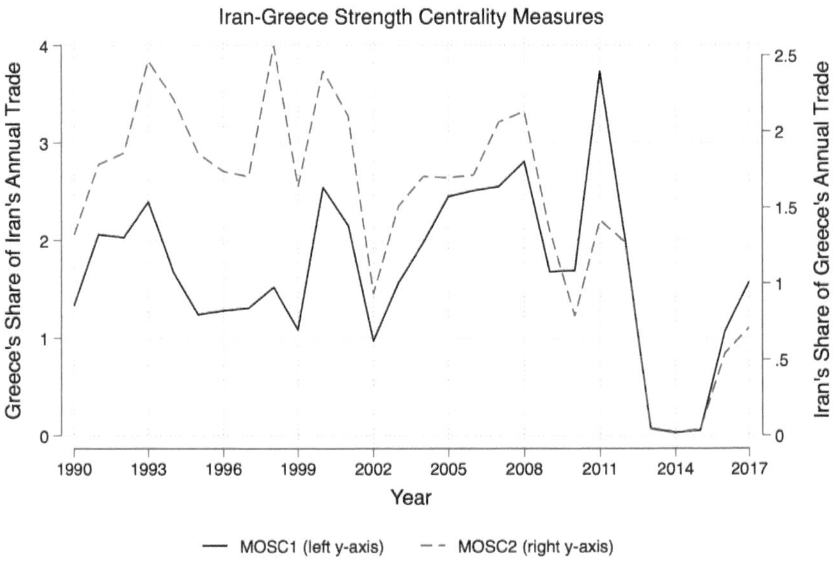

Figure 5.7 Comparison of Strength Centrality Measures for Iran and Greece. *Source:* Created by Authors.

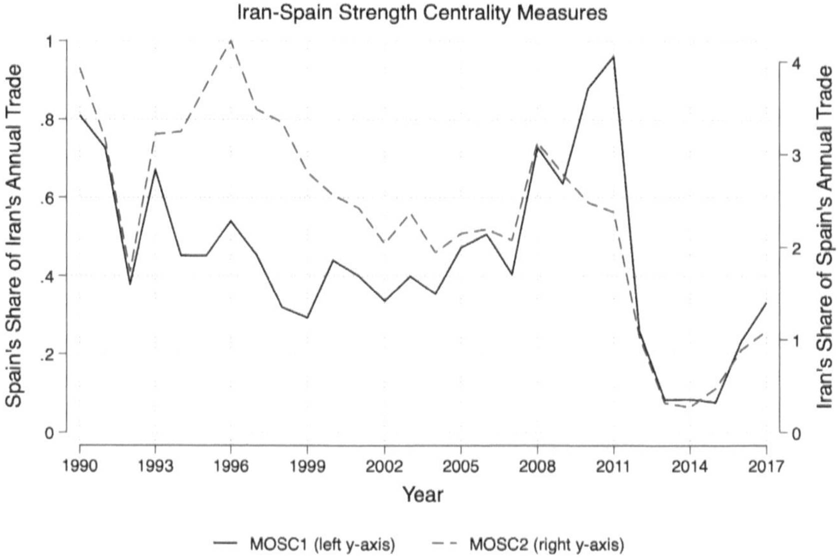

Figure 5.8 Comparison of Strength Centrality Measures for Iran and Spain. *Source*: Created by Authors.

lifting of others contributed to Iran's motivations to negotiate with the P5+1 and come to an agreement about Iran's enrichment of uranium. The bloc's significant engagement in trade with Iran as well as the information and data collected from the generation of panopticon effects provided the Council of the EU with the necessary data to implement effective, targeted economic sanctions. Working in concert with the United States and the economic sanctions imposed by the UN Security Council on Iran, the EU's weaponization of its interdependence with Iran not only deprived Iran of trade with key trading partners, such as Italy, Greece, and Spain, but also limited Iran's economic engagement with the bloc writ large.

Despite United States, EU, and UN sanctions and their effectiveness, the ability of sanctions to deter Iran continued to be challenged by sanctions busting states outside of Europe. The UAE as well as other partners such as Turkey represent distinct challenges to the EU increasing its ability to weaponize its interdependence with Iran to bring about concrete policy change and facilitate negotiations. Traditionally, the UAE has picked up some of the trade that Iran lost with other former partners as further sanctions have been imposed (Early 2015, 96). The two countries also have decades-old "legitimate and illicit commercial networks" (Early 2015, 101). Additionally, Dubai has developed into a transshipment hub, in part due to its geographic location and in part due to its "significant investments in its logistical infrastructure, including the construction of the world's largest human-made port at Jebel Ali"

(Early 2015, 108). Trade between the two countries rose during the mid-1990s and into the 2000s in part due to the proliferation of free trade zones (FTZs) in the UAE (Early 2015, 119). Overall, the UAE represents an important ally to Iran, one who has shown that it is capable and willing to bust sanctions.

CONCLUSION

In our estimation, Iran represents a case where weaponized interdependence is deployed successfully through a combination of policies that generate both panopticon and chokepoint effects. As our analysis demonstrates, Iran proved adept at resisting US unilateral economic sanctions by maintaining robust commercial relationships with European powers, especially Germany despite diplomatic pressure from the United States and Israel (Mousavian 2008).

Once the nuclear issue emerged in 2002, the E3's efforts to engage diplomatically with Iran generated panopticon effects that provided diplomatic resources to the EU through talks and engagement with the pariah state. While the EU was slow to adopt stronger economic sanctions, targeted sanctions in 2010 followed by a total oil embargo on Iran in January 2012 were critical actions that allowed the EU to weaponize its interdependence with Iran. While the oil embargo likely proved costly to Europe, the credible commitment of imposing the embargo and holding member states accountable to it had a significantly detrimental effect on Iran's economy. As noted earlier, the combination of US economic sanctions, particularly secondary sanctions that made trading Iranian oil difficult, coupled with EU sanctions was the "perfect storm" that caused the Iranian economy considerable damage (El-Katiri and Fattouh 2012). After Iran was cut off from one of its most lucrative markets, it had little room to maneuver as countries both inside and outside the EU eschewed Iranian oil to avoid US sanctions regulators. Iran could no longer avoid the multilateral layer of economic sanctions. The only respite for Iran would be to negotiate with the P5+1 for a diplomatic solution that loosened the sanctions noose and provided much-needed sanctions relief to Iran's beleaguered economy.

As Tarja Cronberg rightly notes (2017a, 2017b), EU efforts at engaging diplomatically with Iran and then later working with the United States proved pivotal in the successful (if sadly short-lived) agreement with Iran that would be cast aside after President Obama left office. Yet, this case shows that economic sanctions have the potential to be both effective *and* successful at bringing about change when interdependence is weaponized by the right actors in a target state's network, especially when major trading partners cooperate with economic sanctions (Mclean and Whang 2010). US unilateral efforts to punish Iran sought to achieve policy and behavioral changes from Iran without implementing the necessary policies that could capture critically important information and data to monitor Iran via panopticon effects. Such data monitoring and gathering policies were incompatible with the US's efforts to isolate Iran. Such policies would have also required engagement and access to the US financial system and markets or the normalization of ties establishing embassies and diplomatic infrastructure in both states. As this and the other cases have shown, political and economic isolation limits the effectiveness of economic sanctions and reduces the likelihood of behavioral change.

Chapter 6

Further Applications and the Potential for Weaponized Interdependence

In this chapter, we apply our theoretical and methodological framework to two additional cases: Russia and Cuba. No work on sanctions would be complete without discussing the sanctions against Russia for its violation of international norms through its annexation of Crimea (2014) and invasion of Ukraine (2022-) and Cuban efforts to withstand blistering unilateral US economic sanctions. Future research should explore the theory and hypotheses presented here to show how network structures and locations in those structures matter to understand the effectiveness and success of economic sanctions. Both cases reflect the "logic of choice," especially in highlighting that economic sanctions do not operate alone or in a vacuum but work in tandem and interact with other foreign policies (Baldwin 1999). Yet, how that logic plays out is contingent on network structures and the ability of nodes (or states) in those networks to adapt dynamically as new panopticon and chokepoint effects are generated by more powerful nodes in those networks. We end the chapter with a discussion of the main conclusions of our study and their policy implications as well as our final thoughts.

RUSSIA'S NEW *PARIAHTUDE?*

When Russia invaded Ukraine in 2022, the United States, the EU, and a multitude of states joined forces to impose some of the harshest and most comprehensive economic sanctions ever seen. The Russian invasion of Ukraine signaled Russia's further descent to international pariah status, which began in earnest in 2014 when it annexed Crimea after the Maidan Revolution ousted the former Ukrainian president Viktor Yanukovych, who, even as protests erupted, would make no concessions without Putin's assent

(Marples 2017; Plokhy 2023). The illegal acquisition of territorial title, the use of force contrary to the UN Charter, the raft of human rights abuses both inside Russia and Ukraine, and the humanitarian catastrophe the Russians have unleashed on Ukraine have severely isolated Putin and the Russian state. The war between Russia and Ukraine (ongoing since 2022 at the writing of this work) shows no signs of a ceasefire or peace treaty. As Russia continues its disastrous war where it has endured significant setbacks and failures, Russia is quickly becoming an international pariah.

The application of economic sanctions against Russia emerged slowly since the annexation of Crimea in 2014. The initial muted policy response from Western countries did not match their discourse of condemnation and support for Ukraine. While the economic sanctions in 2014 are often seen as having been highly impactful, the impact of economic sanctions is likely an interactive effect between the imposition of these chokepoint effects coupled with a decline in world oil prices and a weakening of Russia's currency, the ruble. Yet the economic sanctions imposed for Russia's annexation against Crimea did little to hurt the actors targeted by Western sanctions, Russia's powerful elite (Ashford 2016). Extensive economic planning by Russian authorities and sanctions proofing (Glenn 2023) has moved the Russian economy away from trade settlements in dollars and euro to China's yuan (Nikoladze and Mrugank 2023), a trend that reflects increasing political risk of utilizing the US dollar and anti-dollar policymaking from US rivals (McDowell 2023, 21).

If North Korea is a hard target, Russia is equally so despite its greater interdependence with many states in the West where Russian energy finds willing markets for its energy exports. While North Korea has found ways to isolate and limit its exposure to Western sanctions, the Russian "secret weapon" is its ability to impose severe threats of and actual countersanctions on both potential and actual senders. The sanctions imposed after the annexation of Crimea brought attention to a major threat that Russia poses, namely its ability to impose countersanctions (Connolly 2019). Russia is a highly developed economy and has been able to weather the impact of economic sanctions, likely the result of sanctions-proofing over the last nine years since Russia's annexation of Crimea from Ukraine (Glenn 2023; Prokopenko and Gabuev 2023). Its economy is one of the largest in the world, and numerous states around the world rely on not only its energy exports but also its grain exports and exports of fertilizers and other commodities necessary for agricultural production. While both food and fertilizer are exempt from the slate of sanctions to date against Russia by the United States and EU, trade has still been impacted as vessels carrying Russian goods are often targeted with economic sanctions (Alexander et al. 2022, 85). Through its energy exports, Russia has been able to weaponize its economic power against states where interdependence exists, especially with the EU.

While the EU has sought to reduce its reliance on Russian gas, carveouts have been added to EU sanctions for various member states in an effort to maintain intra-European unity against Russian aggression (The Economist 2022; Perkins and Griffin 2023). Despite differences among EU member states, significant political support persists that has allowed the EU to find the consensus to renew restrictive measures (Portela et al. 2021).

The pathway of weaponized interdependence, of course, operates in both directions. The EU's reliance on Russian energy proved to be a liability for the bloc, but it also provided the bloc with a powerful economic weapon by depriving Russia of much-needed revenues as it fought a war in Ukraine that has lasted longer than many analysts had predicted. The creation of a price cap on Russian oil (Wolfram, Johnson, and Rachel 2022) as well as EU efforts to diversify its energy supplies and seek new partnerships, especially with the United States (Kardaś 2023), are not likely to provide immediate relief but, as the war continues, these developments are likely to further isolate Russia and confirm its status as the newest member of the club of pariah states.

While international condemnation that emerged around the 2022 Russian invasion showed significant variation, especially among firms operating in Russia (Sonnenfeld 2022), it remains to be seen how long global firms will remain outside the Russian market. While some firms have sold off their assets and have abandoned the market altogether, other firms have simply taken a pause or have dug in and profited from the absence of Western firms. Many firms have sought to balance reputational harms with commercial necessity, and many firms operating in Russia have preferred to self-sanction due to consumer and shareholder pressures (Early and Preble 2024). Economic sanctions are known for their propensity to generate lucrative commercial opportunities (Early 2015), and, in the case of Russian sanctions, these opportunities have emerged, especially in the former Soviet Republics, all of which have seen tremendous increases in trade and economic growth from the diversion of trade through their borders to and from the Russian market (Gavin and Aarup 2023).

The role of economic sanctions in creating commercial opportunities for firms underlies much of our analysis. We acknowledge that we are not the first scholars to identify or classify this phenomenon (van Bergeijk 1989; Early 2011, 2015). What our research seeks to highlight is that the emergence of these commercial opportunities and likely sanctions busters is a function of the structure of networks in which states find themselves. Further, the success and effectiveness of sanctions is highly dependent upon the structure of these networks, as well. For example, Myanmar's regional footprint and network of trade remains largely regionally focused, which limits the extent and reach of Western senders in coercing Myanmar to change. Russia, on the other hand, was, like Iran, much more exposed economically and financially to the West, especially the EU. Like North Korea, Russia quickly pivoted its economy through internally balancing against Western powers by mobilizing its resources at home or by embracing trade relationships with countries unwilling or unable to enforce economic sanctions, such as China and Turkey. Russia's reliance on China, in particular, has demonstrated not only the willingness of China's firms to capitalize on economic opportunities Western sanctions have provided but also the political support that Beijing offers to Moscow. While Russia relies heavily on the European market to sell its energy, the loss of that market has not been as devastating as analysts have presumed (Ashford 2016).[1]

Sanctions busting remains a perennial problem in international relations, and sanctions against Russia are no different. While firms globally are wary of the Office of Foreign Assets Control (OFAC) and its aggressive approach at fining violators of US economic sanctions, OFAC must first determine who these violators are, which has been challenged by resource issues within the Department of Treasury (Desiderio 2018; Klimasinska, Campbell, and Katz 2014; Preble 2021). The more prominent the economic sanctions and the greater the public attention, the higher the probability that OFAC will punish violators of US economic sanctions, though. While the EU could renounce its connections to Russia, many firms remain in business in Russia. An analysis conducted by Early and Preble (2024) showed that firms whose home countries had extensive trade ties with Russia were far less likely to self-sanction and leave the Russian market. Yet, as Early and Preble (2024) demonstrated in their analysis, public awareness of firms' involvement in Russia has pushed many firms globally to renounce their interests and engagement in the Russian market. Public pressure has played a key role in states' imposition of sanctions as well, including the US sanctions against Myanmar, a country that the United States has traditionally not had a lot of commercial interests (Nyun 2008, 484–5).

The sanctions episode involving Russia highlights again how the implementation and enforcement of economic sanctions show how coordination among allies matters greatly. While UN sanctions are an impossibility given Russia's veto power on the Security Council, sanctions coalitions of the willing can be formed outside the auspices of the UN or even the EU. Those countries with the greatest leverage, especially countries with strong commercial ties to Russia and strong financial connections, could be tasked with leading the charge. As de-dollarization trends (Liu and Papa 2022) and other sanctions evasion measures (Preble 2022a, 2022b) are developed by countries (although it may be decades before the United States need seriously worry), the United States and other senders of economic sanctions will need to rely on more creative approaches, especially for economically better-placed states like Russia with its vast oil and energy reserves.

While the impact of chokepoint effects has been limited, the decline in diplomatic relations between the West and Russia has limited the ability of diplomats and consular activity to capture and gather information on Russia. This decline began in 2017 prior to Russia's invasion of Ukraine and has only accelerated in that six-year period as Russian and Western embassies in consulates downsize or close (Associated Press 2023; Reuters 2023; US Mission, Russia 2021). Downsized embassies, fewer if any diplomatic discussions or engagements, and no high-level contacts between Russia and many Western powers complicates finding a resolution to the war between Russia and Ukraine.

The implication for the Russian sanctions regime is that sanctions' effectiveness depends partially on who is imposing the sanctions. The nature of the Russian regime itself may also highlight the difficulties in using economic sanctions to impact decision-makers in the Russian government (van Bergeijk 2022), decision-makers who have no qualms about passing on the pain of the economic sanctions to a populace that has been successfully controlled by the Russian government's extensive security apparatus. While the sanctions against Russia involve a multitude of actors, the combined US-EU sanctions against Russia may be insufficient as Russia seeks to find ways to minimize its interdependence and connectivity with the West (Glenn 2023; Preble and Willis 2024a). While the dollar's diminishing role globally may be overstated (McDowell 2023), in specific cases like Russia, the ability of the West to weaponize its interdependence will continue to decline considerably as Russian planner and policymakers make a concerted effort to avoid allowing economic sanctions to harm the Russian economy.

EVER RESILIENT CUBA

Cuba represents an interesting case of both agency and network adjustments that have appeared in the other case studies. Soviet "black knight" support for Cuba throughout the Cold War simply delayed the impact of US economic sanctions whereby Cuba could rely upon Soviet economic and military aid to mitigate the impact of US economic sanctions. When the Soviet Union collapsed, the United States' economic sanctions compelled Cuban leadership, faced with the loss of support from its primary benefactor, to develop new trade linkages to replace Soviet support. Unlike Myanmar, North Korea, and Iran, only the United States has imposed sanctions and embargoes on Cuban trade with only short periods of multilateral cooperation. The case of Cuba is an example of the failure of unilateral sanctions to achieve meaningful policy change.

Cuba provides us with an example of a state that successfully delayed the effects of economic sanctions and then purposefully sought out new trade linkages to replace lost Soviet support. Cuba in the post-Soviet period (1990-), for example, when faced with the loss of Soviet trade and aid at the end of the Cold War, created new economic linkages with new trading partners. In this case, the likelihood of network changes is higher as Cuba is faced with few options as no other "black knight" could replace Soviet support.

During the post-Soviet period, Cuba sought to diversify its portfolio of trading partners rather than seek support from a single major trading partner, which likely did not exist. Cuba relies on the Soviet Union as its primary benefactor while engaging in commercial relationships with countries like Canada and Spain. Before the Soviet Union's demise, Cuba could rely on third-party countries looking to chart independent foreign policies (Rodriguez Rodriguez 2018) or countries that disagreed with the economic sanctions for additional commercial support in addition to Soviet support (Doxey 1980, 37; Hufbauer et al. 2011). As Early (2011) notes in his work distinguishing commercially driven sanctions busting and "black knights," where the costs of the economic sanctions are high and outweigh the benefits, the sender should capitulate and give up sanctioning. In situations where any benefits outweigh the pain of economic sanctions, the target should capitulate and give in to the sender's demands. The costs for Cuba were lessened by the "black knight" support of the Soviet Union as well as commercial trade from Canada and Spain, who both wanted to chart independent foreign policies from the United States.

The United States has imposed economic sanctions against Cuba for over seven decades (1960-) after the former canceled Cuba's sugar quota, which saw nearly 3 million tons of Cuban sugar go to the United States annually. The cancellation of the quota by the Eisenhower Administration led to the expropriation of nearly $1 billion by the Castro regime in US property and the banning of US imports into Cuba (Hufbauer et al. 2011; Krinsky and Golove 1993; LeoGrande 1982, 128). The United States responded by imposing a near complete embargo of all exports to Cuba with exemptions for food and medicine (Doxey 1980, 35; Hufbauer et al. 2011; Doxey 1980, 35; Hufbauer et al. 2011) and later closed loopholes entirely, save for the provision of humanitarian goods (Hufbauer et al. 2011; Krinsky and Golove 1993, 114).

While the United States blanketed Cuba with a litany of economic sanctions and a near-total embargo on trade, US policymakers did not stop generating chokepoint effects through the use of economic sanctions against target states. One development was the United States' use of secondary sanctions and the extraterritorial application of those sanctions. The Cuban Democracy Act (CDA, 1992) created stiff secondary sanctions that prohibited foreign subsidiaries of US companies from engaging in economic transactions with Cuba, which President H.W. Bush signed into law after initially opposing it. Secondary sanctions differ from primary sanctions in that they target US individuals and US firms from doing business with third parties that engage in trade with Cuba rather than Cuba itself. Secondary sanctions are now routinely employed against a target state's trading partners across a number of US sanctions regimes. Legislating secondary sanctions built off of earlier attempts by the United States (with the Foreign Assistance Act of 1962) to stop third-party assistance to Cuba by restricting development assistance to any country that assisted the Cuban government. The United States further strengthened its secondary sanctions with provisions under the Helms-Burton Act (Cuban Liberty and Democratic Solidarity (LIBERTAD) Act, 1995; Hufbauer et al. 2011; Roy 1997).

The Organization of American States (OAS) also imposed economic sanctions in response to the Cuban Revolution and later with additional sanctions during the Cuban Missile Crisis. OAS extended multilateral sanctions further in 1964 after the discovery of arms from Cuba in Venezuela, imposing comprehensive sanctions on all trade except food and medicine along with the severing of diplomatic relations save for Chile, Bolivia, Mexico, and Uruguay. The organization lifted its multilateral sanctions in 1975 and ended Cuba's isolation from the group in 2015, but US unilateral sanctions have remained (Hufbauer et al. 2011; *TeleSUR* 2015).

The formulation of sanctions policies against Cuba does not reside only in the domain of the GOP. In 2000, President Clinton, a Democrat, signed the Trade Sanctions Reform and Export Enhancement Act (TSRA, Title IX of Public Law 106 387), which allows the US president to terminate unilateral economic sanctions that disrupt agricultural trade and medical goods as long as the termination of such trade would not lead to increases in controlled goods to sanctioned states (US Department of Treasury 2000). This reform to the implementation and enforcement of US economic sanctions is not surprising given efforts by agricultural lobbies seeking greater access to the Cuban market. As testimony before the Senate Finance Committee demonstrated, US agricultural producers had sought greater access to Cuba's market with over $285 million in agricultural goods being exported to Cuba from 2000 to the first six months of 2003.

Panopticon effects play an important role in the sanctions against Cuba, which led to the United States isolating Cuba both economically and diplomatically. Despite a near embargo on most trade and Cuban access to US financial markets, the US maintenance of an Interests Section in Cuba likely provided the United States with a means to monitor the Cuban government's activities (the US embassy re-opened in 2015) (U.S. Embassy in Cuba 2024). Many of these changes to the application of economic sanctions against Cuba also involved relaxing the travel ban and permitting other forms of economic engagement. The opening up of higher remittances and permitting chartered flights to and from Miami and Havana (Hufbauer et al. 2011) also provide the United States with a means to generate chokepoint effects, especially when the

United States threatens to restrict or actually restrict the number of remittances permitted or if flights can take place between Cuba and the United States.

This relaxation of economic sanctions built off previous efforts by US administrations to permit some transfer of remittances from the United States to Cuba as well as providing an opening for US companies to engage in some form of economic engagement with Cuba (Hufbauer et al. 2011). As Figure 6.1 suggests, from 1980 to 2017 much of Cuba's trade originated outside of the region, which we term extra-regional trade. In 1980, for example, twelve of Cuba's top twenty trading partners came from outside the Western Hemisphere with Spain (0.51 percent), Algeria (0.46 percent), Hungary (0.45 percent), and Poland (0.40 percent) making up the largest trade shares. By 1990, eleven of Cuba's top twenty trading partners came from outside the Western Hemisphere, followed by nine in 2000 and 2010, and then eight by 2017. Figure 6.1 depicts Cuban trade in 1990, around the end of the Cold War and the collapse of the Soviet Union. The figure shows that Cuba indeed had a diverse trading portfolio with trading partners across the globe, with a concentration of trade with European states.

Geospatial Network

International Trade with Cuba, 1990

Based on code created by Brendan Knapp; with special assistance from Dr. Nakissa Jahanbani

Figure 6.1 Trading Partner Distribution. Ties between Cuba and trading partners capture all trading partners in 1990. The ties between Cuba and its trading partners are indicated with solid black lines. We only consider Cuba's trading relationships when total aggregate trade exchanged is greater than or equal to $1 million current USD, which we argue are more significant trading ties. Filled black circles are nodes or states in the international system. The size of the node increases as that country's trade share with Cuba increases. *Source*: Created by Authors.

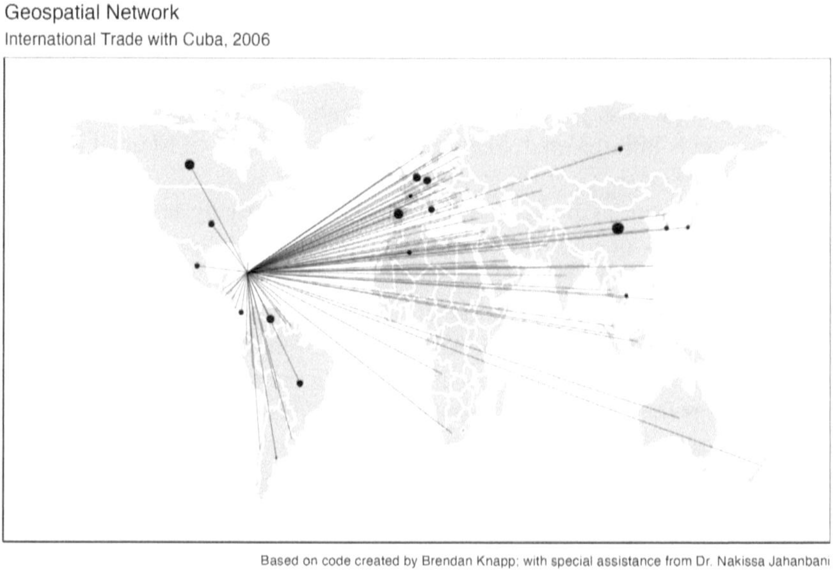

Figure 6.2 Trading Partner Distribution. Ties between Cuba and trading partners capture all trading partners in 2006. The ties between Cuba and its trading partners are indicated with solid black lines. We only consider Cuba's trading relationships when total aggregate trade exchanged is greater than or equal to $1 million current USD, which we argue are more significant trading ties. Filled black circles are nodes or states in the international system. The size of the node increases as that country's trade share with Cuba increases. *Source*: Created by Authors.

Between 1990 and 2006, the apex of Cuba's trade partner diversification, Cuba's distribution of trading partners increased not only in number but also in the way that its trading network became more globally dispersed and interconnected (Figure 6.2). Cuba serves as an interesting case whereby increasing interdependence globally occurs but with trading partners that are unlikely to weaponize such interdependence by joining US international sanctions. By 1975, OAS sanctions disappeared and short-lived West German sanctions by the 1960s had little impact. When the going got tough with US economic sanctions, Cuba looked beyond its regional trading partners who were highly susceptible to US "carrots and sticks." Over time, Cuba's focus on trade has looked beyond the Western Hemisphere. By 2006, nearly 70 percent of Cuba's major trading partners reside outside of the Western Hemisphere, which provides evidence of how Cuban trade interests shifted away from the United States's crosshairs to avoid the United States's ability to weaponize interdependence against other states in Central and South America. And while the United States is one of Cuba's top trading partners, its trade is not central to Cuba's trading network. In 1980, France, Japan, and

Spain, all of which lie outside of the Western Hemisphere, were the most central to Cuba's trade network. Panama, which provided assistance to Cuba in combating US sanctions (and itself a target of US sanctions), remained a major trading partner, yet the strength of Panama's centrality to Cuba's network of trade is infinitesimal, likely related to the ousting of Manuel Noriega by 1989.

Economic sanctions imposed against Cuba have largely been a US affair with brief periods of multilateral sanctions through OAS or one-off senders (like West Germany). The effects of these multilateral sanctions, though, suffered from typical coordination problems in international organizations (Kahler 1988; Stein 1982), and OAS sanctions were undermined by Mexico and other countries refusing to participate. Economic sanctions provided added impetus for Cuba to seek broader economic relations outside the Western Hemisphere away from countries in Central and South America where the United States could more effectively influence Cuban economic relations. With significant support from the Soviet Union throughout the Cold War as well as European, Canadian, and Japanese trade and investment, the United States' sanctions had little impact. Cuba provides evidence that for sanctions to be effective, there must be existing leverage and credibility to the sender's commitments to the sanctions.

POLICY IMPLICATIONS

The pariah states profiled in our study are still heavily sanctioned, yet economic sanctions have done little to resolve the issues that led to the imposition of sanctions in the first place. Economic sanctions should be understood within the larger networks of trade, finance, and international relations. These networks are not only highly dynamic but may provide insights into the overall potential effectiveness and success of economic sanctions. Further, an analysis of such networks may shed light on the ability of target states to evade sanctions as well as create a list of potential sanctions busting states that may advertently and inadvertently diminish the potential of economic sanctions to bring about lasting policy changes. What our study has highlighted is that coordination of economic sanctions not only works, but it is likely a precondition for success against "hard targets" like North Korea, Myanmar, and Iran, each of which present unique challenges in their own right. Our study raises policy implications related to each of our cases.

The elephant in the room with respect to North Korea is that North Korea still remains a nuclear state and shows no signs of relinquishing its nuclear weapons nor does it seem willing to slow down its ballistic missile testing programs. Similarly, human rights abuses are hardly on the decline in North Korea either. While sanctions may have slowed North Korea's nuclear weapons program, the program has continued to develop and grow.

North Korea's nuclear weapons and ballistic missile research are highly problematic for international peace and security in East Asia. Yet, the development of these weapons should hardly surprise analysts and policymakers. North Korea is faced with a daunting security situation that is not amenable to talks without conditions with US forces a stone's throw away in the DMZ and throughout East Asia. Nuclear weapons provide North Korea with assurances that its regime will not be decapitated by South Korean or US military operations while also providing the regime with a powerful bargaining chip. North Korea is a classic "pariah" state in the sense that it has developed nuclear weapons to counter what it perceives as high levels of external security threats (Harkavy 1981; Chow and Easley 2019). Economic and financial sanctions and diplomatic isolation have been ineffective. While economic and financial sanctions may have slowed DPRK's progress in developing weapons of mass destruction, slow progress is still progress. Economic and financial sanctions have been unable to deter or compel the North Koreans to stop or give up their nuclear weapons ambitions, and diplomatic isolation has only limited the ability of states to gather information on the Hermit Kingdom.

The need for the United States and its regional allies to meet North Korea at the negotiation table is perhaps greater than ever before to ensure the stability of the region, rather than rely upon increasing economic and financial sanctions or statements of condemnation. As Kim Jong Un recently stated himself, North Korea will not cease its nuclear weapons program "even if the country faced 100 years of sanctions" (J. Smith 2022). The South Korean capital of Seoul is only a stone's throw from the DMZ, and the prospects for the mass loss of life, untold environmental devastation from the use of nuclear and conventional weapons, as well as unfathomable economic damage are beyond staggering. The United States and its allies can no longer ignore the potential of a nuclear attack and must engage with the regime.

One of the major reasons why the sanctions regime against North Korea has been unsuccessful in its goals of stopping the Kim regime from developing nuclear weapons and delivery systems and regime change is noncompliance by UN member states. Analysts have notably called for the sanctioning of China and Russia, both of which have violated UN sanctions against North Korea on numerous occasions (Arnold 2022) and whose sanctions busting has undermined the impact, effectiveness, and success of the multilateral UN sanctions. As our analysis has shown, North Korean dependence on China for both political and economic support provides China an opportunity to weaponize this interdependence for meaningful change on the Korean Peninsula. China has the potential to make a notable difference in the security situation in East Asia. For its part, the sanctions imposed on Russia since its invasion of Ukraine in 2022 may have pushed Moscow and Pyongyang closer together, as evidenced by their highly publicized summit in September 2022 (Cha and Kim 2023).

The use of economic sanctions by the West against Myanmar shares much in common with North Korea. While North Korea actively refashioned its revenue streams to avoid the impact of US economic sanctions to the greatest extent possible, Myanmar is a "hard target" by happenstance, a regional economy that trades mainly with its neighbors in Southeast Asia, China (with whom it shares a border), India, and Japan. Sanctions against Myanmar have largely been symbolic, especially in the first few rounds, with apparently little expectation from the West that such sanctions would lead to meaningful change. With most of the economic leverage coming from other states in the Indo-Pacific, Myanmar represents a challenge to Western powers with few interests in the country and few opportunities for weaponized interdependence. Given US interests in Southeast Asia, the United States could prioritize cooperation with ASEAN member states on this issue. Given Myanmar's ASEAN membership, Southeast Asian member states may be better placed to work toward meaningful policy change within Myanmar, which is even more important given the recent democratic backsliding that has taken place, putting Aung San Suu Kyi back in prison.

As each of our cases has shown, isolating target states may be counterproductive, and target states reside in a complex network of interactions that involve more than trade and finance with powerful sender states like the United States. The United States's deployment of resources may be misplaced through the use of economic sanctions that have little impact. Symbolic sanctions that are imposed for the sake of imposing them make very little sense from a foreign policy perspective. Given the United States' vast resources, employing US resources in working with allies and rivals who can make a difference may be *the* recipe for sanctions success. The case of Iran and negotiations for the JCPOA is an excellent example of how economic sanctions, when well-coordinated with the right senders, can bring about important policy changes. Such cooperation, of course, represents collective action and coordination problems long identified in the literature, yet such approaches, while more costly, may lead to *better* potential outcomes than the unilateral use of comprehensive economic sanctions against international pariahs. The idea that senders like the United States have an advantage in using economic sanctions is a function of the United States' economic and political engagement with the target state. The United States' unilateral approach to the use of economic sanctions, especially against Iran, has been problematic. Our study suggests that the deployment of economic sanctions can and should focus on the right set of actors rather than additive approaches across time (in the US case, often decades) that seek only to layer sanctions regimes, actions which can lead to de-risking (Moret 2021), overcompliance (Breen 2021), and humanitarian negative externalities typical of economic sanctions (Daher and Moret 2020; Geiss 2005; Moret 2015, 2021).

FINAL THOUGHTS

Our study has sought to demonstrate how network structures that reflect the interconnectedness of nodes or states provide a unique lens for understanding the inability of economic sanctions to be effective. We argue that the structure of networks helps to explain why economic sanctions fail against less powerful states, specifically so-called "pariah" states. Within our case explorations of North Korea, Myanmar, and Iran, we showed how network connectedness through two measures common in social network analysis, degree centrality and strength centrality (for which we created two measures) helped explain why North Korea and Myanmar have been able to avoid economic sanctions while also showing how network configurations played a role in the success in bringing Iran to the negotiating table with Western powers over its nuclear program.

As our analysis indicated, economic sanctions, in some cases, can influence the structure of these networks by changing a state's *connectedness* to other nodes within the network. As states generate chokepoint effects through policies that create economic sanctions, a balance must be struck between cutting off offending nodes from accessing others in the network as the loss of connectivity can lead to a loss of data, information, and monitoring that is captured by policies generating panopticon effects.

The case of North Korea showed that it remained highly adaptable to comprehensive US unilateral sanctions. Even later, after the UN Security Council began imposing economic sanctions on North Korea with the passing of Resolution 1718 in October 2006 after North Korea conducted its first nuclear test, North Korea's network of trade shifted significantly as it sought to isolate itself from the impact of these sanctions. North Korea's agency in response to economic sanctions does not rely solely on shifting its trading relationships. North Korea also makes use of illicit trade and other illicit activities to finance and support the regime and its WMD programs. The extent of illicit trading activities coded from UN Panel of Expert reports from 2012 to 2022 showed a concentration of activities in China and Japan, but sanctions evasion involves a multitude of states in the international system. Beyond licit and illicit trade, the North Koreans have also resorted to cyber heists and cryptocurrency to evade US sanctions after being isolated from much of the global financial system. The ability of nodes in the network to weaponize interdependence through the generation of panopticon and chokepoint effects diminishes. The only actors that could exert influence, namely China and Russia, DPRK's two major licit and illicit trading partners, are unlikely to enforce economic sanctions or utilize their leverage gained through trade, opting instead for foreign policies that generate panopticon effects.

While North Korea represents a near abject failure of economic sanctions in reining in the illegal activities of a state, the case of Myanmar shows the limits of economic sanctions when a state's trading network is largely regional and "unglobalized" in many respects. Sanctions in this case are largely symbolic and kept the junta's human rights violations front and center. Our investigation of Myanmar's experience with Western sanctions builds on research from Pedersen (2007, 2013), Nyun (2008), and Jones (2015), who document the travesty of economic sanctions on Myanmar that failed to achieve their goals while also inflicting a humanitarian crisis on the population. We build upon those insights and argue that weaponized independence remained largely an impossibility given Myanmar's lack of connectedness to global networks of trade and finance.

We instead pivot to the very actors *who might have made a difference with economic sanctions*: ASEAN member states that sought to draw Myanmar into the regional organization. We posit that bringing Myanmar into ASEAN, while not only reflecting the ASEAN Way, also provided ASEAN member states with access to information and data through channels of global governance. What fails to occur is that ASEAN members are unwilling to leverage this information and instead prefer diplomatic and economic engagement. Myanmar as a "success case" for economic sanctions is misplaced as efforts to isolate the military junta were highly counterproductive (Early 2016).

The case of Iran serves as the positive case in our study. While unilateral and comprehensive economic sanctions against Iran by the United States have been highly criticized (Bazoobandi 2015; Brockmann and Preble 2021; Peterson 2012), the cooperation between the United States and EU and the efforts to impose sanctions through the UN Security Council created difficult conditions for Iran, which impacted its domestic politics in such a way that the need to negotiate became a reality for the beleaguered regime.

In the case of Iran, sanctions *worked* and were *effective* because of Iran's *connectedness* to key trading partners in the EU who were able to weaponize interdependence successfully. Not only could the EU generate unrelenting chokepoint effects through its imposition of economic sanctions, but its sanctions combined with the United States' own sanctions (as well as those of the UN) imposed economic costs that were unsustainable. The EU's sanctions were effective not because of their comprehensiveness but because of the way in which the Council of Europe and European Commission designed the economic sanctions (along with the help of working groups within the

EU bureaucracy) that leveraged information and monitoring captured by the generation of panopticon effects. While the JCPOA ultimately failed when the United States withdrew from the agreement (a final opportunity for US foreign policy), coordination and cooperation on economic sanctions worked, but they were successful because Iran's *connectedness* made them susceptible to the deprivation caused by the chokepoint effects.

Pariah states represent a challenge for sanctioning or sender states as they seek to design economic sanctions to bring about lasting behavior change in the target state. As sanctions regimes persist, the likelihood of sanctions busting increases; by some estimates, sanctions busting onset begins, on average, after nearly seven years although in some cases sanctions busting begins almost immediately (Preble 2023). In some cases, like that of Myanmar, the use of sanctions was less about generating meaningful change through chokepoint generating policies and more about sending signals, a form of "foreign policy PR" that draws attention to the pariah state regime's transgressions of international norms. The use of economic sanctions may also represent a form of path dependence, as the imposition of economic sanctions in the US context as part of a larger package of legislation, regulations, and executive orders plays a strong role in influencing future impositions of economic sanctions against targets, especially pariah states. Because pariah states are sanctioned for many years, in some cases several decades or more, the opportunity to add additional layers of sanctions increases, although in many cases the application of economic sanctions fails to consider the nature and structure of networks of licit and illicit trade as well as of finance in which target states find themselves situated.

While our study only considered three pariahs (with a brief discussion of an additional two) and the effectiveness and success of economic sanctions in these cases, future research could explore the networks and contexts of other pariahs in the international system in understanding the role that networks and connectedness play in the potential for more effective and successful sanctions. Lastly, we briefly considered two shadow cases—Russia and Cuba—that stress the importance of trade networks and the limits of isolation in understanding not only if sanctions will work but also whether senders have the necessary connectivity to the target (and vice versa) to effectively weaponize interdependence.

NOTE

1. While we cannot access comprehensive trade data due to the relativity of this round of sanctions, we would likely see several connections between Russia and countries in Eastern Europe, Central Asia, and East Asia, as well as other parts of the globe.

References

Aggestam, Lisbeth, and Adrian Hyde-Price. 2019. "Double Trouble: Trump, Transatlantic Relations and European Strategic Autonomy." *JCMS: Journal of Common Market Studies* 57 (S1): 114–27. doi:10.1111/jcms.12948.

Albert, Eleanor. 2020. "North Korea's Military Capabilities." *Council on Foreign Relations*. https://www.cfr.org/backgrounder/north-koreas-military-capabilities.

Alexander, Peter, Almut Arneth, Roslyn Henry, Juliette Maire, Sam Rabin, and Mark D. A. Rounsevell. 2022. "High Energy and Fertilizer Prices Are More Damaging than Food Export Curtailment from Ukraine and Russia for Food Prices, Health and the Environment." *Nature Food* 4 (1): 84–95. doi:10.1038/s43016-022-00659-9.

Alexanian, Janet A. 2011. "Eyewitness Accounts and Political Claims: Transnational Responses to the 2009 Postelection Protests in Iran." *Comparative Studies of South Asia, Africa and the Middle East* 31 (2): 425–42. doi:10.1215/1089201X-1264334.

Alikhani, Hossein. 2000. *Sanctioning Iran: Anatomy of a Failed Policy*. London: I.B.Tauris.

Amnesty International. 2022. "Amnesty International Annual Report 2021/22." *Amnesty International*. https://www.amnesty.org/en/latest/research/2022/03/annual-report-202122/.

Ang, Adrian U-Jin, and Dursun Peksen. 2007. "When Do Economic Sanctions Work? Asymmetric Perceptions, Issue Salience, and Outcomes." *Political Research Quarterly* 60 (1). [University of Utah, Sage Publications, Inc.]: 135–45.

Anguelov, Nikolay, and Kristin Bryant. 2015. "Myanmar—20 Years of Sanctions and Their Lasting Effect." In *Economic Sanctions vs. Soft Power: Lessons from North Korea, Myanmar, and the Middle East*, edited by Nikolay Anguelov, 21–32. New York: Palgrave Macmillan US. doi:10.1057/9781137523761_3.

Arnold, Aaron. 2016. "The True Costs of Financial Sanctions." *Survival* 58 (3): 77–100. doi:10.1080/00396338.2016.1186981.

———. 2022. "To Sanction North Korea, Sanction Those That Won't—Russia and China." *Bulletin of the Atomic Scientists*. July 14. https://thebulletin.org/2022/07/to-sanction-north-korea-sanction-those-that-wont-russia-and-china/.

Aryani, Nabilla Syahaya Putri. 2019. "Constructive Engagement as Indonesia's Foreign Policy Strategy in Promoting Democratization in Myanmar." *Indonesian Journal of International Relations* 3 (2): 1–16. doi:10.32787/ijir.v3i2.84.

Ashford, Emma. 2016. "Not-So-Smart Sanctions: The Failure of Western Restrictions Against Russia." *Foreign Affairs* 95 (1). Council on Foreign Relations: 114–23.

Associated Press. 2009. "Some Memorable Quotes from Kim Dae-Jung," August 18. https://www.seattletimes.com/nation-world/some-memorable-quotes-from-kim-dae-jung/.

———. 2023. "Danes Orders Russia to Reduce Embassy Staff to the Same Number That Denmark Has in Moscow." *AP News*. September 1. https://apnews.com/article/russia-denmark-embassy-intelligence-diplomats-699358f80b359abaa97858bd2ccea44b.

Attia, Hana, and Julia Grauvogel. 2023. "International Sanctions Termination, 1990–2018: Introducing the IST Dataset." *Journal of Peace Research* 60 (4). SAGE Publications Ltd: 709–19. doi:10.1177/00223433221087080.

Bae, Jong-Yun. 2010. "South Korean Strategic Thinking toward North Korea: The Evolution of the Engagement Policy and Its Impact upon U.S.-ROK Relations." *Asian Survey* 50 (2). University of California Press: 335–55. doi:10.1525/as.2010.50.2.335.

Bae, Jong-Yun, and Chung-in Moon. 2014. "South Korea's Engagement Policy." *Critical Asian Studies* 46 (1). Routledge: 15–38. doi:10.1080/14672715.2014.863576.

Baldwin, David A. 1985. *Economic Statecraft*. Princeton, N.J: Princeton University Press.

———. 1999. "The Sanctions Debate and the Logic of Choice." *International Security* 24 (3): 80–107.

———. 2020. *Economic Statecraft*. New edition. Princeton: Princeton University Press.

Baldwin, David A., and Robert A. Pape. 1998. "Evaluating Economic Sanctions." *International Security* 23 (2). The MIT Press: 189–98. doi:10.2307/2539384.

Bapat, Navin A., and Bo Ram Kwon. 2015. "When Are Sanctions Effective? A Bargaining and Enforcement Framework." *International Organization* 69 (1): 131–62. doi:10.1017/S0020818314000290.

Barber, James. 1979. "Economic Sanctions as a Policy Instrument." *International Affairs* 55 (3): 367–84. doi:10.2307/2615145.

Barry, Colin M., and Katja B. Kleinberg. 2015. "Profiting from Sanctions: Economic Coercion and US Foreign Direct Investment in Third-Party States." *International Organization* 69 (04): 881–912. doi:10.1017/S002081831500017X.

Batmanghelidj, Esfandyar, and Erica Moret. 2022. "The Hidden Toll of Sanctions." *Foreign Affairs*. https://www.foreignaffairs.com/articles/world/2022-01-17/hidden-toll-sanctions.

Bazoobandi, Sara. 2015. "Sanctions against Iran: Winners and Losers." In *On Target? EU Sanctions as Security Policy Tools*, edited by Iana Dreyer and José Luengo-Cabrera, 57–65. Paris: EU Institute for Security Studies.

BBC News. 2010. "North Korean Artillery Hits South Korean Island," November 23, sec. Asia-Pacific. https://www.bbc.com/news/world-asia-pacific-11818005.
———. 2021. "Myanmar: Who Are the Rulers Who Have Executed Democracy Campaigners?," February 2, sec. Asia. https://www.bbc.com/news/world-asia-55902070.
Bergeijk, Peter A. G. van. 1989. "Success and Failure of Economic Sanctions." *Kyklos* 42 (3): 385–404.
———. 2015. "Sanctions against Iran -- A Preliminary Economic Assessment." In *On Target? EU Sanctions as Security Policy Tools*, edited by Iana Dreyer and José Luengo-Cabrera, 49–56. Paris: EU Institute for Security Studies.
———. 2022. "Sanctions Against the Russian War on Ukraine: Lessons from History and Current Prospects." *Journal of World Trade* 56 (4): 571–86.
Biersteker, Thomas J., Sue E. Eckert, and Marcos Tourinho, eds. 2016. *Targeted Sanctions: The Impacts and Effectiveness of United Nations Action*. Cambridge: Cambridge University Press.
Blomquist, Rachel, and Daniel Wertz. 2015. "An Overview of North Korea-Japan Relations." *The National Committee on North Korea*. https://www.ncnk.org/resources/briefing-papers/all-briefing-papers/overview-north-korea-japan-relations.
Borgatti, Stephen, Martin Everett, Jeffrey Johnson, and Filip Agneessens. 2022. *Analyzing Social Networks Using R*. Thousand Oaks: SAGE.
Borszik, Oliver. 2016. "International Sanctions against Iran and Tehran's Responses: Political Effects on the Targeted Regime." *Contemporary Politics* 22 (1). Routledge: 20–39. doi:10.1080/13569775.2015.1112951.
Breen, Emmanuel. 2021. "Corporations and US Economic Sanctions: The Dangers of Overcompliance." In *Research Handbook on Unilateral and Extraterritorial Sanctions*, edited by Charlotte Beaucillon, 256–69. Research Handbooks in International Law Series. Cheltenham, UK ; Northampton, Massachusetts, USA: Edward Elgar Publishing.
Brewer, Eric, and Sue Mi Terry. 2021. "It Is Time for a Realistic Bargain With North Korea." *Foreign Affairs*. https://www.foreignaffairs.com/articles/north-korea/2021-03-25/it-time-realistic-bargain-north-korea.
Brockmann, Kolja, and Keith A. Preble. 2021. *Rethinking EU Sanctions on Iran: Non-Proliferation and the Mitigation of Humanitarian Impact*. Stockholm: Stockholm International Peace Research Institute. https://www.sipri.org/publications/2021/other-publications/mitigating-humanitarian-impact-complex-sanctions-environment-european-union-and-sanctions-regimes.
Brown, William Andreas. 1998. Interview with Ambassador William Andreas Brown. The Association for Diplomatic Studies and Training Foreign Affairs Oral History Project.
Buncombe, Andrew, and Joseph Allchin. 2012. "'People's Triumph' Heralds New Age of Democracy, Claims Exultant Suu Kyi." *The Independent*, April 3.
Bünte, Marco, and Clara Portela. 2012. "Myanmar: The Beginning of Reforms and the End of Sanctions," GIGA Focus International Edition, 3.
Bush, George W. 2002. "Address Before a Joint Session of the Congress on the State of the Union." *American Presidency Project*. https://www.presidency.ucsb.edu/documents/address-before-joint-session-the-congress-the-state-the-union-22.

Buszynski, Leszek. 2009. "Russia and North Korea: Dilemmas and Interests." *Asian Survey* 49 (5). University of California Press: 809–30. doi:10.1525/as.2009.49.5.809.

Callahan, Mary P. 1996. "Burma in 1995: Looking Beyond the Release of Aung San Suu Kyi." *Asian Survey* 36 (2). University of California Press: 158–64. doi:10.2307/2645813.

———. 2005. *Making Enemies: War and State Building in Burma*. Ithaca, N.Y.: Cornell University Press.

Caruso, Raul. 2003. "The Impact of International Economic Sanctions on Trade: An Empirical Analysis." *Peace Economics, Peace Science and Public Policy* 9 (2): 1–37.

———. 2005. "The Impact of International Economic Sanctions on Trade: Empirical Evidence over the Period 1960-2000." *Rivista Internazionale Di Scienze Sociali* 113 (1). Vita e Pensiero – Pubblicazioni dell'Università Cattolica del Sacro Cuore: 41–66.

Castle, Stephen. 2010. "Europe Imposes New Sanctions on Iran." *The New York Times*, July 26, sec. Middle East. https://www.nytimes.com/2010/07/27/world/middleeast/27iran.html.

Cha, Victor. 2010. "The Sinking of the Cheonan," April. https://www.csis.org/analysis/sinking-cheonan.

Chalermpalanupap, Termsak. 1999. "ASEAN-10: Meeting the Challenges." https://asean.org/asean-10-meeting-the-challenges-by-termsak-chalermpalanupap/.

Chang, Semoon. 2006a. "Should U.S. Economic Sanctions against North Korea Be Lifted?" *North Korean Review* 2 (2). McFarland & Company: 36–46.

———. 2006b. "The Saga of U.S. Economic Sanctions Against North Korea." *The Journal of East Asian Affairs* 20 (2). Institute for National Security Strategy: 109–39.

Charron, Andrea, and Clara Portela. 2015. "The UN, Regional Sanctions and Africa." *International Affairs (Royal Institute of International Affairs 1944-)* 91 (6). [Wiley, Royal Institute of International Affairs]: 1369–85.

———, eds. 2022. *Multilateral Sanctions Revisited: Lessons Learned from Margaret Doxey*. McGill-Queen's/Brian Mulroney Institute of Government Studies in Leadership, Public Policy, and Governance 9. Montreal Kingston London Chicago: McGill-Queen's University Press.

Chen Weiss, Jessica. 2013. "Authoritarian Signaling, Mass Audiences, and Nationalist Protest in China." *International Organization* 67 (1): 1–35. doi:10.1017/S0020818312000380.

Chow, Jonathan T., and Leif-Eric Easley. 2019. "Renegotiating Pariah State Partnerships: Why Myanmar and North Korea Respond Differently to Chinese Influence." *Contemporary Security Policy* 40 (4). Routledge: 502–25. doi:10.1080/13523260.2019.1660483.

Chung, Chien-peng. 2003. "Democratization in South Korea and Inter-Korean Relations." *Pacific Affairs* 76 (1). Pacific Affairs, University of British Columbia: 9–35.

Connolly, Richard. 2019. *Russia's Response to Sanctions: How Western Economic Statecraft Is Reshaping Political Economy in Russia*. Cambridge: Cambridge University Press.

Cortright, David, and George A. Lopez, eds. 1995. *Economic Sanctions: Panacea or Peacebuilding in a Post-Cold War World?* Boulder: Westview Press.

———. 2000. *The Sanctions Decade: Assessing UN Strategies in the 1990s*. Boulder, Colo: Lynne Rienner Publishers.

———. 2002. *Smart Sanctions: Targeting Economic Statecraft*. Lanham, Maryland: Rowman & Littlefield.

Council of the European Union. 2012. *Council Regulation (EU) No 267/2012 of 23 March 2012 Concerning Restrictive Measures against Iran and Repealing Regulation (EU) No 961/2010. OJ L.* Vol. 088. http://data.europa.eu/eli/reg/2012/267/oj/eng.

Council of the European Union. 2023. "Myanmar/Burma: Council Adds 4 Persons and 2 Entities to EU Sanctions List in Eighth Round of Sanctions." https://www.consilium.europa.eu/en/press/press-releases/2023/12/11/myanmar-burma-council-adds-4-persons-and-2-entities-to-eu-sanctions-list-in-eighth-round-of-sanctions/.

Cronberg, Tarja. 2017a. *Nuclear Multilateralism and Iran: Inside EU Negotiations*. London; New York, NY: Routledge.

———. 2017b. "No EU, No Iran Deal: The EU's Choice between Multilateralism and the Transatlantic Link." *The Nonproliferation Review* 24 (3–4): 243–59. doi:10.1080/10736700.2018.1432321.

Daher, Joseph, and Erica Moret. 2020. *Invisible Sanctions: How Over-Compliance Limits Humanitarian Work on Syria: Challenges of Fund Transfer for Non-Profit Organizations Working on Syria*. Berlin: IMPACT - Civil Society Research and Development e.V.

Dasgupta, Sravasti. 2022. "All the Countries Not Invited to Queen's Funeral." *The Independent*. September 19. https://www.independent.co.uk/news/uk/queen-funeral-who-is-not-invited-countries-b2170159.html.

Davenport, Kelsey. 2022a. "The Six-Party Talks at a Glance." *Arms Control Association*. https://www.armscontrol.org/factsheets/6partytalks.

———. 2022b. "Chronology of U.S.-North Korean Nuclear and Missile Diploma." *Arms Control Association*. https://www.armscontrol.org/factsheets/dprkchron.

———. 2023. "Timeline of Nuclear Diplomacy with Iran." *Arms Control Association*. January. https://www.armscontrol.org/factsheets/Timeline-of-Nuclear-Diplomacy-With-Iran.

De Benedictus, L., S. Nenci, G. Santoni, L. Tajoli, and C. Vicarelli. 2013. "Network Analysis of World Trade Using the BACI-CEPII Dataset." *Centre d'Etudes Prospectives et d'Informations Internationales*. http://www.cepii.fr/pdf_pub/wp/2013/wp2013-24.pdf.

Demarais, Agathe. 2022. *Backfire: How Sanctions Reshape the World against U.S. Interests*. New York: Columbia University Press.

Desiderio, Andrew. 2018. "Trump Administration's 'Nerve Center' for Sanctions Policy Is 'Depleted' at the Worst Possible Time." *Daily Beast*, May 8. https://www.thedailybeast.com/trump-administrations-nerve-center-for-sanctions-policy-is-depleted-at-the-worst-possible-time.

Doxey, Margaret P. 1980. *Economic Sanctions and International Enforcement*. 2nd ed. London: Oxford University Press.

———. 1987. *International Sanctions in Contemporary Perspective*. London: MacMillian.

Drezner, Daniel W. 2011. "Sanctions Sometimes Smart: Targeted Sanctions in Theory and Practice." *International Studies Review* 13 (1): 96–108. doi:10.1111/j.1468-2486.2010.01001.x.

Drulakova, Radka, Jan Martin Rolenc, Zuzana Travnickova, and Stepanka Zemanova. 2010. "Assessing the Effectiveness of EU Sanctions Policy." *Central European Journal of International and Security Studies* 4 (1): 101–22.

Drury, A. Cooper. 2001. "Sanctions as Coercive Diplomacy: The U. S. President's Decision to Initiate Economic Sanctions." *Political Research Quarterly* 54 (3): 485–508. doi:10.2307/449267.

Early, Bryan R. 2009. "Sleeping With Your Friends' Enemies: An Explanation of Sanctions-Busting Trade." *International Studies Quarterly* 53 (1): 49–71. doi:10.1111/j.1468-2478.2008.01523.x.

———. 2011. "Unmasking the Black Knights: Sanctions Busters and Their Effects on the Success of Economic Sanctions." *Foreign Policy Analysis* 7 (4): 381–402. doi:10.1111/j.1743-8594.2011.00143.x.

———. 2012. "Alliances and Trade with Sanctioned States: A Study of U.S. Economic Sanctions, 1950–2000." *Journal of Conflict Resolution* 56 (3): 547–72. doi:10.1177/0022002711420961.

———. 2015. *Busted Sanctions: Explaining Why Economic Sanctions Fail*. Stanford: Stanford University Press.

———. 2016. "Busting the Myth That Myanmar Is a Sanctions Success Story." *Policy Forum*. November 30. https://www.policyforum.net/busting-myth-myanmar-sanctions-success-story/.

———. 2021. "Making Sanctions Work: Promoting Compliance, Punishing Violations, and Discouraging Sanctions Busting." In *Research Handbook on Economic Sanctions*, edited by Peter Van Bergeijk, 167–86. Cheltenham: Edward Elgar.

Early, Bryan R., and Amira Jadoon. 2016. "Do Sanctions Always Stigmatize? The Effects of Economic Sanctions on Foreign Aid." *International Interactions* 42 (2): 217–43. doi:10.1080/03050629.2016.1093477.

Early, Bryan R., and Dursun Peksen. 2019. "Searching in the Shadows: The Impact of Economic Sanctions on Informal Economies." *Political Research Quarterly* 72 (4). SAGE Publications Inc: 821–34.

Early, Bryan R., and Keith Preble. 2021. "Grand Strategy and the Tools of Economic Statecraft." In *The Oxford Handbook of Grand Strategy*, edited by Thierry Balzacq and Ronald R. Krebs, 369–88. Oxford: Oxford University Press. https://oxfordhandbooks.com/view/10.1093/oxfordhb/9780198840299.001.0001/oxfordhb-9780198840299-e-24.

Early, Bryan R., and Keith A. Preble. 2020a. "Enforcing US Economic Sanctions: Why Whale Hunting Works." *The Washington Quarterly* 43 (1). Routledge: 159–75. doi:10.1080/0163660X.2020.1736881.

———. 2020b. "Going Fishing versus Hunting Whales: Explaining Changes in How the US Enforces Economic Sanctions." *Security Studies* 29 (2): 231–67. doi:10.1080/09636412.2020.1722850.

———. 2024. "For Fear or Positive PR? Exploring Firms' Self-Sanctioning Responses to Ukraine." In *The Effect of Economic Sanctions within the Russia-Ukraine Conflict*, edited by Morad Bali. Hauppauge, NY: Nova Science.

Early, Bryan R., and Robert Spice. 2015. "Economic Sanctions, International Institutions, and Sanctions Busters: When Does Institutionalized Cooperation Help Sanctioning Efforts?" *Foreign Policy Analysis* 11 (3): 339–60. doi:10.1111/fpa.12038.

East-West Center, and National Committee on North Korea. 2019. "Total Inter-Korean Trade." *North Korea in the World: North Korea's External Relations*. https://northkoreaintheworld.org/inter-korean/inter-korean-trade.

Egreteau, Renaud. 2020. "Foreign Policy and International Engagement: Strategic Realities, Domestic Priorities." In *Myanmar: Politics, Economy and Society*, edited by Adam Simpson and Nicholas Farrelly, 1st edition. Abingdon, Oxon ; New York, NY: Routledge.

EIA. 2022. *Country Analysis Executive Summary: Iran*. Washington, DC: U.S. Energy Information Administration. https://www.eia.gov/international/content/analysis/countries_long/Iran/pdf/iran_exe.pdf.

El-Katiri, Laura, and Bassam Fattouh. 2012. *On Oil Embargos and the Myth of the Iranian Oil Weapon*. Oxford: Oxford Institute for Energy Studies. https://www.oxfordenergy.org/publications/on-oil-embargos-and-the-myth-of-the-iranian-oil-weapon-2/.

Elliott, Kimberly Ann. 1998. "The Sanctions Glass: Half Full or Completely Empty?" *International Security* 23 (1): 50–65. doi:10.2307/2539262.

Eriksson, Mikael. 2011. *Targeting Peace: Understanding UN and EU Targeted Sanctions*. Farnham, Surrey, England ; Burlington, VT: Ashgate.

Esfandiary, Dina, and Mark Fitzpatrick. 2011. "Sanctions on Iran: Defining and Enabling 'Success.'" *Survival* 53 (5): 143–56. doi:10.1080/00396338.2011.621639.

European Commission. 2022. "EU Trade Relations with Iran." https://policy.trade.ec.europa.eu/eu-trade-relationships-country-and-region/countries-and-regions/iran_en.

European Parliament and Council of the European Union. 2019. "Directive (EU) 2019/1153 of the European Parliament and of the Council of 20 June 2019 Laying down Rules Facilitating the Use of Financial and Other Information for the Prevention, Detection, Investigation or Prosecution of Certain Criminal Offences, and Repealing Council Decision 2000/642/JHA." June 20. https://eur-lex.europa.eu/eli/dir/2019/1153/oj.

Farrell, Henry, and Abraham L. Newman. 2019. "Weaponized Interdependence: How Global Economic Networks Shape State Coercion." *International Security* 44 (1): 42–79. doi:10.1162/isec_a_00351.

Féron, Henri, Ewa Eriksson Fortier, Kevin Gray, Suzy Kim, Marie O'Reilly, Kee B. Park, and Joy Yoon. 2019. "The Human Costs and Gendered Impact of Sanctions on North Korea." *Korea Peace Now*. https://koreapeacenow.org/wp-content/uploads/2019/10/human-costs-and-gendered-impact-of-sanctions-on-north-korea.pdf.

Felbermayr, Gabriel, Aleksandra Kirilakha, Constantinos Syropoulos, Erdal Yalcin, and Yoto V. Yotov. 2020. "The Global Sanctions Data Base." *European Economic Review* 129 (October): 103561. doi:10.1016/j.euroecorev.2020.103561.

Financial Information Unit. 2018. "National Risk Assessment of Mongolia on Financing of Terrorism and Proliferation Financing of Weapons of Mass Destruction." *Government of Mongolia.* https://www.mongolbank.mn/documents/cma/0904_03eng.pdf.

Frank, Ruediger. 2006. "The Political Economy of Sanctions Against North Korea." *Asian Perspective* 30 (3). Lynne Rienner Publishers: 5–36.

———. 2015. "North Korea's Foreign Trade." *38 North.* October 22. https://www.38north.org/2015/10/rfrank102215/.

Fuller, Thomas. 2012. "From Prisoner to Parliament in Myanmar." *The New York Times*, April 1, sec. World. https://www.nytimes.com/2012/04/02/world/asia/myanmar-elections.html.

Funabashi, Yoichi. 2007. *The Peninsula Question: A Chronicle of the Second Korean Nuclear Crisis.* Washington, D.C: Brookings Institution Press.

Gavin, Gabriel, and Sarah Anne Aarup. 2023. "Leaking Russia Sanctions Send Floods of Cash to Ex-Soviet Countries." *POLITICO.* April 26. https://www.politico.eu/article/lithuania-russia-vladimir-putin-stop-turning-blind-eye-to-back-doors-for-russian-trade-top-diplomat-tells-eu/.

Geiss, Robin. 2005. "Humanitarian Safeguards in Economic Sanctions Regimes: A Call for Automatic Suspension Clauses, Periodic Monitoring, and Follow-up Assessment of Long-Term Effects." *Harvard Human Rights Journal* 18: 167–99.

Gerami, Nima, and Pierre Goldschmidt. 2012. "The International Atomic Energy Agency's Decision to Find Iran in Non-Compliance, 2002-20." *Center for the Study of Weapons of Mass Destruction.* https://wmdcenter.ndu.edu/Publications/Publication-View/Article/627151/the-international-atomic-energy-agencys-decision-to-find-iran-in-non-compliance/https%3A%2F%2Fwmdcenter.ndu.edu%2FPublications%2FPublication-View%2FArticle%2F627151%2Fthe-international-atomic-energy-agencys-decision-to-find-iran-in-non-compliance%2F.

Gijs, Camille. 2022. "US Issues Visas to Russia's UN Delegation for General Assembly, Moscow Says." *Politico.* September 13. https://www.politico.eu/article/us-issued-russia-visas-for-sergey-lavrov-and-russian-delegation-to-attend-unga-moscow-says/.

Giumelli, Francesco. 2011. *Coercing, Constraining, and Signalling: Explaining UN and EU Sanctions after the Cold War.* Colchester: ECPR Press.

Giumelli, Francesco. 2013a. "How EU Sanctions Work: A New Narrative." 129. Chaillot Papers. Paris: European Union Institute for Security Studies. https://www.iss.europa.eu/sites/default/files/EUISSFiles/Chaillot_129.pdf.

———. 2013b. *The Success of Sanctions: Lessons Learned from the EU Experience.* 1st edition. Farnham, Surrey, England: Routledge.

———. 2023. "Sticking to the Big Brother: An Analysis of the EU's Response to Revitalised US-North Korea Relations." In *Multilateralism in Peril: The Uneasy Triangle of the US, China and the EU*, edited by Chien-Huei Wu, Frank Gaenssmantel, and Francesco Giumelli, 373–99. Abingdon: Routledge.

Giumelli, Francesco, and Paul Ivan. 2013. "The Effectiveness of EU Sanctions: An Analysis of Iran, Belarus, Syria, and Myanmar (Burma)." *EPC Issue Paper 76*. Brussels: European Policy Center. https://www.epc.eu/documents/uploads/pub_3928_epc_issue_paper_76_-_the_effectiveness_of_eu_sanctions.pdf.

Giumelli, Francesco, and Michal Onderco. 2021. "States, Firms, and Security: How Private Actors Implement Sanctions, Lessons Learned from the Netherlands." *European Journal of International Security* 6 (2): 190–209. doi:10.1017/eis.2020.21.

Glass, Andrew. 2019. "President Bush Cites 'Axis of Evil,' Jan. 29, 2002." *POLITICO*. January 29. https://www.politico.com/story/2019/01/29/bush-axis-of-evil-2002-1127725.

Glenn, Caileigh. 2023. "Lessons in Sanctions-Proofing from Russia." *The Washington Quarterly* 46 (1): 105.120. doi: 10.1080/0163660X.2023.2188829.

Google. 2012. "Countries.csv." *Dataset Publishing Language*. https://developers.google.com/public-data/docs/canonical/countries_csv.

Grauvogel, Julia, and Christian von Soest. 2014. "Claims to Legitimacy Count: Why Sanctions Fail to Instigate Democratisation in Authoritarian Regimes." *European Journal of Political Research* 53 (4): 635–53. doi:10.1111/1475-6765.12065.

Growth Lab at Harvard University. 2021. "Atlas of Economic Complexity." http://atlas.cid.harvard.edu/.

Haacke, Jürgen. 2006. *Myanmar's Foreign Policy: Domestic Influences and International Implications*. Adelphi Paper 381. London: International Institute for Strategic Studies.

Habib, Benjamin. 2016. "The Enforcement Problem in Resolution 2094 and the United Nations Security Council Sanctions Regime: Sanctioning North Korea." *Australian Journal of International Affairs* 70 (1). Routledge: 50–68. doi:10.1080/10357718.2015.1095278.

Haggard, Stephan, and Marcus Noland. 2007. *Famine in North Korea: Markets, Aid, and Reform*. Columbia: Columbia University Press.

———. 2010. "Sanctioning North Korea: The Political Economy of Denuclearization and Proliferation." *Asian Survey* 50 (3). University of California Press: 539–68. doi:10.1525/as.2010.50.3.539.

———. 2017. *Hard Target: Sanctions, Inducements, and the Case of North Korea*. Studies in Asian Security. Stanford, California: Stanford University Press.

Hagström, Linus, and Marie Söderberg. 2006. "Taking Japan-North Korea Relations Seriously: Rationale and Background." *Pacific Affairs* 79 (3). Pacific Affairs, University of British Columbia: 373–85.

Harkavy, Robert E. 1981. "Pariah States and Nuclear Proliferation." *International Organization* 35 (1). [MIT Press, University of Wisconsin Press, Cambridge University Press, International Organization Foundation]: 135–63.

Harold, Scott W., and Alireza Nader. 2012. "China and Iran: Economic, Political, and Military Relations." Occasional Papers. RAND Corporation. https://www.rand.org/pubs/occasional_papers/OP351.html.

Harvard Growth Lab. 2021. "About the Data." *Atlas of Economic Complexity*. https://atlas.cid.harvard.edu/about-data.

Hiraiwa, Shunji. 2020. "Japan's Policy on North Korea: Four Motives and Three Factors." *Journal of Contemporary East Asia Studies* 9 (1). Routledge: 1–17. doi:10.1080/24761028.2020.1762300.

Houghton, David Patrick. 2017. "The Pueblo Hostage Crisis." *The Wilson Center.* March 20. https://www.wilsoncenter.org/blog-post/the-pueblo-hostage-crisis.

Hovi, Jon, Robert Huseby, and Detlef F. Sprinz. 2005. "When Do (Imposed) Economic Sanctions Work?" *World Politics* 57 (4): 479–99. doi:10.1353/wp.2006.0011.

Hu, Elise. 2016. "The 'Livelihood Loophole' And Other Weaknesses Of N. Korea Sanctions." *NPR*, September 15, sec. Conflict Zones. https://www.npr.org/sections/parallels/2016/09/15/493889932/the-livelihood-loophole-and-other-weaknesses-of-n-korea-sanctions.

Hudson, John, and David Francis. 2016. "Why Did Sanctions Fail Against North Korea?" *Foreign Policy.* https://foreignpolicy.com/2016/09/09/why-did-sanctions-fail-against-north-korea/.

Hufbauer, Gary Clyde, Jeffrey J. Schott, Kimberly Ann Elliott, and Milica Cosic. 2011. "Case Studies in Economic Sanctions and Terrorism: US v. Cuba (1960-: Castro)." *Peterson Institute for International Economics.* https://www.piie.com/sites/default/files/publications/papers/sanctions-cuba-60-3.pdf.

Hufbauer, Gary Clyde, Schott, Jeffrey J., Kimberly Ann Elliott, and Barbara Oegg. 2009. *Economic Sanctions Reconsidered.* Washington, DC: Peterson Institute for International Economics.

Huhtala, Marie T. 2005. Interview with Ambassador Marie Therese Huhtala. The Association for Diplomatic Studies and Training Foreign Affairs Oral History Project.

Hui, Mun Dong. 2020. "N. Korean Laborers Continue to Earn Foreign Currency Abroad." *Daily NK.* November 20. https://www.dailynk.com/english/north-korean-laborers-continue-earn-foreign-currency-abroad/.

Idris, Nor Azizan, and Zarina Othman. 2008. "From 'Non-Interference' to 'Constructive Engagement': Contemporary Malaysia-Myanmar Relations." *Tamkang Journal of International Affairs* 12 (4): 1-41. https://www.airitilibrary.com/Article/Detail?DocID=10274979-200904-12-4-1-41-a

Inskit Group and Recorded Future. 2020. "How North Korea Revolutionized the Internet as a Tool for Rogue Regimes." CTA-2020-0209. Boston, MA: Recorded Future. https://www.recordedfuture.com/north-korea-internet-tool/.

International Monetary Fund. 2022. "Mongolia: Staff Concluding Statement of the 2022 Article IV Mission." *IMF.* October 25. https://www.imf.org/en/News/Articles/2022/10/25/mcs102522-mongolia-staff-concluding-statement-of-the-2022-article-iv-mission.

Iran Watch. 2002. "Remarks by Alireza Jafarzadeh on New Information on Top Secret Projects of the Iranian Regime's Nuclear Program | Iran Watch," April 14. https://www.iranwatch.org/library/ncri-new-information-top-secret-nuclear-projects-8-14-02.

———. 2021. "Why Companies around the World Are Reversing Course on Iran Business | Iran Watch," May 18. https://www.iranwatch.org/our-publications/policy-briefs/how-companies-around-world-are-reversing-course-iran-business.

Izenman, Kayla, and Katherine Norton-Williams. 2020. "Crypto in the Hermit Kingdom: Understanding the Objectives of the Pyongyang Blockchain and Cryptocurrency Conference." *RUSI*. https://rusi.org/commentary/crypto-hermit-kingdom-understanding-objectives-pyongyang-blockchain-and-cryptocurrency.

Jacobson, Michael. 2008. "Sanctions against Iran: A Promising Struggle." *The Washington Quarterly* 31 (3): 69–88.

Jervis, Robert. 2017. *Perception and Misperception in International Politics: New Edition*. Revised edition. Princeton, New Jersey: Princeton University Press.

Jervis, Robert, and Mira Rapp-Hooper. 2018. "Perception and Misperception on the Korean Peninsula." *Foreign Affairs*, June. https://www.foreignaffairs.com/articles/north-korea/2018-04-05/perception-and-misperception-korean-peninsula.

Jones, Lee. 2015. *Societies Under Siege: Exploring How International Economic Sanctions (Do Not) Work*, Oxford: Oxford University Press. doi:10.1093/acprof:oso/9780198749325.003.0004.

Jun, Jenny. 2013. "Dealing with a Sore Lip: Parsing China's 'Recalculation' of North Korea Policy." *38 North*. March 29. https://www.38north.org/2013/03/jjun032913/.

Kahler, Miles. 1988. "Organization and Cooperation: International Institutions and Policy Coordination." *Journal of Public Policy* 8 (3/4): 375–401.

Kang, Jin Woong. 2007. "Historical Changes in North Korean Nationalism." *North Korean Review* 3 (1). McFarland & Company: 86–104.

Kardaś, Szymon. 2023. "Keeping the Lights on: The EU's Energy Relationships since Russia's Invasion of Ukraine." *European Council on Foreign Relations (ECFR)*. May 4. https://ecfr.eu/publication/keeping-the-lights-on-the-eus-energy-relationships-since-russias-invasion-of-ukraine/.

Kavaklı, Kerim Can, J. Tyson Chatagnier, and Emre Hatipoğlu. 2020. "The Power to Hurt and the Effectiveness of International Sanctions." *The Journal of Politics* 82 (3). The University of Chicago Press: 879–94. doi:10.1086/707398.

KCNA. 1997. "U.S. Sanction May Hamper Implementation of DPRK-U.S. Agreement," August 8. https://kcnawatch.org/newstream/.

———. 1998a. "'Sanctions' Must Be Abandoned," March 27. https://kcnawatch.org/newstream/1452000159-783636522/sanctions-must-be-abandoned/.

———. 1998b. "Sanctions Useless," August 15. https://kcnawatch.org/newstream/1452000309-684874070/sanctions-useless/.

———. 1998c. "U.S. Warned Not to Provoke DPRK," October 13. https://kcnawatch.org/newstream/.

———. 1999. "U.S. Lifts Economic Sanctions against DPRK," September 21. https://kcnawatch.org/newstream/.

———. 2017. "U.S.-Led Campaign for Sanctions on DPRK Is Doomed to Failure," August 3. https://kcnawatch.org/newstream/.

Kaempfer, William H., and Anton D. Lowenberg. 1999. "Unilateral versus Multilateral International Sanctions: A Public Choice Perspective." *International Studies Quarterly* 43 (1): 37–57.

Kim, Claudia Junghyun. 2023. *Base Towns: Local Contestation of the U.S. Military in Korea and Japan*. Oxford Studies in Culture and Politics. Oxford, New York: Oxford University Press.

Kim, Haeyoung. 2014. "Stifled Growth and Added Suffering: Tensions Inherent in Sanctions Policies Against North Korea." *Critical Asian Studies* 46 (1). Routledge: 91–112. doi:10.1080/14672715.2014.863579.

Kim, Hong Nack. 1991. "Japan's Relations with North Korea." *Current History* 90 (555): 164–67, 180.

Kim, Hyung-Jin. 2021. "Leaders of North Korea, China Vow to Strengthen Ties." *Associated Press*. July 11. https://apnews.com/article/health-china-coronavirus-pandemic-north-korea-8fc7a269318c481035c43b030754cbf0.

Kim, Inhan. 2017. "No More Sunshine: The Limits of Engagement with North Korea." *The Washington Quarterly* 40 (4). Routledge: 165–81. doi:10.1080/0163660X.2017.1406716.

Kim, Insoo, and Minyong Lee. 2011. "Has South Korea's Engagement Policy Reduced North Korea's Provocations?" *North Korean Review* 7 (2). McFarland & Company: 57–65.

Kim, Tong-Hyung. 2019. "Russian-North Korean Relations since the Korean War." *Associated Press*, April 25, sec. North Korea. https://apnews.com/article/24932ed50a424a12a243cc1434c71b49.

Klimasinska, Kasia, Dakin Campbell, and Ian Katz. 2014. "Banks Woo Treasury Sanctions Pros to Navigate Complex U.S. Rules." *Bloomberg.Com*. https://www.bloomberg.com/news/articles/2014-08-13/banks-woo-treasury-sanctions-pros-to-navigate-complex-u-s-rules.

Knapp, Brendan. 2017. "Plotting a Geospatial Network." *RPubs*. December 7. https://rpubs.com/BrendanKnapp/GeospatialNetworkPlotting.

Knoke, David, and Song Yang. 2020. *Social Network Analysis*. Third edition. Quantitative Applications in the Social Sciences 154. Thousand Oaks, California: SAGE.

Kokabisaghi, Fatemeh. 2018. "Assessment of the Effects of Economic Sanctions on Iranians' Right to Health by Using Human Rights Impact Assessment Tool: A Systematic Review." *International Journal of Health Policy and Management* 7 (5): 374–93. doi:10.15171/ijhpm.2017.147.

Krinsky, Michael, and David Golove. 1993. *United States Economic Measures Against Cuba: Proceedings in the United Nations and International Law Issues*. Northampton, MA: Aletheia Press.

Kroenig, Matthew. 2018. "The Return to the Pressure Track: The Trump Administration and the Iran Nuclear Deal." *Diplomacy & Statecraft* 29 (1): 94–104. doi:10.1080/09592296.2017.1420529.

Kudo, Toshihiro. 2011. "Results of the 2010 Elections in Myanmar: An Analysis." *Institute of Developing Economies*. January. https://www.ide.go.jp/English/Research/Region/Asia/20110104.html.

Laney, James T. 2011. "Interview with The Honorable James T. Laney , 2011." The Association for Diplomatic Studies and Training Foreign Affairs Oral History Project.

Lee, Yong Suk. 2018. "International Isolation and Regional Inequality: Evidence from Sanctions on North Korea." *Journal of Urban Economics* 103 (January): 34–51. doi:10.1016/j.jue.2017.11.002.

Lektzian, David J., and Mark Souva. 2007. "An Institutional Theory of Sanctions Onset and Success." *Journal of Conflict Resolution* 51 (6): 848–71. doi:10.1177/0022002707306811.

LeoGrande, William. 1982. "Relations with Cuba." In *From Gunboats to Diplomacy: New Policies for Latin America*, edited by Richard Newfarmer, 126–39. Democratic Policy Committee, US Senate. https://www.google.com/books/edition/From_Gunboats_to_Diplomacy/ZjdwAAAAMAAJ?hl=en&gbpv=1&printsec=frontcover.

Leopold, Jason, Anthony Cormier, John Templon, Tom Warren, Jeremy Singer-Vine, Scott Pham, Rihcard Holmes, et al. 2020. "The FinCEN Files." *BuzzFeed News*, September 20. https://www.buzzfeednews.com/article/jasonleopold/fincen-files-financial-scandal-criminal-networks.

Lerner, Mitchell. 2023. "The USS Pueblo Incident." *The Wilson Center*. Accessed February 8. https://digitalarchive.wilsoncenter.org/essays/uss-pueblo-incident-0.

Lewis, Simon, and Daphne Psaledakis. 2023. "US Targets Myanmar's State Oil and Gas Enterprise with Form of Sanctions." *Reuters*, November 1. https://www.reuters.com/business/energy/us-targets-myanmars-state-oil-gas-enterprise-with-form-sanctions-2023-10-31/.

Liu, Zongyuan Zoe, and Mihaela Papa. 2022. *Can BRICS De-Dollarize the Global Financial System?* Cambridge: Cambridge University Press. https://www.cambridge.org/core/elements/can-brics-dedollarize-the-global-financial-system/0AEF98D2F232072409E9556620AE09B0.

Lobell, Steven E. 2018. "A Granular Theory of Balancing." *International Studies Quarterly* 62 (3): 593–605. doi:10.1093/isq/sqy011.

Loh, Dylan M. H. 2018. "The Disturbance and Endurance of Norms in ASEAN." *Australian Institute of International Affairs*. November 11. https://www.internationalaffairs.org.au/australianoutlook/the-disturbance-and-endurance-of-norms-in-asean/.

Lord, Winston. 1998. "Interview with Winston Lord." The Association for Diplomatic Studies and Training Foreign Affairs Oral History Project.

Lukin, Artyom, and Liudmila Zakharova. 2018. "Russia-North Korea Economic Ties: Is There More Than Meets the Eye?" *Orbis* 62 (2): 244–61. doi:10.1016/j.orbis.2018.02.005.

MacNamara, Kelly. 2012. "Myanmar on Cusp of New Era: Suu Kyi; Veteran Activist's Election to Political Office Marks Key Democratic Step Forward." *The Gazette (Montreal)*, April 3.

Mallard, Gregoire, Farzan Sabet, and Jin Sun. 2020. "The Humanitarian Gap in the Global Sanctions Regime." *Global Governance* 26 (1): 121–53. doi:10.1163/19426720-02601003.

Marples, David R. 2017. "Russia's Perceptions of Ukraine: Euromaidan and Historical Conflicts." In *Ukraine in Crisis,* edited by Nicolai Petro, 4–17. London: Routledge.

Martin, Curtis H. 2002. "Rewarding North Korea: Theoretical Perspectives on the 1994 Agreed Framework." *Journal of Peace Research* 39 (1). Sage Publications, Ltd.: 51–68.

———. 2007. "G.W. Bush and North Korea: A Levels of Analysis View." *Pacific Focus* 22 (1): 111–36. doi:10.1111/j.1976-5118.2007.tb00196.x.

Maung Thawnghmung, Ardeth, and Paul Sarno. 2006. "Myanmar Impasses: Alternatives to Isolation and Engagement?" *Asian Journal of Political Science* 14 (1). Routledge: 40–63. doi:10.1080/02185370600832497.

Mazarr, Michael J. 1995. "Going Just a Little Nuclear: Nonproliferation Lessons from North Korea." *International Security* 20 (2). The MIT Press: 92–122. doi:10.2307/2539230.

McLean, Elena V., and Taehee Whang. 2010. "Friends or Foes? Major Trading Partners and the Success of Economic Sanctions." *International Studies Quarterly* 54 (2): 427–447. doi: 10.1111/j.1468-2478.2010.00594.x.

McDonald, Mark. 2012. "Now, Will She Kick the Hornet's Nest?" *New York Times*, April 2, sec. World. https://archive.nytimes.com/rendezvous.blogs.nytimes.com/2012/04/02/now-a-question-of-tactics-in-myanmar/.

McDowell, Daniel. 2023. *Bucking the Buck: US Financial Sanctions and the International Backlash against the Dollar*. New York: Oxford University Press.

Moret, Erica. 2015. "Humanitarian Impacts of Economic Sanctions on Iran and Syria." *European Security* 24 (1): 120–40. doi:10.1080/09662839.2014.893427.

———. 2021. "Unilateral and Extraterritorial Sanctions in Crisis: Implications of Their Rising Use and Misuse in Contemporary World Politics." In *Research Handbook on Unilateral and Extraterritorial Sanctions*, edited by Charlotte Beaucillon, 19–36. Cheltenham: Edward Elgar Publishing.

Morgan, T. Clifton, Navin Bapat, and Yoshiharu Kobayashi. 2014. "Threat and Imposition of Economic Sanctions 1945–2005: Updating the TIES Dataset." *Conflict Management and Peace Science* 31 (5): 541–58. doi:10.1177/0738894213520379.

Morgan, T. Clifton, Navin Bapat, and Valentin Krustev. 2009. "The Threat and Imposition of Economic Sanctions, 1971—2000." *Conflict Management and Peace Science* 26 (1): 92–110. doi:10.1177/0738894208097668.

Morning Edition. 2015. "A U.S. Negotiator Says There's Still Pending Business With Iran." *NPR*, October 9. https://www.npr.org/sections/parallels/2015/10/09/446983211/a-u-s-negotiator-says-theres-still-pending-business-with-iran.

Mousavian, Seyyed Hossein. 2008. *Iran-Europe Relations: Challenges and Opportunities*. Durham Modern Middle East and Islamic World Series 11. New York: Routledge.

Murray, Donette. 2010. *US Foreign Policy and Iran: American-Iranian Relations since the Islamic Revolution*. London: Routledge.

Nada, Garrett, Connor Bradbury, Jason Starr, Helia Ighani, and Alex Yacoubian. 2023. "Timeline of U.S. Sanctions." *The Iran Primer*. https://iranprimer.usip.org/resource/timeline-us-sanctions.

Nephew, Richard. 2019. "China and Economic Sanctions: Where Does Washington Have Leverage?" Global China: Assessing China's Growing Role in the World. Washington, D.C.: Brookings Institution. https://www.brookings.edu/wp-content/uploads/2019/09/FP_20190930_china_economic_sanctions_nephew.pdf.

Niblock, Tim. 2002. *"Pariah States" & Sanctions in the Middle East: Iraq, Libya, Sudan*. Boulder, Colo.: Lynne Rienner Pub.

Nikoladze, Maia, and Bhusari Mrugank. 2023. "Russia and China Have Been Teaming up to Reduce Reliance on the Dollar. Here's How It's Going." *Atlantic Council*. February 22. https://www.atlanticcouncil.org/blogs/new-atlanticist/russia-and-china-have-been-teaming-up-to-reduce-reliance-on-the-dollar-heres-how-its-going/.

Nincic, Miroslav. 2007. *Renegade Regimes: Confronting Deviant Behavior in World Politics*. New York: Columbia University Press.

Noland, Marcus. 2009. "The (Non-) Impact of UN Sanctions on North Korea." *Asia Policy* 7. National Bureau of Asian Research (NBR): 61–88.

Nyun, Thihan Myo. 2008. "Feeling Good or Doing Good: Inefficacy of the U.S. Unilateral Sanctions Against the Military Government of Burma/Myanmar." *Washington University Global Studies Law Review* 7 (3): 455–518.

Office of the Historian. 2001. "History of the Department of State during the Clinton Presidency (1993-2001)." *U.S. Department of State*. Department Of State. The Office of Electronic Information, Bureau of Public Affairs. https://2001-2009.state.gov/r/pa/ho/pubs/8519.htm.

Okano-Heijmans, Maaike. 2010. "Troubled Neighbours: Japan's Negative Economic Diplomacy Towards North Korea." *European Journal of East Asian Studies* 9 (2). Brill: 363–94.

Onderco, Michal. 2015. "Money Can't Buy You Love: The European Union Member States and Iranian Nuclear Programme 2002–2009." *European Security* 24 (1). Routledge: 56–76. doi:10.1080/09662839.2014.948865.

Pak, Jung H. 2020. *Becoming Kim Jong Un: A Former CIA Officer's Insights into North Korea's Enigmatic Young Dictator*. First edition. New York: Ballantine Books.

———. 2010. "Report of the Panel of Experts Established Pursuant to Resolution 1874 (2009)." S/2010/571. New York: United Nations. https://www.un.org/securitycouncil/sanctions/1718/panel_experts/reports.

———. 2012. "Final Report of the Panel of Experts Submitted Pursuant to Resolution 1985 (2011)." S/2012/337. New York: United Nations. https://www.un.org/securitycouncil/sanctions/1718/panel_experts/reports.

———. 2013. "Final Report of the Panel of Experts Submitted Pursuant to Resolution 2050 (2012)." S/2013/337. New York: United Nations. https://www.un.org/securitycouncil/sanctions/1718/panel_experts/reports.

———. 2014. "Final Report of the Panel of Experts Submitted Pursuant to Resolution 2094 (2013)." S/2014/131. New York: United Nations. https://www.un.org/securitycouncil/sanctions/1718/panel_experts/reports.

———. 2015. "Final Report of the Panel of Experts Submitted Pursuant to Resolution 2141 (2014)." S/2015/131. New York: United Nations.

———. 2016. "Final Report of the Panel of Experts Established Pursuant to Resolution 2207 (2015)." S/2016/157. New York: United Nations.

———. 2017a. "Final Report of the Panel of Experts Established Pursuant to Resolution 2276 (2016)." S/2017/150. New York: United Nations.

———. 2017b. "Midterm of the Panel of Experts Established Pursuant to Resolution 2345 (2017)." S/2017/142. New York: United Nations.

———. 2018. "Final Report of the Panel of Experts Established Pursuant to Resolution 2345 (2017)." S/2018/171. New York: United Nations.

———. 2019. "Final Report of the Panel of Experts Submitted Pursuant to Resolution 2407 (2018)." S/2019/171. New York: United Nations. https://www.un.org/securitycouncil/sanctions/1718/panel_experts/reports.

———. 2020. "Final Report of the Panel of Experts Established Pursuant to Resolution 2464 (2019)." S/2020/151. New York: United Nations.

Pape, Robert A. 1997. "Why Economic Sanctions Do Not Work." *International Security* 22 (2): 90–136.

———. 1998. "Why Economic Sanctions Still Do Not Work." *International Security* 23 (1): 66–77. doi:10.2307/2539263.

Park, John, and Jim Walsh. 2016. *Stopping North Korea, Inc.: Sanctions Effectiveness and Unintended Consequences.* Cambridge: Massachusetts Institute of Technology.

Park, Kyung Ae, and Sung-Chull Lee. 1992. "Changes and Prospects in Inter-Korean Relations." *Asian Survey* 32 (5). University of California Press: 429–47. doi:10.2307/2644975.

Pattison, Pete. 2014. "Countries Hosting North Korean Workers May Be Breaching UN Sanctions." *The Guardian.* December 31. http://www.theguardian.com/global-development/2014/dec/31/countries-hosting-north-korean-workers-may-be-breaching-un-sanctions.

Pedersen, Morten B. 2007. *Promoting Human Rights in Burma: A Critique of Western Sanctions Policy.* Lanham: Rowman & Littlefield Publishers.

———. 2013. "How to Promote Human Rights in the World's Most Repressive States: Lessons from Myanmar." *Australian Journal of International Affairs* 67 (2). Routledge: 190–202. doi:10.1080/10357718.2013.764581.

Peksen, Dursun. 2011. "Economic Sanctions and Human Security: The Public Health Effect of Economic Sanctions." *Foreign Policy Analysis* 7 (3): 237–51. doi:10.1111/j.1743-8594.2011.00136.x.

———. 2019a. "When Do Imposed Economic Sanctions Work? A Critical Review of the Sanctions Effectiveness Literature." *Defence and Peace Economics* 30 (6): 635–47. doi:10.1080/10242694.2019.1625250.

———. 2019b. "Autocracies and Economic Sanctions: The Divergent Impact of Authoritarian Regime Type on Sanctions Success." *Defence and Peace Economics* 30 (3). Routledge: 253–68. doi:10.1080/10242694.2017.1368258.

Peksen, Dursun, and Timothy M. Peterson. 2016. "Sanctions and Alternate Markets: How Trade and Alliances Affect the Onset of Economic Coercion." *Political Research Quarterly* 69 (1): 4–16. doi:10.1177/1065912915620049.

Perkins, Robert, and Rosemary Griffin. 2023. "EU to Tackle Russian Sanctions 'busting' as Lawmakers Call for Tighter Enforcement." *S&P Global Insights.* November 9. https://www.spglobal.com/commodityinsights/en/market-insights/latest-news/oil/110923-eu-to-tackle-russian-sanctions-busting-as-lawmakers-call-for-tighter-enforcement.

Peterson, Sabrina M. 2012. "Iran's Deteriorating Economy: An Analysis of the Economic Impact of Western Sanctions." *International Affairs Review.* October 9. http://www.iar-gwu.org/node/428.

Plaisted, Joan M. 2001. Interview with Ambassador Joan M. Plaisted. The Association for Diplomatic Studies and Training Foreign Affairs Oral History Project.

Plokhy, Serhii. 2023. *The Russo-Ukrainian War: The Return of History*. New York: W. W. Norton & Company.

Poh, Angela. 2017. "The Myth of Chinese Sanctions over South China Sea Disputes." *The Washington Quarterly* 40 (1). Routledge: 143–65. doi:10.1080/0163660X.2017.1302744.

Portela, Clara. 2005. "Where and Why Does the EU Impose Sanctions?" *Politique Européenne* 17 (3): 83–111.

———. 2011. *European Union Sanctions and Foreign Policy: When and Why Do They Work?* London: Routledge.

———. 2015. "EU Strategies to Tackle the Iranian and North Korean Nuclear Issues." In *The EU and Non-Proliferation of Nuclear Weapons*, edited by Spyros Blavoukos, Dimitris Bourantonis, and Clara Portela, 188–204. Basingstoke, Hampshire: Palgrave MacMillan.

Portela, Clara, Paulina Pospieszna, Joanna Skrzypczyńska, and Dawid Walentek. 2021. "Consensus against All Odds: Explaining the Persistence of EU Sanctions on Russia." *Journal of European Integration* 43 (6). Routledge: 683–99. doi:10.1080/07036337.2020.1803854.

Portela, Clara, and Chiara Ruffa. 2015. "The Politics of Coercion: Assessing the EU's Use of Military and Economic Instruments." In *The SAGE Handbook of European Foreign Policy*, edited by Knud Erik Jorgenseon, Asne Kalland Aarstad, Edith Drieskens, Katie Laatikainen, and Ben Tonra, 2: 545–58. London: SAGE. https://doi.org/10.4135/9781473915190.

Preble, Keith A. 2020. "Affordable Adjustments and Exploitable Opportunities: The Search for Alternatives to Sanctions Busting." https://papers.ssrn.com/sol3/papers.cfm?abstract_id=3684065.

———. 2021. "Sanctions Reform Should Start with the Treasury Office Enforcing Them." *War on the Rocks*. November 9. https://warontherocks.com/2021/11/sanctions-reform-should-start-with-the-treasury-office-enforcing-them/.

Preble, Keith A. 2022a. "Sanctions Run Amok: The Undermining of U.S. Power." *Fletcher Security Review* 9 (1): 60–65.

Preble, Keith A. 2022b. "'If You Can't Beat 'em, Join 'em': An Argument for US Support of and Participation in INSTEX." *Global Trade and Customs Journal* 17 (9). https://kluwerlawonline.com/journalarticle/Global+Trade+and+Customs+Journal/17.7/GTCJ2022051.

———. 2023. "'Just Right': The Goldilocks Theory of Sanctions Busting's Causes." *Foreign Policy Analysis* 19 (4). doi:https://doi.org/10.1093/fpa/orad020.

Preble, Keith A., and Charmaine N. Willis. 2024a. "How Russia Has Managed to Shake Off the Impact of Sanctions -- with a Little Help from its Friends." *The Conversation*, February 29. https://theconversation.com/how-russia-has-managed-to-shake-off-the-impact-of-sanctions-with-a-little-help-from-its-friends-223632

Preble, Keith A., and Charmaine N. Willis. 2024b. "Trading with Pariahs: North Korean Sanctions and the Challenge of Weaponized Interdependence." *Global Studies Quarterly* 4 (2). doi: https://doi.org/10.1093/isagsq/ksae031.

Prokopenko, Alexander, and Alexander Gabuev. 2023. "Podcast: What's the Secret of the Russian Economy's Resilience?" *Carnegie Endowment for International Peace*. December 14. https://carnegieendowment.org/politika/91235.

Putnam, Robert D. 1988. "Diplomacy and Domestic Politics: The Logic of Two-Level Games." *International Organization* 42 (3): 427–60.

Reilly, James. 2012. "China's Unilateral Sanction." *The Washington Quarterly* 35 (4). https://www.tandfonline.com/doi/abs/10.1080/0163660X.2012.726428?journalCode=rwaq20.

Reuters. 2023. "Netherlands Orders Russian Embassy to Downsize, Moscow Says It Will Respond." *Reuters*, February 18, sec. Europe. https://www.reuters.com/world/europe/netherlands-orders-russian-embassy-downsize-closes-st-petersburg-consulate-2023-02-18/.

Rice, Matthew. 2000. "Clinton Signs 'Iran Nonproliferation Act' | Arms Control Association." *Arms Control Association*. April. https://www.armscontrol.org/act/2000-04/iran-nuclear-briefs/clinton-signs-iran-nonproliferation-act.

Rodriguez Rodriguez, Raúl. 2018. "Canada and Cuba: Historical Overview of Their Political and Diplomatic Relations." In *Other Diplomacies, Other Ties: Cuba and Canada in the Shadow of the US*, edited by Luis René Fernández Tabío, Cynthia Wright, and Lana Wylie, 39–63. Toronto ; Buffalo ; London: University of Toronto Press.

Roegiers, Brett, and Kyle Almond. 2018. "In Pictures: The Historic Korean Summit." *CNN*, April. https://www.cnn.com/interactive/2018/04/world/korea-summit-cnnphotos/.

Roy, Joaquin. 1997. "The Helms-Burton Law: Development, Consequences, and Legacy for Inter-American and European-US Relations." *Journal of Interamerican Studies and World Affairs* 39 (3): 77–108. doi:10.2307/166486.

Salisbury, Daniel. 2017a. "Why UN Sanctions against North Korea's Missile Program Failed." *The Conversation*. http://theconversation.com/why-un-sanctions-against-north-koreas-missile-program-failed-83554.

———. 2017b. "Why Do Entities Get Involved in Proliferation? Exploring the Criminology of Illicit WMD-Related Trade." *The Nonproliferation Review* 24 (3–4): 297–314. doi:10.1080/10736700.2018.1423718.

Samuels, Richard J. 2004. "Payback Time: Japan–North Korea Economic Relations." In *A New International Engagement Framework for North Korea?: Contending Perspectives*, edited by Choong-yong Ahn, Nicholas Eberstadt, and Young-sun Lee, 317–34. Washington: Korea Economic Institute of America.

Sanger, David E. 2020. "North Korea's Internet Use Surges, Thwarting Sanctions and Fueling Theft." *The New York Times*, sec. U.S. https://www.nytimes.com/2020/02/09/us/politics/north-korea-internet-sanctions.html.

Sang-Hun, Choe. 2021. "North Korea Fires 2 Ballistic Missiles as Rivalry With the South Mounts." *The New York Times*, September 15, sec. World. https://www.nytimes.com/2021/09/15/world/asia/north-korea-ballistic-missiles.html.

Sauer, Tom. 2011. "The Impact of the European Union on Iran's Nuclear Program." In *Iran and the West: Regional Interests and Global Controversies*, edited by Rouzbeh Parsi and John Rydqvist, 93–106. Stockholm: FOI, the Swedish Defense Research Agency.

Schelling, Thomas C. 1977. *Arms and Influence.:* Westport, Conn: Praeger.

Seeberg, Peter. 2016. "The EU and the International Sanctions against Iran: European and Iranian Foreign and Security Policy Interests, and a Changing Middle East." *Palgrave Communications* 2 (November): 1–9. doi:10.1057/palcomms.2016.80.

Seekins, Donald M. 2005. "Burma and U.S. Sanctions: Punishing an Authoritarian Regime." *Asian Survey* 45 (3). University of California Press: 437–52. doi:10.1525/as.2005.45.3.437.

Sicker, Martin. 1987. *The Making of a Pariah State: The Adventurist Politics of Muammar Qaddafi.* New York: Praeger.

Sieff, Kevin. 2017. "North Korea's Surprising, Lucrative Relationship with Africa." *Washington Post*, July 10, sec. Africa. https://www.washingtonpost.com/world/africa/north-koreas-surprising-lucrative-relationship-with-africa/2017/07/10/c4e6f65d-30fe-4bd2-b178-d90daaac3007_story.html.

Sikkink, Kathryn. 2008. "From Pariah State to Global Protagonist: Argentina and the Struggle for International Human Rights." *Latin American Politics and Society* 50 (1). [University of Miami, Wiley, Center for Latin American Studies at the University of Miami]: 1–29.

Slavin, Barbara. 2011. *Iran Turns to China, Barter to Survive Sanctions.* Washington, DC: Atlantic Council. https://www.files.ethz.ch/isn/137386/111011_ACUS_IranChina.pdf.

Smith, Josh. 2022. "New North Korea Law Outlines Nuclear Weapons Use, Including Pre-Emptive Strikes." *The Japan Times.* https://www.japantimes.co.jp/news/2022/09/09/asia-pacific/north-korea-nuclear-weapons-policy/.

Smith, Sheila A. 2006. "Shifting Terrain: The Domestic Politics of the U.S. Military Presence in Asia." 8. East-West Center Special Reports. East-West Center. https://www.eastwestcenter.org/publications/shifting-terrain-the-domestic-politics-the-us-military-presence-in-asia.

Snyder, Scott. 2009a. "Lee Myung-Bak's Foreign Policy: A 250-Day Assessment." *Korean Journal of Defense Analysis* 21 (1). Routledge: 85–102. doi:10.1080/10163270902745711.

———. 2009b. *China's Rise and the Two Koreas: Politics, Economics, Security.* New ed. edition. Boulder, Colo: Lynne Rienner Pub.

Son, Key-young. 2006. *South Korean Engagement Policies and North Korea: Identities, Norms and the Sunshine Policy.* 1st edition. London: Routledge.

Sonnenfeld, Jeffrey. 2022. "Over 400 Companies Have Withdrawn from Russia—But Some Remain." *Yale School of Management.* March 17. https://som.yale.edu/story/2022/over-400-companies-have-withdrawn-russia-some-remain.

Sorensen, Lucy, Charmaine Willis, Victor Asal, and Melissa Breger. 2024. "Paddling the Pupils: The Legality (or not) of Corporal Punishment in Schools." In *Children's Rights in Crisis: Multidisciplinarity, Transnational, and Comparative Perspectives*, edited by Salvador Santino F. Regilme, 23-45. Manchester: Manchester University Press.

Stein, Arthur A. 1982. "Coordination and Collaboration: Regimes in an Anarchic World." *International Organization* 36 (2): 299–324.

Steinberg, David I. 2007. "The United States and Its Allies: The Problem of Burma/Myanmar Policy." *Contemporary Southeast Asia* 29 (2). Institute of Southeast Asian Studies (ISEAS): 219–37.

Su, Yi-hao. 2020. "Trade Plants the Flag: Sanctions-Busting and the Signing of New Preferential Trade Agreements." *Foreign Policy Analysis*: 1–19. doi:10.1093/fpa/oraa009.

Sun, Yun. 2014. "Iran and Asia 1: China Is The Quiet Giant." *The Iran Primer*. https://iranprimer.usip.org/blog/2014/jan/29/iran-and-asia-1-china-quiet-giant.

Swift. 2022a. "Swift and Data." *Swift*. https://www.swift.com/about-us/swift-and-data.

———. 2022b. "Swift and Sanctions." *Swift*. https://www.swift.com/about-us/legal/compliance-0/swift-and-sanctions.

Tabatabai, Ariane. 2017. "Negotiating the 'Iran Talks' in Tehran: The Iranian Drivers That Shaped the Joint Comprehensive Plan of Action." *The Nonproliferation Review* 24 (3–4). Routledge: 225–42. doi:10.1080/10736700.2018.1426180.

Tabrizi, Aniseh Bassiri, and Ruth Hanau Santini. 2012. "EU Sanctions against Iran: New Wine in Old Bottles?" *ISPI Analysis* 97 (March): 1–7.

Taliaferro, Jeffrey W. 2006. "State Building for Future Wars: Neoclassical Realism and the Resource-Extractive State." *Security Studies* 15 (3). Routledge: 464–95. doi:10.1080/09636410601028370.

Tarock, Adam. 2016. "The Iran Nuclear Deal: Winning a Little, Losing a Lot." *Third World Quarterly* 37 (8): 1408–24. doi:10.1080/01436597.2016.1166049.

TeleSUR. 2015. "OAS Admits They Owe Cuba Apology for 50 Years of Exclusion," December 17. https://www.telesurenglish.net/news/OAS-Admits-They-Owe-Cuba-Apology-for-50-Years-of-Exclusion-20151217-0026.html.

Teo, Cheng Wee. 2012. "Suu Kyi Defends Decision to Contest; Making Citizens Part of Democratic Process Vital, She Replies to Those Who Claim Govt Is Using Her." *The Straits Times*, March 31.

The Australian. 2012. "A Step on the Road to Democracy," April 3.

The Economist. 2022. "The EU's Unity over Ukraine Has given It Surprising Heft." *The Economist*, March 26. https://www.economist.com/europe/the-eus-unity-over-ukraine-has-given-it-surprising-heft/21808306.

U.S. Department of State. 2002. "The Global War on Terrorism: The First 100 Days." Washington, D.C., Bureau of Public Affairs. https://2001-2009.state.gov/s/ct/rls/wh/6947.htm.

U.S. Embassy in Cuba. 2024. "Policy & History: U.S. & Cuba." Havana, Cuba. https://cu.usembassy.gov/embassy/policy-history.

The New York Times. 2005. "Text of Joint Statement," September 19, sec. World. https://www.nytimes.com/2005/09/19/world/asia/text-of-joint-statement.html.

Toloraya, Georgy. 2011. "Changing Lanes: The Russian Alternative." *38 North*. September 8. https://www.38north.org/2011/09/gtoloraryа090811/.

Town, Jenny, and Sally Yozell. 2020. "Chinese Fishing Near North Korea Is a Symptom of a Bigger Problem." *The Diplomat*, July 13. https://thediplomat.com/2020/07/chinese-fishing-near-north-korea-is-a-symptom-of-a-bigger-problem/.

U. S. Mission, Russia. 2021. "Message to U.S. Citizens: U.S. Mission Russia - Reduction of Consular Services." *U.S. Embassy & Consulates in Russia*. April 30.

https://ru.usembassy.gov/message-to-u-s-citizens-u-s-mission-russia-reduction-of-consular-services/.

United Nations. 2021. *UN Comtrade Database*. New York: United Nations. http://comtrade.un.org.

United Nations Security Council. 2006a. *Resolution 1718*. http://unscr.com/en/resolutions/1718.

———. 2006b. *Resolution 1695*. http://unscr.com/en/resolutions/1695.

U.S. Department of Treasury. 2020. "Treasury Sanctions Entities Involved in Exporting Workers from North Korea." *U.S. Department of Treasury*. November 19. https://home.treasury.gov/news/press-releases/sm1189.

Vale, Peter, and Ian Taylor. 1999. "South Africa's Post-Apartheid Foreign Policy Five Years on - from Pariah State to 'Just Another Country'?" *The Round Table* 88 (352). Routledge: 629–34. doi:10.1080/750459615.

Wagner, Alex. 2002. "Bush Labels North Korea, Iran, Iraq an 'Axis of Evil.'" *Arms Control Association*. https://www.armscontrol.org/act/2002-03/press-releases/bush-labels-north-korea-iran-iraq-axis-evil.

Warrick, Joby. 2018. "High Seas Shell Game: How a North Korean Shipping Ruse Makes a Mockery of Sanctions." *Washington Post*, March 3. https://www.washingtonpost.com/world/national-security/high-seas-shell-game-how-a-north-korean-shipping-ruse-makes-a-mockery-of-sanctions/2018/03/03/3380e1ec-1cb8-11e8-b2d9-08e748f892c0_story.html.

Watterson, Christopher J. 2020. "Maximum Pressure Made Permeable: The Trouble with Washington's North Korea Sanctions." *War on the Rocks*. https://warontherocks.com/2020/01/maximum-pressure-made-permeable-the-trouble-with-washingtons-north-korea-sanctions/.

Weeks, Jessica L. 2008. "Autocratic Audience Costs: Regime Type and Signaling Resolve." *International Organization* 62 (1). Cambridge University Press: 35–64. doi:10.1017/S0020818308080028.

Wertz, Daniel. 2013. "The Evolution of Financial Sanctions on North Korea." *North Korean Review* 9 (2). McFarland & Company: 69–82.

———. 2020. "Understanding U.S. and International Sanctions on North Korea." *NCNK*. November 20. https://www.ncnk.org/resources/briefing-papers/all-briefing-papers/understanding-u.s.-and-international-sanctions-north.

Whang, Taehee, and Hannah June Kim. 2015. "International Signaling and Economic Sanctions." *International Interactions* 41 (3): 427–52. doi:10.1080/03050629.2015.1024242.

Willis, Charmaine. 2018. "Trump's Big North Korea Giveaway Isn't A New Tactic." *Huffington Post*, June 15, sec. Opinion. https://www.huffingtonpost.com/entry/opinion-willis-trump-north-korea-war-games_us_5b23c245e4b07cb1712dcad4.

Willis, Charmaine N. 2018. "'Great Deceptions' and Midterms: Status of North Korean Denuclearization." *The Globe Post*, November 16. https://theglobepost.com/2018/11/16/status-north-korea-denuclearization/.

Willis, Charmaine N., and Keith A. Preble. 2024. 3 Year on From Coup, Economic Sanctions Look Unlikely to Push Myanmar Back to Democracy." *The*

Conversation, February 1. https://theconversation.com/3-years-on-from-coup-economic-sanctions-look-unlikely-to-push-myanmar-back-to-democracy-221297.

Win, Khin Zaw. 2007. "Reality Check on the Sanctions Policy Against Myanmar." In *Myanmar: State, Society and Ethnicity*, edited by N. Ganesan and Kyaw Yin Hlaing, 278–87. Singapore: Institute of Southeast Asian Studies.

Wit, Joel. 1999. "The Korean Peninsula Energy Development Organization: Achievements and Challenges." *The Nonproliferation Review* 6 (2). Routledge: 59–69. doi:10.1080/10736709908436750.

Wolfram, Catherine, Simon Johnson, and Łukasz Rachel. 2022. *The Price Cap on Russian Oil Exports, Explained.* Cambridge, MA: Harvard Kennedy School, Belfer Center for Science and International Affairs.

Woolley, John, and Gerhard Peters. 1999. "The American Presidency Project." 2022. https://www.presidency.ucsb.edu.

Yan, Erjia, and Ying Ding. 2009. "Applying Centrality Measures to Impact Analysis: A Coauthorship Network Analysis." *Journal of the American Society for Information Science and Technology* 60 (10): 2107–18. doi:10.1002/asi.21128.

Yoon, Dasl. 2019. "North Korean Workers Flock Home as Sanctions Deadline Hits." *Wall Street Journal*, December 20, sec. World. https://www.wsj.com/articles/north-korean-workers-flock-home-as-sanctions-deadline-hits-11576837803.

Yotov, Yoto, Erdal Yalcin, Aleksandra Kirilakha, Constantinos Syropoulos, and Gabriel Felbermayr. 2020. "The Global Sanctions Data Base." *Centre for Economic Policy Research.* August 4. https://cepr.org/voxeu/columns/global-sanctions-data-base.

Zakharova, Liudmila. 2016. "Economic Cooperation between Russia and North Korea: New Goals and New Approaches." *Journal of Eurasian Studies* 7 (2). SAGE Publications Ltd: 151–61. doi:10.1016/j.euras.2016.04.003.

Zarate, Juan. 2013. *Treasury's War.* Public Affairs. https://www.publicaffairsbooks.com/titles/juan-zarate/treasurys-war/9781610391160/.

Zhao, Quansheng. 1996. *Interpreting Chinese Foreign Policy: The Micro-Macro Linkage Approach.* Oxford: Oxford University Press.

Zhebin, Alexander. 1995. "Russia and North Korea: An Emerging, Uneasy Partnership." *Asian Survey* 35 (8). University of California Press: 726–39. doi:10.2307/2645732.

Zwirko, Colin. 2021. "North Korea Tested New Train-Launched Ballistic Missile System: State Media | NK News." *NK News.* September 15. https://www.nknews.org/2021/09/north-korea-tested-new-train-launched-ballistic-missile-system-kcna/.

Index

About the Authors

Keith A. Preble, PhD, is a visiting assistant professor of political science at Miami University (Ohio) and a postdoctoral researcher with the Project on International Security, Commerce, and Economic Statecraft (PISCES) at the Center for Policy Research at the University at Albany, SUNY. He holds a PhD in political science from the University at Albany, SUNY, along with an MA in public policy and administration from Northwestern University and an MA in government and politics from St. John's University. His research focuses on sanctions evasion and circumvention techniques, economic statecraft, and the role of economic power in foreign policy.

Charmaine N. Willis Ward, PhD, is a visiting assistant professor of political science at Skidmore College. She received her PhD and an MA in political science from the University at Albany, SUNY, along with an MA in international affairs from American University's School of International Service. Her research examines the causes and consequences of US foreign policy, with a focus on the US military abroad and economic sanctions. She also studies contentious politics, including social movements and terrorism, with a regional focus on East and Southeast Asia.

www.ingramcontent.com/pod-product-compliance
Ingram Content Group UK Ltd.
Pitfield, Milton Keynes, MK11 3LW, UK
UKHW041838031026
15587UKWH00002B/849

9 781666 903737